LOOK TO THE MOUNTAIN

AN ECOLOGY OF INDIGENOUS EDUCATION

LOOK TO THE MOUNTAIN
AN ECOLOGY OF INDIGENOUS EDUCATION

GREGORY CAJETE, PH.D.

Introduction by Vine Deloria, Jr.

KIVAKÍ
PRESS

Kivaki Press
P.O. Box 1053
Skyland, NC 28776
1-800-578-5904

Publisher's Cataloging in Publication

Cajete, Gregory A.
    Look to the mountain : an ecology of indigenous education / Gregory Cajete ; introduction by Vine Deloria, Jr. — 1st ed.
       p. cm.
    Includes bibliographical references.
    ISBN 1-882308-65-4
    1. Indians of North America--Education--Philosophy. 2. Human ecology--North America.   I. Title.

E96.C35 1994   370'.8997
                                        QBI94-295

First Edition
First Printing, 1994
Second Printing, 1997
Printed in the United States of America
3 4 5 6 — 98 97

A WISE ELDER AMONG MY PEOPLE — the Tewa Pueblo Indians — frequently used the phrase *Pin pé obi*, 'look to the mountaintop.' I first heard it when I was seven years old, as I was practicing for the first time to participate in relay races we run in Pueblo country to give strength to the sun father as he journeys across the sky.

I was at one end of the earth track which ran east to west, like the path of the sun. The old man, who was blind, called me to him and said: "Young one, as you run, look to the mountain top," and he pointed to Tsikomo, the Western sacred mountain of the Tewas. "Keep your gaze fixed on that mountain, and you will feel the miles melt beneath your feet. Do this, and in time you will feel as if you can leap over bushes, trees, and even the river.'"

—Alfonso Ortiz
San Juan Pueblo, 1972

❋ ACKNOWLEDGMENTS ❋

THERE ARE A NUMBER OF PEOPLE whose advice, encouragement, and technical assistance were instrumental in bringing this book to completion. First, I wish to acknowledge the inspiration and support of family, friends, and various members of the Indian community too numerous to mention. The nurturing spirit of these special people provided the rooted ecology that made this work possible. I wish to extend my deepest gratitude to my mother, Clara Cajete, and my grandmother Maria Cajete for their special presence, love and guidance in my life. Also, special thanks to my wife, Patsy, and son, James, for their patience and love.

I extend deep gratitude to Phillip Foss for his expert technical and editorial assistance with critical phases in the production of this book. I also wish to acknowledge Vine Deloria, Edward T. Hall, Simon Ortiz, Roger Buffalohead, Michael Mooris, Elisabet Sahtouris, Peggy MacIntosh, Tomas Atencio, Lloyd New, Rina Swentzel, Dolores LaChapelle, Alfonso Ortiz, Dave Warren, Gloria Emerson and Naomi Tuttle for their support and invaluable advice regarding portions of this work.

Finally, I would like to recognize the hundreds of Native American students that I have encountered over the last twenty years of teaching, learning, and creating. Indeed, this work is a co-creation with them and through them.

This work is also a reflection of the good thoughts — as well as the trials and tribulations — of the many Indian and non-Indian people I have encountered who *care* about Indian education and the continuance of the essential spirit of Indian thought and traditions.

—Gregory Cajete
Santa Fe, 1994

FOR ALL MY RELATIONS
AND CHILDREN EVERYWHERE:

LOOK TO THE MOUNTAIN!
AND
BE WITH LIFE

❀ LIST OF ILLUSTRATIONS ❀

❈ CONTENTS ❈

✸ FOREWORD ✸

Vine Deloria, Jr.

FROM THE BEGINNING OF CONTACT with European culture until the present, education has been a major area of conflict and concern. Early efforts by the Spanish were directed at transforming the Indian culture into an exact replica of church-dominated, administratively-controlled villages, cities and provinces that could be understood as an improved version of European Spanish society. The French saw their task as creating a new society, half indigenous, half-European. So while they educated Indian children in the ways of the church, they also encouraged their leading families to send their children to Indian villages to live as part of a chief or headman's family and absorb the Indian ways. The English, from whom American educational efforts with Indians have been derived, sought only to provide Indians with sufficient familiarity with their culture, particularly with their economic system, so that educated Indians could fit into the rural Protestant agricultural milieu.

Early treaties provided that churches would establish schools for Indian children at their respective missions in exchange for a tract of land for their denomination. As education became more important to white Americans, and public secularized education became the norm, the federal government began to include education, at least a teacher and a school building, as a regular part of treaty provisions. Education was not limited to book-learning, however, and almost every treaty after 1840 provided for vocational training in the form of blacksmiths, carpenters, farmers, and other tradesmen who would instruct both children and adults in the crafts of industrial society.

Richard Pratt, experimenting with Chiracahua Apache prisoners at Fort Marion, conceived of the idea of mass, forced, off-reservation education that, it was supposed, would sweep away the barbarism of the Indians in one generation. Unfortunately the transition from a life of freedom and a healthy diet to regimented uniforms, a bland and civilized diet of fats, and isolation from their families for years at a time proved fatal to the Indian children who were put into the government boarding school system. Those who did survive this ordeal and returned to the reservation had no way to make a decent living and quickly reverted to traditional ways in order to feed themselves and re-establish family ties. A majority of the graduates of the federal boarding schools eventually found employment in the expanding federal bureaucracy that controlled the reservations and helped to create the lethargic administrative apparatus we have today in the Bureau of Indian Affairs.

Day schools, a much more popular version of American education, were created in reservation areas that were isolated from the agency town, and as policies and theories of education changed with the blowing winds of non-Indian education, so did the fate of these institutitons. John Collier expanded the day school concept because he saw the need to involve parents and the local community in the educational activities of the government. Following the Second World War, however, when educational theories about learning began to run rampant, and financial costs of schools started to escalate beyond anyone's wildest predictions, reservation education became a function of consolidation with state public school systems. Finally in the 1960s with the national expansion of educational programs to poverty areas, Indian education was fully attached to federal finances and modern educational theories.

For the past two decades Indians have aggressively moved to establish indigenous educational institutions on their reservations. Beginning with the Navajo Community College and expanding to nearly thirty community colleges and educational institutes, a measure of higher education has been placed within reach of reservation people. Subcontracting alternative schools both on reservations and in urban areas has also become popular in the last twenty years, demonstrating a desire by American Indians to gain full control of their children's education once again.

The progress of the past generation has been clothed primarily in terms of wresting institutional control away from non-Indian educators and school boards. While this transition has been made in many areas of the western United States, it does not portend a fundamental change in the *substance* of Indian education since the schools, whether operated by Indians or non-Indians, must conform to state and federal guidelines as to curricula, test scores, and other trappings of modern American education. Indian-controlled schools may be ready to take the next step, but they are having great difficulty in determining exactly what that step should be.

Teaching methods vary considerably between the traditonal English-American process of intense memorizing of facts and doctrines (regarded as a contemporary expression of truth—political, scientific, historical, religious and philosophical) and the traditional Indian way of learning by doing. The philosophical perspective received in modern non-Indian school courses, that the world is an inanimate mass of matter arranged by chance into a set of shapes and energy patterns, is a matter of belief, not experience, and is the polar opposite of the traditional Indian belief. Indian educators thus face the question of whether they will move the substance of education away from this essentially meaningless proposition toward the more realistic Indian model that sees the world as an intimate relationship of living things.

Moving from one perspective to another is no simple matter, and consequently, Indian education and educators badly need a generation of original thinkers who can scan both points of view. They can build models and interpretations of the world that serve as transitions to enable Indians to communicate with the non-Indian body of knowledge and demonstrate the validity of the Indian understanding. No one is more ideally suited for this task than Gregory Cajete. An Indian educator for more than twenty years, he brings the insights of his Santa Clara Pueblo heritage and research in context of a number of tribal societies to focus on the western body of knowledge, producing new and exciting ways of synthesizing these two disparate bodies of knowledge.

Cajete develops an educational theory of context, something that has been missing, indeed, not even conceived, in American education from the very beginning. Here we have not the narrow focus of pitting one set of cultural values against another, as some of the "politically correct" theoreticians do today, but a recognition that any propositions or doctrines must find a comfortable home in the existing community and age-group context where they are promulgated in order to be effective. This task is exceedingly difficult in modern American society because of the belief that everything we do in this country is the best and most sophisticated way of accomplishing a task. Thus the educator must loosen the moorings of certainty even while he or she points out a different way of securing reliability for the data and their interpretation.

Although he is culturally from the American Southwest, Cajete does not confine his examples to familiar material from the Pueblos. Instead he reaches into a number of tribal traditions and brings their insights to bear on problems of interpretation and the task of arranging the data that are to be examined. From the Lakota religious tradition he includes the idea that we are all related — originally a religious truth but also a methodology for examining the natural world and understanding how things function symbiotically. From other tribal traditions he brings stories that illustrate the necessity of making education a function of the community historical consciousness.

I do not pretend to understand everything in this book . What I do know is that this book represents a new, creative, and sophisticated effort to build intellectual bridges between two entirely different systems of knowing the world. It is the first major work by an American Indian scholar that systematically works through the tangent points that exist between Indian and non-Indian understandings of education. As such it should receive the most serious consideration from Indian and non-Indian alike. Until Indian scholars begin to develop a systematic approach to communication of ideas, as Cajete has done here, very little will change in American Indian education.

We can hope, as we see how Gregory Cajete has developed his outline of knowledge and teaching, that he is the pioneer of the next generation of American Indians in education, that others will rise to these challenges, and that he will continue to blaze new intellectual trails we can follow.

—Vine Deloria, 1994

A Note On Terminology

The terms *Tribal* and *Indigenous* will apply broadly to the many traditional and Tribally oriented groups of people who are identified with a specific place or region and whose cultural traditions continue to reflect an inherent environmental orientation and sense of sacred ecology.

The term *Indigenous* will also describe the culturally based forms of education that are not primarily rooted in modern Western educational philosophy and methodology.

Other terms such as *American Indian* or *Indian* will refer to the specific histories, situations, examples, and activites of Indian people. The terms *Native America* or *Native American* will emphasize the specific connection to the pre-colonial inhabitants of the Americas that have a direct and ancient relationship to, or originate from, the people, ideas, and places of the Americas.

All the terms mentioned will be capitalized to denote greater emphasis and to support the inherent spirit of the theme and presentation of this book.

Note to the Reader

Look to the Mountain represents a 21–year evolution of thinking regarding the nature, guiding thoughts and *spirit* of traditional forms of American Indigenous Education. Deep appreciation and abiding respect are the essential values which have guided the development of this work from start to finish. Given this orientation, quotes, references and examples have been selected with great care and cultural sensitivity. All references to indigenous tribes presented have a substantial history of prior publication or citation in scholarly sources. Only a general overview of selected indigenous concepts is presented to build the necessary philosophical framework for a contemporary expression of "Indian Education" firmly rooted in the principles and values of the most enduring characteristics of traditional education.

This work draws upon diverse examples of traditional American Indian Education that include a quest for self, individual and community survival and wholeness in the context of community and a natural environment. This work advocates for the development of a new educational consciousness. A consciousness which allows indigenous peoples to explore their collective heritage in education and to make the contributions to global education that stem from their deep ecological understandings.

It is my hope that the reader will gain important insights in terms of the creative possibilities of indigenous thought for the revitalization of modern education. In addition, it is my hope that Look to the Mountain will reaffirm the thoughts, intuitions and hope of many Indian people about the future of education for their children and communities.

Look to the Mountain is an honoring of traditional forms of indigenous education. It also presents my vision of where we, as American Indians, have been, where we are and the possibilities of where we may go in our collective journey to reach that place that Indian people talk about.

Best wishes, may the good spirits guide you and remember: *"Look to the Mountain"*.

Gregory Cajete
1997, Santa Fe, NM

❋ PREFACE ❋

ABOUT PARAMETERS AND PROCESS

T HE PERSPECTIVES, ORIENTATIONS, IDEAS, MODELS, interpretations, and beliefs presented herein are a *personal synthesis* based on my own creative process as an Indian educator. This book is a reflection of my particular understanding of the shared metaphors that American Indians hold regarding Tribal education. It is an inclusive exploration of the *nature* of Indigenous education. It reflects upon the creative possibilities inherent in introducing an Indigenous frame of reference as an important consideration in the development of a contemporary philosophy of American Indian education. As a whole, this work outlines key elements of American Indian Tribal orientations to learning and teaching. It represents my perception of "an ecology of indigenous education."

This book is also an *open letter* to Indian educators, those involved with Indian education issues, and other Indigenous people who wish to consider alternative cultural possibilities of education. My approach has been that of a teacher exploring the dimensions of Indigenous teaching and learning in creative ways. The description of this journey, this curriculum, has become this book. Teachers create curricula (circles of learning and teaching) through constantly creating models and applying them to actual teaching situations. Ideally, teachers constantly adjust their models to fit their students and the changing realities of educating. Through such constant and creative adjustment, teachers and students engage in a symbiotic relationship and form feedback loops around what is being learned. In this way, teachers are always creating their stories even as they are telling them.

This work explores a culturally-informed alternative for thinking about and enabling the contemporary education of American Indian people. It is a *translation* of foundational Tribal education principles into a contemporary framework of thought and description. It *advocates* developing a contemporary, culturally based, educational process founded upon traditional Tribal values, orientations, and principles, while *simultaneously* using the most appropriate concepts, technologies, and content of modern education.

Excerpts of Indigenous thought and tradition used in this work represent essential aspects of the ecology of Indigenous education. Each excerpt is presented with my deepest respect, honoring the richness of its Indigenous being. The content represents a small portion of what is available in the vast array of research related to American Indian cultures. American Indian cultures are among the most studied anywhere in the world. Access to this vast sea of content, facilitated by Indian educators and scholars, is an essential step in creating a contemporary epistemology of Indian education. This access to, and revitalization of, the Indigenous bases of education must occur, not only in the contemporary classroom, but in Indian communities as well. All Indian people, young and old, professional and grassroots, should consider themselves participants in a process of moving forward to the Indigenous basics of education. *Indian people themselves must introduce contemporary expressions of Tribal education to their people.* It is up to each Indian community, whether they live in an urban setting or reservation, to decide how their needs regarding cultural maintenance or revitalization may be addressed through education; and it is up to each Indian community to decide what is appropriate to introduce through the vehicle of modern education and what should be imparted with appropriate traditional mechanisms.

Modern education and traditional education can no longer afford to remain historically and contextually separate entities. Every community must integrate the learning occurring through modern education with the cultural bases of knowledge and value orientations essential to perpetuate its way of life. A balanced integration must be created. Over time, the emphasis on Western oriented curricula will erode Indigenous ways of life. Indian educators and Tribal leaders must understand that the unexamined application of Western education can condition people away from their cultural roots. Modern education provides tools essential to the survival of Indian people and communities, but this education must be within the context of a greater cultural whole. In support of cultural preservation, Indian educators and Tribal leaders also need to advocate culturally based education to achieve the foundational goals of self-determination, self-governance, and Tribal sovereignty. Indigenous education offers a highly creative vehicle for thinking about the perpetuation of American Indian cultures as they enter the twenty-first century.

The exploration of Indigenous education presented in this book includes the expression of the universals of the educational process from the perspectives of traditional American Indian thought. Its foundation lies in the applicability of its perspectives to the whole process of teaching and learning—not just that of American Indians. The universals that are explored may be viewed as archetypes of human learning and as part of the Indigenous psyche of all people and cultural traditions. All relevant sources of thought, research, and educational philosophy—from various cultural sources—have been considered, to illuminate the possibilities of a contemporary education that mirrors Indigenous thought and its primary orientation of relationship with the natural world. Therefore, the thesis of this work can be applicable to the Native Hawaiian, the Australian Aborigine, the African bushman and other Indigeneous people seeking to revitalize their guiding stories through education.

The Contemporary Dilemma of American Indian Education

A pervasive problem affecting the contemporary vision of American Indian education is that its definition and evolution have always been dependent on American politics. Much of what characterizes Indian education policy is not the result of research predicated upon American Indian philosophical orientations, but the result of Acts of Congress, the history of treaty rights interpretation through the courts, and the historic Indian/White relations unique to each Tribal group or geographic region. Historically, the views guiding the evolution of modern Indian education have not been predicated upon assumptions that are representative of Indian cultural perspectives.[1] In spite of such policy orientations, traditional educational processes have continued within the context of many Indian families and communities. While there has been progress in the last twenty years, the integration of these two approaches to education has been practically nonexistent.

The basis of contemporary American education is the transfer of academic skills and content that prepares the student to compete in the infrastructure of American society as it has been defined by the prevailing political, social, and economic order. American educational theory is generally devoid of substantial ethical or moral content regarding the means used to achieve its ends. The ideal curriculum espoused through American education ends up being significantly different from the experienced curriculum internalized by students. The American society that many Indian students experience is wrought with contradictions, prejudice, hypocrisy, narcissism, and unethical predispositions at all levels, including the schools. There continue to be educational conflicts, frustrations, and varying levels of alienation experienced by many Indian people because of their encounters with mainstream education.

A fundamental obstacle to cross-cultural communication revolves around significant differences in cultural orientations and the fact that Indian people have been forced to adapt to an educational process not of their making. Traditionally, Indians view life through a different cultural metaphor than mainstream America. It is this different cultural metaphor that frames the exploration of the Indigenous educational philosophy presented in this book.[2]

Traditional Indian education represents an anomaly for the prevailing objectivist theory and methodology of Western education. What is implied in the application of objectivism is that there is one correct way of understanding the dynamics of Indian education, one correct methodology, and one correct policy for Indian education. And that *one way* is the way of mainstream America. The mindset of objectivism, when applied to the field of Indian education, excludes serious consideration of the relational reality of Indian people, the variations in Tribal and social contexts, and the processes of perception and understanding that characterize and form its expressions.[3]

Objectivist research has contributed a dimension of insight, but it has substantial limitations in the multidimensional, holistic, and relational reality of the education of Indian people. It is the affective elements—the subjective experience and observations, the communal relationships, the artistic and mythical dimensions, the ritual and ceremony, the sacred ecology, the psychological and spiritual orientations—that have characterized and formed Indigenous education since time immemorial. These dimensions and their inherent meanings are not readily quantifiable, observable or easily verbalized, and as a result, have been given little credence in mainstream approaches to education and research. Yet, it is these aspects of indigenous orientation that form a profound context for learning through exploring the multidimensional relationships between humans and their inner and outer worlds.

For Indian educators, a key to dealing with the conflict between the objective and relational orientations, the cultural bias, and the cultural differences in perception lies in open communication and creative dialogue, which challenges the tacit infrastructure of ideas that guide Indian education today.

Education is essentially a communal social activity. Educational research that produces the most creatively productive insights involves communication within the whole educational community, not just authorities recognized by mainstream educational interests. Education is a communication process and plays an essential role in every act of educational perception. There must be a flow of communication regarding the educational process among all educators as a result of individual internal dialogue, publication, and the discussion of ideas.[4]

The ideas based on the tacit infrastructure of mainstream American education have been embraced in a relatively unexamined form by many educators. This situation, as it pertains to Indian education, limits creative acts of perception. A free play of thought and opening of the field must occur. It is only in realizing that there is a tacit infrastructure and then questioning it that a high level of creative thought can become possible regarding the potential of Indigenous educational philosophy. Only in realizing that American Indian perceptions of education have traditionally been informed by a different metaphor of teaching and learning can more productive insights into contemporary Indian education be developed.[5]

These traditional metaphors of education derive their meaning from unique cultural contexts and interactions with natural environments. In turn, the collective experiences of Indian people and their cultural adaptations have culminated in a body of shared metaphors regarding the nature of education and its essential ecology.

This exploration of Indigenous education attempts to develop insights into the community of shared metaphors and understandings that are specific to Indian cultures, yet reflect the nature of human learning as a whole. Traditional systems of Indian education represent ways of learning and doing through a Nature-centered philosophy. They are among the oldest continuing expressions of "environmental" education in the world. Taken as a whole, they represent an environmental education process with profound meaning for modern education as it faces the challenges of living in the twenty-first century. These processes have the potential to create deeper understanding of our collective role as caretakers of a world that we have thrown out of balance.

This book is essentially a continuation of my dissertation, *Science: A Native American Perspective (A Culturally Based Science Education Curriculum Model)* produced under the auspices of the New Philosophy Program of International College. The perceived needs that motivated my dissertation continue to form the impetus for this work. These needs are summarized as follows:

1. The need for a contemporary perspective of American Indian education that is principally derived from, and informed by, the thoughts, orientations, and cultural philosophies of Indian people themselves. The articulation and fulfillment of this need are, I believe, essential steps in Indian educational self-determination.

2. The need for exploring alternative approaches to education that directly and successfully address the requirements of Indian populations during this time of educational and ecological crisis. It is essential to open the field and entertain the possibilities of new approaches in a creative quest for viable and complete educational processes.

3. The need to integrate, synthesize, organize, and focus the accumulated materials from a wide range of disciplines about Indian cultures and Indian education toward the evolution of a contemporary philosophy for American Indian education that is Indigenously inspired and ecologically based.[6]

21

Contemporary American Indian education has focused on Indian people learning the skills necessary to be productive—or at least survive—in post-industrial American society. American Indians have been encouraged to be consumers in the tradition of the American dream and all that it entails. Indians have been encouraged to use modern education to progress by being participants in the system and seeking the rewards that success supposedly provides. Yet, in spite of many that have succeeded by embracing Western education, Indian people must question the effects modern education has had on their collective cultural, psychological, and ecological viability. What has been lost and what has been gained by participating in a system of education that does not honor unique Indigenous perspectives? How far can we go in adapting to such a system before that system literally educates Indian people out of cultural existence? Have Indian people reached the limits of what they can do with mainstream educational orientations? How can they re-envision and reestablish the ecology of education that formed and maintained Tribal societies?

Ironically, many creative Western thinkers have embraced essentially Indigenous environmental education views and are vigorously appropriating Indigenous concepts to support the development of their alternative models. For example, cultural historian and philosopher Thomas Berry proposes a new context for education that essentially reinvents the roles and contexts inherent to Indigenous education:

> The primary educator, as well as the primary law giver and primary healer would be the natural world itself. The integral earth community would be a self-educating community within the context of a self-educating universe. Education at the human level would be the conscious sensitizing of humans to the profound communications made by the universe about us, by the sun, the moon, and the stars, the clouds, the rain, the contours of the earth and all its living forms. All music and poetry of the universe would flow into the student; the revelatory presence of the divine, as well as insight into the architectural structures of the continents and the engineering skills whereby the great hydrological cycle functions in moderating the temperature of the earth, in providing habitat for aquatic life, in nourishing the multitude of living creatures would be as natural to the educational process. The earth would also be our primary teacher of sciences, especially biological sciences, and of industry and economics. It would teach us a system in which we would create a minimum of entropy, a system in which there is no unusable or unfruitful junk.

Only in such an integral system is the future viability of humans assured.[7]

Berry's comments mirror contemporized exposition of the Indigenous education processes of Tribal societies. It is within the light of such a vision that *this story* must unfold for Indian and non-Indian alike. If our collective future is to be harmonious and whole, *or* if we are even to have a viable future to pass on to our children's children, it is imperative that we actively envision and implement new ways of educating for ecological thinking and sustainability. The choice is ours, yet paradoxically we may have no choice.

Telling A Special Story

This book is about vision and the creative exploration of choices that American Indian education offers as we collectively "Look to the Mountain" searching for an ecology of education that can sustain us in the twenty-first century. This book explores a vision of education that unfolds through the tracking of a very special Story. The Story is about the unique ways of American Indian teaching and learning. It is honoring a process for seeking life that American Indian people represent and reflect through their special connections to Nature, family, community, and spiritual ecology. It is honoring connections and the place traditional teaching and learning have in American Indian life. This book maps a journey through shared metaphors and stops to recognize, appreciate, and contemplate traditional American Indian education, its implications for the future of American Indian children, and the Tribal cultures that they will carry into the twenty-first century.

In this journey we will focus upon a circle of relationships that mirror the seven orientation processes of preparing, asking, seeking, making, understanding, sharing, and celebrating the special wisdom of American Indian Tribal education. Environmental relationship, myth, visionary traditions, traditional arts, Tribal community, and Nature centered spirituality have traditionally formed the foundations in American Indian life for discovering one's true face (character, potential, identity), one's heart (soul, creative self, true passion), and one's foundation (true work, vocation), all of which lead to the expression of a complete life.

This work *outlines a way of perception and creative thought* as it relates to education. Like the proverbial Kokopeli, I wish to plant seeds of thought and deep reflection regarding the nature of Indigenous education. I wish to draw attention to a way of looking at and understanding a primal process of education grounded in the basics of human nature. It is a way of education that is pregnant

23

with potential, not only for the transformation of what is misnamed "Indian Education," but also for its profound applications toward transforming modern education. We must develop the openness and courage to take a creative leap to find in our lives a transformative vision for the sake of ourselves and our children.

This book expresses the experience of American Indian life that I have come to know. I am writing as an educator to other educators. I am writing in support of American Indian children, people, and communities. I am writing to empower their strength, courage, creativity, and the contributions they will make. I am writing for life's sake and with the understanding that:

Education is an art of process, participation, and making connection. Learning is a growth and life process; and Life and Nature are always relationships in process!

The Asking

❋ 1 ❋

INTRODUCTION

AMERICAN EDUCATION FROM A TRIBAL PERSPECTIVE

LEARNING IS ALWAYS A CREATIVE ACT. We are continuously engaged in the art of making meaning and creating our world through the unique processes of human learning. Learning for humans is instinctual, continuous, and the most complex of our natural traits. Learning is also a key to our ability to survive in the environments that we create and that create us.

Throughout history human societies have attempted to guide, facilitate, and even coerce the instinct for learning toward socially defined ends. The complex of activities for forming human learning is what we call "education." To this end, human societies have evolved a multitude of educational forms to maintain their survival and to use as vehicles for expressing their unique cultural mythos. Cultural mythos also forms the foundation for each culture's guiding vision, that is, a culture's story of itself and its perceived relationship to the world. In its guiding vision, a culture isolates a set of ideals that guide and form the learning processes inherent in its educational systems. In turn, these ideals reflect what that culture values as the most important qualities, behaviors, and value structures to instill in its members. Generally, this set of values is predicated on those things it considers central to its survival.

This book is a journey into the realm of cultural ideals from which the learning, teaching, and systems of education of Native America have evolved. As such, these ideals present a mirror reflecting on the critical dilemma of American education. While the legacy of American education is one of spectacular scientific and technological achievement resulting in abundant material prosperity, the cost has been inexorably high. American prosperity has come at the expense of the environment's degradation and has resulted in unprecedented exploitation of human and material resources worldwide.

Education is in crisis as America finds itself faced with unprecedented challenges in a global community of nations desperately struggling with massive social, economic, and cultural change. Education must find new ways of helping Americans learn and adapt in a multicultural, twenty-first century world. It must come to terms with the conditioning inherent in its educational systems that contribute to the loss of a shared integrative metaphor of *Life*. This loss, which may ultimately lead to a social/cultural/

ecological catastrophe, should be a key concern of every American.

The orchestrated "bottom-line, real world" chorus sung by many in business and government has become the common refrain of those who announce *they lead* the world. Yet, what underlies the crisis of American education is the crisis of modern man's identity and his cosmological disconnection from the natural world. Those who identify most with the bottom line often suffer from an image without substance, technique without soul, and knowledge without context. The cumulative psychological result is usually alienation, loss of community, and a deep sense of incompletness.

In contrast, traditional American Indian education historically occurred in a holistic social context that developed the importance of each individual as a contributing member of the social group. Tribal education sustained a wholesome life process. It was an educational process that unfolded through mutual, reciprocal relationships between one's social group and the natural world. This relationship involved all dimensions of one's being, while providing both personal development and technical skills through *participation* in community life. It was essentially a communally integrated expression of environmental education.

Understanding the depth of relationships and the significance of participation in all aspects of life are the keys to traditional American Indian education. *Mitakuye Oyasin* (we are all related) is a Lakota phrase that captures an essence of Tribal education because it reflects the understanding that our lives are truly and profoundly connected to other people and the physical world. In Tribal education, knowledge gained from first-hand experience in the world is transmitted or explored through ritual, ceremony, art, and appropriate technology. Knowledge gained through these vehicles is then used in everyday living. Education, in this context, becomes education for life's sake. Education is, at its essence, learning about life through participation and relationship in community, including not only people, but plants, animals, and the whole of Nature.

This ideal of education directly contrasts with the dominant orientation of American education that continues to emphasize objective content and experience detached from primary sources and community. This conditioning, to exist as a marginal participant and perpetual observer, is a foundational element of the crisis of American education and the alienation of modern man from his own being and the natural world.

In response to such a monumental crisis, American education must forge educational processes that *are* for Life's Sake and honor the Indigenous roots of America. A true transition of today's American educational orientations, to more sustainable and connected foundations, requires serious consideration of other cultural, life-enhancing, and ecologically viable forms of education.

Traditional American Indian forms of education must be considered conceptual wellsprings for the "new" kinds of educational thought that can address the tremendous challenges of the twenty-first century. Tribal education presents models and universal foundations to transform American education and develop a "new" paradigm for curricula that will make a difference for Life's Sake.

To begin such a process, American education must move from a focus on specialization to holistic knowledge; from a focus on structures to understanding processes, from objective science, to systemic science, and from building to networking.[1]

American education must rededicate its efforts to assist Americans in their understanding and appreciation of spirituality as it relates to the Earth and the place in which they live. It must engender a commitment to service rather than competition, promote respect for individual, cultural and biological diversity, and engage students in learning processes that facilitate the development of their human potential through creative transformation.

American Indians have struggled to adapt to an educational process that is not their own. Yet, American Indian cultural forms of education contain seeds for new models of educating that can enliven American education as a whole, and allow American Indians to evolve contemporary expressions of education tied to their cultural roots. For American Indians, a new Circle of education must begin, rooted in Tribal education and reflecting the needs, values, and socio/political issues Indian people perceive.

As Indian educator Eber Hampton so aptly states, this new circle must encompass the importance Indian people place on the continuance of their ancestral traditions, respect individual uniqueness in spiritual expression, facilitate an understanding within the context of history and culture, develop a strong sense of place and service to community, and forge a commitment to educational and social transformation that recognizes and further empowers the inherent strength of Indian people and their cultures.[2]

To accomplish this, Indian people must open avenues of communication and establish a reflective dialogue toward evolving a contemporary theory for Indian education that originates from them and their collective experience.

Politicians and institutions have largely defined Indian education through a volume of legislative acts at the state and federal levels. For decades, this has entangled Indian leaders, educators and whole communities in the government's social/political bureaucracy.

Historically, Indian education stems more from the U.S. government's self-serving political relationship with Indian tribes than any cultural process rooted in Tribal philosophies and social values. No recognizable contemporary theory of Indian education exists to guide the implementation or direction of educational curriculum development. Instead what is called "Indian education" today is a "compendium of models, methodologies and techniques gleaned from various sources in mainstream American education and adapted to American Indian circumstances, usually with the underlying aim of cultural assimilation."[3]

It is time for Indian people to define Indian education in their own voices and in their own terms. It is time for Indian people to enable themselves to explore and express the richness of their collective history in education. Education for Indian people has been, and continues to be, a grand story, a search for meaning, an essential food for the soul.

Building On Earlier Realities

The Mayan practice of building one pyramidal structure by encasing a pervious one provides an appropriate metaphor for the developmental building process of Indigenous education.

At the end of each Mayan dynasty, the nobles of the ascending dynasty would commemorate their new order by erecting a symbolic new reality. They would build a new ceremonial pyramid by encasing an older one.

This new structure became the visible symbolic expression through which they espoused the new reality. As is evident from current excavations, these successive facades recycled many of the materials used previously in the structures. A constant building upon earlier realities is a basic characteristic of Indigenous process. The newest reality may seem different from earlier ones, but its essence and foundation remain tied to the earlier realities it encases. The pyramids are restructured and enlarged, but their ancient foundations remain.

Many temple pyramids served as tombs for the noble elite of each dynasty. The practice of burrowing into the heart of a pyramid to place a tomb metaphorically connected the deceased noble to the realities of both past and present.

Building on the realities of past generations and expressing new realities, while remaining true to basic principles, reflects the structuring process natural to the evolution of Indigenous education. Extending the metaphor of the Mayan pyramids to building a contemporary Indigenous education, we engineer the new reality built upon earlier ones, while simultaneously addressing the needs, and acting in the sun, of our times.

Education is always in process and is being built from the stones, and upon the foundations, of prior structures. Indigenous education has prior structures, i.e., stones and foundations from which it can again be built. The following chapters describe these foundations of Indigenous education and some of the "stones" from which they are made.

Foundational Characteristics of Indigenous Education

There are a number of elements that characterize Indigenous educational processes. These elements characterize Indigenous education wherever and however it has been expressed. They are like the living stones, the "Inyan" as the Lakota term it, which animate and support the expressions of Indigenous education. A few of these characteristics are included here to provide landmarks for the reader.[4]

- A sacred view of Nature permeates its foundational process of teaching and learning.

- Integration and interconnectedness are universal traits of its contexts and processes.

- Its elements, activities, and knowledge bases of teaching and learning radiate in concentric rings of process and relationship.

- Its processes adhere to the principle of mutual reciprocity between humans and all other things.

- It recognizes and incorporates the principle of cycles within cycles (there are deeper levels of meaning to be found in every learning/teaching process).

- It presents something for everyone to learn, at every stage of life.

- It recognizes the levels of maturity and readiness to learn in the developmental processes of both males and females. This recognition is incorporated into the designs and situations in which Indigenous teaching takes place.

- It recognizes language as a sacred expression of breath and incorporates this orientation in all its foundations.

- It recognizes that each person and each culture contains the seeds that are essential to their well-being and positive development.

- Art is a vehicle of utility and expression. It is recognized as an expression of the soul and a way of connecting people to their inner sources of life.

- The ritual complex is both structure and process for teaching key spiritual and cultural principles and values.

- It recognizes that the true sources of knowledge are found within the individual and the entities of Nature.

- It recognizes that true learning occurs through participation and honoring relationships in both the human and natural communities.

- It honors the ebb and flow of learning as it moves through individuals, community, Nature, and the cosmos.

- It recognizes that learning requires letting go, growing, and re-integrating at successively higher levels of understanding.

- Its purpose is to teach a way of life that sustains both the individual and the community.

- It unfolds within an authentic context of community and Nature.

- It uses *story* as a way to root a perspective that unfolds through the special use of language.

- *Story*, expressed through experience, myth, parables, and various forms of metaphor is an essential vehicle of Indigenous learning.

- It recognizes the power of thought and language to create the worlds we live in.

- It creates maps of the world that assist us through our life's journey.

- It resonates and builds learning through the Tribal structures of the home and community.

- Indigenous thinking adheres to the most subtle, yet deeply rooted, universals and principles of human learning.

- It integrates human individuality with communal needs..

- It is founded upon successive stages of learning, i.e., how to see, feel, listen, and act.

- It honors each person's way of being, doing, and understanding.

- It recognizes that we learn by watching and doing, reflecting on what we are doing, then doing again.

- It is always grounded in the natural basics of life.

- Indigenous thinking recognizes that learning is complete only if it starts from the beginning and follows through. One skill builds on another, but the basics must always be honored. Learning is step by step.

- It recognizes that learning and teaching require overcoming doubt.

- It honors the fact that learning requires seeing what is real about a situation, a thing, or an entity.

- It recognizes that learning is about seeing the whole through the parts.

- It honors the fact that true learning builds your self-confidence by coming to understand who you really are and living to your full potential.

- Indigenous thinking honors the reality that there are always two sides to the two sides. There are realities and realities. Learning how they interact is real understanding.

- It recognizes that thinking and learning who one is can be accomplished by learning who one is not!

- We learn through our bodies and spirits as much as through our minds.

- From the Indigenous perspective, the purpose of training in learning and thinking is to bring forth your personal power; training develops your personal power through focused attention, repetition, and context.

- Indigenous people recognize that personal power, learning and thinking are expressed through doing. Therefore, learning the doing is an essential process.

- It recognizes that culture and its reality are invested anew with each generation.

- Indigenous teaching mirrors thinking back to the learner.

- Indigenous teaching emphasizes seeing things comprehensively: seeing things through and through.

- The *orientation* of Indigenous learning flows from expectation, through exchange and context, to application of experience and vision.

These essential points are reflected throughout the contexts, methods, and expressions of Indigenous education presented in this book. They can provide building stones for new structures, new foundations, and new realities in contemporary Indian education. The key lies in our collective ability to create the contexts and to erect a new expression of Indian education in a twenty-first century world. We are the architects of our future!

FINDING FACE, FINDING HEART, AND FINDING A FOUNDATION

AN OVERVIEW OF TRIBAL EDUCATION

THE EXPRESSIONS OF AMERICAN INDIAN EDUCATION reflect traits shared by the Indigenous cultures of the world. They are expressions of the ancestral Tribal roots of all the families of man.

In exploring the Tribal foundations of American Indian education we are tracking the earliest sources of human teaching and learning. These foundations teach us that learning is a subjective experience tied to a place environmentally, socially, and spiritually. Tribal teaching and learning were intertwined with the daily lives of both teacher and learner. Tribal education was a natural outcome of living in close communion with each other and the natural environment.

The living place, the learner's extended family, the clan and tribe provided the context and source for teaching. In this way, every situation provided a potential opportunity for learning, and basic education was not separated from the natural, social, or spiritual aspects of everyday life. Living and learning were fully integrated.

The ideals of this process were naturally founded on the continuous development of self-knowledge, on finding life through understanding and participating in the creative process of living, on direct awareness of the natural environment, on knowledge of one's role and responsibility to community, and on cultivating a sensitivity to the spiritual essences of the world. To attain such ideals required participation in a shared cultural metaphor and the continuity of knowledge, perception, experience, and wisdom afforded through the understanding and experience of Tribal elders.

The cultivation of all one's senses through learning how to listen, observe, and experience holistically by creative exploration was highly valued. In addition, the ability to use language through storytelling, oratory, and song was highly regarded by all tribes as a primary tool for teaching and learning. This was because the spoken or sung word expressed the spirit and breath of life of the speaker, and thus was considered sacred.

Informality characterized the greater part of American Indian teaching and learning, since most traditional knowledge was within the context of the day-to-day life experience of the people. However, formal learning was usually required in the transfer of sacred knowledge. Therefore, various ceremonial practices, founded upon experience and participation in Tribal culture, formed a complex for the formal teaching and learning of this knowledge. Initiation rites occurred at graduated stages of growth and maturation. Important initiation ceremonies and accompanying formal education were integrated with the natural physical and psychological transitions occurring at the end of early childhood, puberty, early, middle, late adulthood, and old age. Ceremony was a life-long introduction to sacred and environmental knowledge, graduated so individuals were presented new levels of knowledge when they were physically, psychologically, and socially ready to learn them.[1]

Hah oh is a Tewa word sometimes used to connote the process of learning.[2] Its closest English translation is to "breathe in." *Hah oh* is a shared metaphor describing the perception of traditional Tribal teaching—a process of breathing in—that was creatively and ingeniously applied by all tribes. As a whole, traditional Tribal education revolved around experiential learning (learning by doing or seeing), storytelling (learning by listening and imagining), ritual/ceremony (learning through initiation), dreaming (learning through unconscious imagery), tutoring (learning through apprenticeship), and artistic creation (learning through creative synthesis). Through these methods the integration of inner and outer realities of learners and teachers was fully honored, and the complementary educational processes of both realities were fully engaged.[3]

The legacy of the traditional forms of American Indian education is significant because it embodies a quest for self, individual and community survival, and wholeness in the context of a community and natural environment. Tribal/Indigenous education is really endogenous education, in that it educates the inner self through enlivenment and illumination from one's own being and the learning of key relationships. Therefore, the foundations for Tribal/Indigenous education naturally rest upon increasing awareness and development of innate human potentials. Based on this orientation, American Indians and other Indigenous groups used ritual, myth, customs, and life experience to integrate both the process and content of learning into the fabric of their social organizations. This promoted wholeness in the individual, family, and community.[4]

This approach to educating is represented metaphorically in a phrase used by nearly all American Indians that, roughly translated, means 'seeking life' or 'for life's sake'. The ideal purpose of education is to attain knowledge, seek truth, wisdom, completeness, and life as perceived by traditional philosophies and cultures around the world.

Education As Flower and Song: A Tribal Metaphor

In the tradition of the Nahuatl speaking Aztec of Mexico, the ideal purpose of education was to: "find one's face, find one's heart" and search for a "foundation", a truth, a support, a way of life and work through which one could express one's Life. The Aztec developed schools called the "Calmecac" in which the tlamatinimine, the philosopher poets of Aztec society, taught by using poetic chants called "flower and song". Through formal and informal methods, the tlamatinimine encouraged their students to find their face (develop and express their innate character and potential); to find their heart (search out and express their inner passion); and to explore foundations of life and work (find the vocation that allowed the student the fullest expression of self and truth). The tlamatinimine led his students on many paths of study, including astronomy, architecture, religion, martial arts, medicine, philosophy, and various other cultural art forms.[5]

The tlamatinimine explored with their students the mystery of life after death. They studied man as a creator of a way of life, and man as the creator of educational, ethical, legal, and aesthetic principles. They explored the nature of the social and personal ideals that gave rise to the divine spark in man's heart and transformed him into an artist, a poet, a sage.[6]

The Aztec quest for expressing each student's gift in service to their community made them capable of creating divine things and being a complete man or woman. This recurring theme of Indigenous education has variations in ancient cultures around the world.

Just as the Greek concept of *paideia* or educating for wholeness through teaching and learning of *arete* (enabling expressions of human life), the Aztecs molded their young according to an ideal. While this ideal was culturally defined by Aztec thought and tradition, it engendered an approach to educating commonly practiced by Indian people throughout the Americas. The Aztec Calmecac exemplified an essence of Tribal/Indigenous education that serves as both an ideal and a challenge for the design and development of modern educational curricula. Other examples of Tribal educational metaphors exist reflecting a richness and depth of understanding of human learning. Whether one views traditional Iroquois, Sioux, Pueblo, Navajo, or Huichol ways of knowing and learning, the pattern is the same: unity through diversity. Indian people are all related. Tribal ways reflect a natural diversity of expression of basic principles and foundations. Regardless of Tribal culture, Indians of the Americas share common metaphors of Indigenous knowledge and education. It is because of such shared metaphors that the development of a contemporary Indigenous philosophy of Indian Education is possible. Developing an understanding of what the shared metaphor is, with its common foundations and ideals, marks the first step in this new stage of the ancient journey of Indian people in America.

Foundations of American Indigenous Education

Indians throughout the Americas incorporate many symbolic expressions reflecting the metaphysical, ecological, and cultural constructs of Tribal education. These include symbolic expressions representing the: Tree of Life, Earth Mother, Sun Father, Sacred Twins, Mother of Game or Corn, Old Man, Trickster, Holy Wind, For Life's Sake, We Are All Related, Completed Man/ Woman, The Great Mystery, Life Way, and Sacred Directions. These expressions, which occur in a variety of forms in many American Indian languages, reflect common understandings and shared foundations for traditional ways of learning. Behind these mythic metaphors are the philosophical infrastructures and fields of Tribal knowledge that lie at the heart of American Indian epistemologies. For instance, among the Iroquois, the "Tree of Life" and its "white roots of peace" form a rich matrix of interrelated myths that present not only Iroquoian traditional knowledge but truths recognized by other tribes. The Iroquoian myth of the "Great Turtle" is an archetypal "Earth Mother" tale that embodies the understanding of the whole Earth as a living, breathing, and knowing entity who nourishes and provides for every living thing through its own magnificent life process. Earth Mother's counterpart in maintaining life, the Sun Father, appears in key roles in such myths as Scar Face among the Blackfoot and the Old Man of the Crystal House among the Chumash.

In the myth of Scar Face, the Sun places a horrible scar on the face of his grandson as punishment for his daughter's (the Moon) disobedience. Sun banishes the child from the Star World to live on earth with human beings. The child is found and raised by a kindly couple who have no children of their own. Scar Face grows into a fine young man, kind, courageous, and compassionate. Yet, he is a lonely boy set apart from other boys by his scar and his knowledge that he is an orphan. Upon learning that his father lives far to the West in the land of the Star People, he embarks on an epic journey through which he finds not only his father, Morning Star, and his mother, the Moon, but so impresses his grandfather, the Sun, with his feats of courage, that he is given the knowledge and rituals of the Sweat Lodge and the Sun Dance. Scar Face returns to Earth and shares the sacred knowledge of the Sweat Lodge with his people, takes a wife, and returns to live in the land of the Star People.[7]

The tale of Scar Face is an archetypal hero myth that reflects the perception of the Sun as the cosmic father, as a giver of life, health, and knowledge. The Sun inseminates, illuminates, nourishes, and sustains life. The myth of Scar Face personifies the central role of the Sun as a life giver while reflecting the Sun's power to destroy and punish if not properly respected.

Among the Chumash, the Sun, or as they refer to him, Old Man of the Crystal House, was considered a powerful spiritual being who carried a torch across the sky to light and warm the earth. He lived in the East in a house made of crystal with his two daughters, Morning and Evening Star, who could be seen sometime in the pre-dawn morning waking him, or the evening bidding him to return. Although the Sun ensured life with his light and warmth, he was also known to cause death. During his travel across the sky, he would collect people, plants, and animals to eat for his supper. Every Winter, the Sun would grow weary and want to stop his traveling. He could be seen moving further and further south and giving less light and warmth. Chumash astronomer/priests would gather their people and hold elaborate ceremonies to pull the sun back for another year and thereby restore the world to its rightful orientation.[8]

These myths, and the variety of myths related to other symbolic complexes, present the Nature centered orientation of Indigenous education in the Americas. *Rightful orientation* to the natural world is the primary message and intent of the mythic perception symbolized by the sacred directions among American Indians. The majority of American Indian tribes recognize seven sacred or elemental directions. These directions include East, West, North, South, Zenith, Nadir, and the Center. Through deep understanding and expression of the metaphoric meaning of these orientations, American Indians have intimately defined their *place* in the Universe.

By perceiving themselves in the *middle* of these directions, they oriented themselves to the multidimensional field of knowledge and the phenomena of their physical and spiritual worlds. Individual tribes named and associated symbols with each direction that characterized their perceptions and experience. These symbols included natural phenomena, colors, animals, plants, spirits, and holy winds (kinds of thought).

Extending the environmental orientation inherent in these sacred directions to education, there are elemental, yet highly integrated, kinds of thought founding the vehicles and contexts of Indigenous education.

These orienting foundations of spiritual ecology include: the Environmental, the Mythic, the Artistic/Visionary, and the Affective/ Communal.

In traditional life, these foundations intimately relate to act relativistically at all levels of their expression. In every sense, they *contain* each other so that exploration of any one can *take* you into the heart of the Tribal educational experience. There is a balance occurring in the interplay of these foundations. This balance is illustrated by the interplay of foundations within the environmental and spiritual fields of experience. An ebb and flow characterizes the interplay among foundations. The structure of these interactions is represented in the following diagram.

The Ebb and Flow of Tribal Education

The Mythic, Visionary and Artistic foundations form a triad which interacts with the triad formed by the Environmental, Affective and Communal Foundations. These two triads are integrated by the seventh foundation of the Spiritual/ Ecological. The ebb and flow of these foundations unfolds through the environmental context and cycles of winter and summer.

Foundations of Tribal Education

The *Spiritual Ecology* of Tribal education is both a foundational process and field through which traditional American Indian education occurs. For Indigenous people, Nature and all it contains formed the parameters of the school. Each foundation of Tribal education is exquisitely complex. Dynamic contexts develop from a unique and creative process of teaching and learning.

The Mythic, Visionary, and Artistic foundations form a natural triad of tools, practices, and ways of teaching/learning. Through their interaction and play, they form a fourth dimension for the deep understanding of our inner being. This triad of foundations springs forth from teaching/learning and the innate knowledge of our inner self. It is the Winter Element or the deeply inward aspect of Indigenous education. The Affective, Communal, and Environmental foundations complement the understanding of the other triad of tools, practices, and ways of teaching/learning. These foundations are the Summer Element or the outward, highly interactive and external dimension of Tribal education.

In traditional American Indian life, the foremost context for understanding is the *Spiritual*, the orienting foundation of Indigenous knowledge and process. It is the spiritual that forms not only the foundation for religious expression, but also the ecological psychology underpinning the other foundations.

The *Environmental* foundation forms a context to observe and integrate those understandings, bodies of knowledge, and practices resulting from direct interaction with the natural world. This foundation *connects* a tribe to their *place*, establishing their relationship to their land and the earth in their minds and hearts. To say American Indians were America's first practical ecologists is a simplification of a deep sense of ecological awareness and state of being. The environmental foundation of Tribal education reflects a deeper level of teaching and learning than simply making a living from the natural world. For American Indians, as with other Nature centered Indigenous cultures around the world, the natural environment *was* the essential reality, the "place of being". Nature was taught and understood *in* and *on* its own terms.

Based on the environmental foundation of Tribal education, a mutual-reciprocal relationship was established and perpetuated between Tribal people and their environment. "Nature was used—beaver, bison, etc.—for sustenance, but richness of ends was achieved with material technology that was elegant, sophisticated, appropriate, and controlled within the context of the traditional society."[9]

The *Mythic* foundation rests upon the archetypal stories that describe the cosmology in the tribe's language and cultural metaphors. This foundation explores the guiding thoughts, dreams, explanations, and orientations to the world. It represents the world view of the tribe and, through the process of storytelling, presents the script for teaching, learning, and participating in stories that guide the people. Ultimately, all education is the expression of storytelling.

The *Visionary* foundation rests upon individual psychological and spiritual experiences that lead to, or result from the practices, rituals, and ceremonies of a tribe. Such practices and contexts provide a framework for individuals and groups to teach and learn through exploring their inner psychology and their collective unconscious. American Indians applied the visionary foundation to access knowledge from primary sources deep within themselves and the natural world.

The *Artistic* foundation and the Visionary contain the external practices, mediums, and forms through which we express the understandings we have come to see. Art allows us to symbolize knowledge, understanding, and feeling through image, thus making it possible to transcend a finite time and culture. Art becomes a primary source of teaching since it integrates and documents an internal process of learning. Art was such an integral part of American Indian life that it was not perceived as an isolated, self-sufficient, phenomenon. Consequently, there are no words in the Indian languages that can be translated exactly to mean "Art". The closest translations into English usually refer to "making" or "completing". The Artistic foundation also acts as a bridging/translating foundation for the Mythic and Visionary foundations. That is, the Artistic *mediates* the other two.

The *Affective* foundation of Tribal education forms a second context containing the internal emotional response to learning, living, growing, and understanding in relationship to the world, ourselves, and each other. This is the foundation on which we establish rapport with what we are learning and come to understand why we are learning. It reflects our whole gamut of emotion relating to the educational process. It is the seat of our primary motivation and the way we establish personal or group meaning for our learning. It is the foundation through which we cultivate our intention, choice, trust, responsibility, and heart for learning. Like the Artistic foundation, the Affective foundation acts as a bridge between the environmental and communal foundations. It mediates our feelings for our place and our community. For American Indians, love for one's land and people has always been a primary motivation for learning and service to one's tribe.

The *Communal* foundation is paired with the Affective and forms a third context that contains the external responses and experiences reflecting the social/communal dimension of Tribal education. The life of the community and its individuals are the primary focus of Tribal education. The community is the primary context, through the family, clan or other Tribal social structures, where the first dimensions of education unfold for all human beings. All humans are social animals who directly depend on each other, not only for their mutual survival but their identity as well. The Communal experience is the seat of human cultures, and there is nothing in human life that it does not influence. The Communal experience is tied through history and tradition to the oldest instinctual human mediums of education. The structure, process, and content of teaching and learning resulting from traditional American Indian Tribal/communal experience are inherently Human. Learning and teaching are occurring at all times, at all levels, and in a variety of situations. For American Indian Tribal education, the community is a primary context for learning to be "a human, one of the People."

A value many Indian people share is that their stories, languages, customs, songs, dances, and ways of thinking and learning must be preserved because they sustain the life of the individual, family, and community. It is especially the stories that integrate the life experience and reflect the essence of the people's sense of spiritual being; it is the mythic stories of a people that form the script for cultural process and experience.

Culture is the face, myth is the heart, and traditional education is the foundation for Indigenous life. All cultures have Indigenous roots bedded in the rich soil of myth from which the most elemental stories of human life spring.

Indian elders often remind young people to *live the myths* by saying, "These stories, this language, these ways, and this land are the only valuables we can give you — but life is in them for those who know how to ask and how to learn."

The metaphor for this seeking is coded in the Tewa phrase, *Pin Peyé Obe*: 'Look to the Mountain!' Reconnecting contemporary Indian education to its mythic roots begins with looking to the cardinal mountains of thought from which our stories come and to which they return.

With or without our conscious participation, a new story of education is emerging. Understanding the plot of this new story is an important task for forging an Indigenous philosophy of American Indian education that will ensure cultural survival in the twenty-first century.

❋ III ❋

FOR LIFE'S SAKE

THE SPIRITUAL ECOLOGY OF INDIGENOUS EDUCATION

Introduction

INDIGENOUS EDUCATION, AT ITS INNERMOST CORE, is education about the life and nature of the spirit that moves us. Spirituality evolves from exploring and coming to know and experience the nature of the living energy moving in each of us, through us, and around us. The ultimate goal of Indigenous education was to be fully knowledgeable about one's innate spirituality. This was considered completeness in its most profound form. It is no accident that learning and teaching unfolded in the context of spirituality in practically every aspect of traditional American Indian education. Nowhere else in the study of American Indian cultures is the principle of unity in diversity more clearly illustrated than in American Indian spiritual traditions. Though American Indian tribes represent diverse expressions of spirituality, there are elemental understandings held in common by all. It is these shared understandings that allow development of a foundation for Indian education, including contemporary philosophy, whose principles can generally be accepted by all tribes. A shared set of structures and tools for learning about spirit was used in similar ways by different tribes. The roles and structures of shamanism, the making of sacred art, the use of the sweat lodge, the reflection of the cosmos in a tribe's central ceremonial structures, vision questing, ceremonies, rituals, and dances tied to Nature's cycles are a few examples. Added to these are a group of shared metaphors and concepts that found unique expressions in different regions and tribes, but were derived from a similar understanding and orientation to life.

For example, American Indians believe it is the breath that represents the most tangible expression of the spirit in all living things. Language is an expression of the spirit because it contains the power to move people and to express human thought and feeling. It is also the breath, along with water and thought, that connects all living things in direct relationship. The interrelationship of water, thought (wind), and breath personifies the elemental relationship emanating from "that place that the Indians talk about," that place of the Center where all things are created.

I can remember the first time I heard the phrase, "that's the place

Indians talk about." It was a phrase repeated by Acoma Pueblo poet, Simon Ortiz, in a wonderful story about the spiritual connections Indian people feel to the special places in their lands and their lives. By talking about those special places, they connected their spirit to them through their words, thoughts, and feelings. I remember thinking how beautifully simple, yet how profound, this metaphor was. It illustrates the special quality and power the spirit has to orient us through the breath of its manifestations in language, song, prayer, and thought.

Imbued with the perception that all things are sacred, traditional education, from the moment of conception to beyond the moment of death, was learning the true nature of one's spirit. This learning began by reflecting upon the nature of human and community expression through the understanding and use of breath in all its forms. This understanding went beyond the physical nature of breath to include the perception of thought as a "wind" that was a unique variation of breath. Language and song were other forms of breath that formed a holistic foundation for communication. Breath—consciously formed and activated through language, thought, prayer, chanting, ritual, dance, sport, work, story, play, and art—comprised the parameters of communication in Tribal education.

This tradition of communicating about and for spiritual ecology has continued evolving for thousands of years as a way to seek and find one's life, one's completeness. Among American Indians this tradition of educating and expressing the spiritual has evolved into many forms reflecting the transformations of the People. Given the diversity and richness of American Indian spiritual traditions, it is impossible and misleading to reduce them to simple descriptions. However, they come from primal roots and continue to express universal perceptions and concepts.

This chapter explores some basic concepts of American Indian spiritual traditions that connect all tribes at the level of spiritual ecology. As mentioned earlier, American Indian traditions revolve around seeking life and communicating with the various manifestations of breath to realize a higher level of completeness in life's journey. What is called education today was, for American Indians, a journey for learning to be fully human. Learning about the nature of the spirit in relationship to community and the environment was considered central to learning the full meaning of life.

There are five elements that generally characterized American Indian spiritual traditions. First, there is the lack of an espoused doctrine of religion. Indian languages lack a word for "religion." The words used refer to a "way" of living, a tradition of the people. This reflects the orientation of American Indian spiritual traditions to a process rather than to an intellectual structure. These are tools for learning and experiencing rather than ends in themselves.

Second, there is the idea that spoken words and language have a quality of spirit because they are an expression of human breath. Language as prayer and song has a life energy that can influence other energy and life forms toward certain ends. For American Indians, language used in a spiritual, evocative, or affective context is sacred and is to be used responsibly.

Third, the creative act of making something with spiritual intent, what today is called art, has its own quality and spiritual power that needs to be understood and respected. Art is a result of a creative process that, traditionally for American Indians, was an act and expression of the spirit. Art was sacred.

Fourth, life and spirit, the dual faces of the Great Mystery, move in never-ending cycles of creation and dissolution. Therefore, ceremonial forms, life activities, and the transformations of spirit are cyclical. These cycles follow the visible and invisible patterns of Nature and the cosmos. In response to this creative principle, ritual cycles are used to structure and express the sacred in the communal context of traditional Native American life.

Fifth, is the shared understanding that Nature is the true ground of spiritual reality. The natural forms and forces are expressions of spirit whose qualities interpenetrate the life and process of human spirituality. For American Indians and Indigenous people as a whole, Nature is Sacred and its Spiritual Ecology is reflected throughout.[1]

Most Indian tribes share basic understandings about sacred knowledge. These include the understanding that a universal energy infuses everything in the cosmos and expresses itself through a multitude of manifestations. This also includes the recognition that all life has power that is wondrous and full of spirit. This is the Great Soul or the Great Mystery or the Great Dream that cannot be explained or understood with the intellect, but can be perceived only by the spirit of each person.

The next perception is that all things and all thoughts are related through spirit. Personal and direct communication with all the manifestations of spirit through prayer and ritual reinforces the bond of the individual, family, clan, and community to the unseen power of the Great Mystery. Knowledge and understanding of morals and ethics are a direct result of spiritual experiences. Sacred traditions and the elders who possess special teachings act as bridges to spiritual experiences and as facilitators for learning about spiritual matters. This is the basis of the elders' standing and respect in the tribe or community, as long as they use their knowledge for the good of the people.

Finally, people must constantly be aware of their weakness and strive to become wise in the ways that they live their lives. Through story, humor, and ritual, people "remember to remember" who they are, where they come from, and the spirit they share with all of creation.[2]

In relation to these characteristics, this chapter will explore four basic concepts that informed the expression of the spiritual dimension of Indigenous education. These are: the interrelated concepts of "seeking life" and "becoming complete", the concept of the "highest thought", the concept of "orientation", and the concept of "pathway".

To illustrate these concepts an aspect of a selected tribe will describe and place in context the essential features of each. These are descriptive examples and are not comprehensive. Tribal people and scholars of American Indian traditions will no doubt perceive similar expressions in their own cultural traditions or those they have studied. Each example provides a glimpse of a core dynamic of learning about spiritual ecology, seeking life, and "that place the Indians talk about."

Seeking Life and Becoming Complete

The way we talk about a place or another entity reflects how we feel, how we see, how we understand, and most importantly, how we think about it. Language is a reflection of how we organize and perceive the world. In every language there are key words, phrases, and metaphors that act as sign posts to the way we think about the world and ourselves.

Indian languages are richly diverse in their expressions related to how they structure the world. As is true with all languages, Indian metaphors reflect the nature of the reality they see and to which their mind has been set through experience and cultural understanding. In spite of the diversity of Indian languages and the potential for infinite ways of thinking about reality, there are metaphors that can be consistently translated to mean a similar thought.

The phrases seeking life, for life's sake, to find life, to complete, to become complete, of good heart, of good thought, with harmony, and a host of related combinations, have translations in all Indian languages. These are the metaphors that Indian people use in talking about themselves, their places, and their relationships. They are phrases used to begin and end communal events, in ritual prayers, in stories, in oratory, as greetings, in conversation, and in teaching. They are phrases for "remembering to remember" why things are done individually and in community. These shared metaphors reflect an underlying continuity of thought and perception that have a profound influence on the aims of traditional Indian education. They imply a journey of learning to know life in all its manifestations—especially those of the spirit—and through this journey experience a state of wholeness. Seeking, finding, being with, and celebrating spiritual ecology is the essential meaning of the phrase "that's the place Indian people talk about."

As a guiding concept, "seeking life and becoming complete" pervades the expressions of Native American spirituality to such an extent that it is seldom discussed or questioned. Historically, this was the world view that guided thought and behavior. The extent to which this guiding concept was internalized compares with the pervasive internalization of capitalism and the consumer mindset of modern Americans. Capitalism and consumerism are so ingrained in the American "real world" that they are seldom questioned as foundations of human life. Materialism and an objective sense of physical reality predominate the mindset of most modern people. For many moderns, this orientation has become a theology of money, treated as sacred and strived for religiously. For American Indians and other Indigenous people, Spirit and Nature were the real world, the ground of existence upon which they formed a theology of Nature that has evolved and matured over the last forty thousand years.

The theology of Nature based on "seeking life and becoming complete" forms the boundaries of this exploration of the spiritual ecology of Indigenous education.

Thinking the Highest Thought

The Indigenous ideal of living "a good life" in Indian traditions is at times referred to by Indian people as striving "to always think the highest thought." This metaphor refers to the framework of a sophisticated epistemology of community based ecological education. This is an epistemology in which the community and its mythically authenticated traditions support a way of life and quality of thinking that embodies an ecologically-informed consciousness.

Thinking the highest thought means thinking of one's self, one's community, and one's environment richly. This thinking in the highest, most respectful, and compassionate way systematically influences the actions of both individuals and the community. It is a way to perpetuate "a good life," a respectful and spiritual life, a wholesome life. Thus, the community becomes a center for teaching and a context for learning how to live ecologically.

In Indigenous societies, living ecologically is also about living in harmonious relationship to "a place." The origins of this special and essentially ecological relationship are usually represented in the guiding story, the central myth which the group holds sacred. The community embodies the essence of that "place," which is really the place of the spirit referred to in the guiding myth. Through their central myth, each Indigenous community identifies itself as a sacred place, a place of living, learning, teaching, and renewal; a place where the "People" share the breath of their life and thought. The community is a living, spiritual entity that is supported by every responsible adult.

In striving to think the highest thought and reach that place the "People" talk about, each adult becomes a teacher and a student. Because learning to think the highest thought and reconnect with that special "place" of mythic times is a step-by-step process that begins at birth; each individual, from the youngest to oldest, has a role to play.

There are types of thinking and knowing that are developmental and form the essential steps to thinking the highest thought. Each step must be learned and honored in order to reach that special place of ecological understanding and relationship. Learning about each step is life-long and one overlaps the other through time and levels of knowing. Each contains the others and shares concentric rings of relationship. Yet, each has its unique lessons.

Based on this perspective, the first way of thinking and knowing has to do with one's physical place. That is, one has to come to terms with where one physically lives. One has to know one's home, one's village, and then the land, the earth upon which one lives. These are the hills, canyons, valleys, forests, mountains, streams, rivers, plains, deserts, lakes, and seas—the place where you live, awareness of your physical environment.[3]

For Indigenous people, this first type of thought begins the extension and integration of connections with Nature and other people in the community. It is thinking that orients them to the ecology of the place immediately surrounding them. As a way of knowing, thinking, and orienting, it proceeds in concentric rings from the location of the family household, to the segment of the village the household is located in, to the village as a whole, to the land immediately surrounding the village, then to the mountains or other geographic features that form the recognized boundaries of each Indigenous group's territory.

Indigenous villages generally have a Center and several sections that define where its various family or clan groups live. These groupings represent the basic mythic and social divisions of each village. Each village household is a unique expression of a family and an orientation shared by members of each family. The clans and village proper form an orientation and way of thinking and learning about place that is represented by each successively larger group. The experiences and thinking in relation to the immediate natural environment are also shared. These are the basic dimensions of the first way of thinking and knowing. For Indigenous people, thinking and knowing about the spiritual ecology begins in the family, village, and its natural location.

A second kind of Indigenous thought occurs in relationship to other people, plants, animals, natural elements, and phenomena. This type of thought and knowing revolves around consciously understanding the nature of one's relationships to other people, other life, and the natural world. This is a way of self-knowing and defining of spirit that is based in our senses and our emotions. It is a way of thinking that allows us to experience and understand the differences and similarities between the life in ourselves, other living things, and other entities of the natural world.

This way of thinking is based on the physical senses and developing the ability to hear, observe, perceive, and emotionally feel the spirit moving in all its manifestation in the world around us. For traditional Indigenous people around the world, *Spirit is real.* It is physically expressed in everything that exists in the world.

A third way of Indigenous thought has to do with reflective contemplation, speaking, and acting. This involves applying the capacity to think things through completely, to make wise choices, to speak responsibly for purpose and effect, and to act decisively to produce something that is useful and has spirit. This kind of thought also has to do with the expression of respect, ethics, morals, and proper behavior—all of which lead to the development of humility. This way of thinking brings forth the best and most desirable aspect of humanness as a proper response to learning about and dealing with the natural world.

A fourth way of thought regards the kind of knowing that has long experience with all aspects of human life. This way of thought requires a learning that comes only from maturity. It leads to a knowing that includes, but also moves beyond knowing just through the physical senses towards wisdom. Wisdom is a complex state of knowing founded on accumulated experience. In Tribal societies, wisdom is the realm of the elderly. By virtue of their long life experience, they were deemed most capable of maintaining the essential structures of the spiritual life and well-being of the community. They maintain the Tribal memories of the stories, rituals, and social structures that ensured the "good life" of the community through the spirit. They are also, by virtue of their age, the members of the community closest to that revered state of being "complete" men and women.

There is a fifth dimension of thinking characteristic of Indigenous societies that starts with wisdom and evolves beyond it to understanding and knowing the spirit directly with all one's senses. It is a multisensory consciousness, a way of knowing associated with the mystic or spiritual leaders in their most fully developed state of being. It is most often associated with the most elderly of an Indigenous society. This is not always the case, for this way of thinking can develop earlier in life from visionary experiences of people at any age. This is the level of thinking most closely associated with myth and dream. It is the threshold to "that place Indian people talk about." It is the place through which a sense of spiritual ecology develops, the center place of thought, the place of the deepest respect and sacredness, the place of good life, the place of the Highest Thought.

Moving through each of these five ways of thought allows a person's awareness of their "spiritual ecology" to become riper, more mature. It is a pathway of knowledge and seeking life referred to in metaphoric ways in various Indigenous guiding myths.

The Concept of Orientation

Education is essentially a learned external orientation to family, community, places, societies, and cultures. Education is also learning an internal orientation to self and, in its metaphysical sense, to spirit.

Orientation is more than physical context and placement. In its deeper meanings it is about mindset, ways of thinking and knowing, origins of communication and a sense of direction. It is about how the human spirit understands itself. Traditional forms of Indian education have many expressions of the concept of orientation or "directions" as it is sometimes called. For Indian people, orientation, with relationship, forms the field for understanding the interaction between the human spirit and other expressions of spirit. Spiritual orientation and breath are sometimes explained in conjunction with the origins of wind in the creation/emergence myths among Indigenous people around the world. Mountains and the Winds associated with them appear among some tribes as symbols of orientation.

The Navajo perspectives related to wind, pathway, and hunting provide some of the most elegant written examples of the dynamic concept of Indigenous orientation. The following narrative descriptions of elements of Navajo Natural Philosophy as recorded and described by James McNeley mirror orientations in other American Indian tribes. They are presented here with deep respect and honor for the Navajo way of "Indigenous" thinking, knowing, and being.

The concept of Holy Wind and its role in the Navajo cultural philosophy exemplifies the nature of orientation and its connection to spiritual thought. Orientation embodies the essence of Navajo traditional belief. Upon his emergence from the fourth world, First Man's task was to recreate the four Earth Mounds that had been found in the fourth world. This initial task was to orient things in this, the fifth world, which was devoid of form and boundaries. Metaphysically speaking, First Man had to create a context in which to make the fifth world. This is the essence of spiritual orientation and "that place the Indians talk about."

In Navajo Philosophy, the First or Supreme Wind played a key role in creating the world. This First Wind has manifestations in all living and non-living things. In humans the manifestation of the First Wind is called *nilch'i hwii'siziinii* or 'the wind within one', or 'wind soul'. It is a unique expression of the breath of life—part of the First Wind, the source of all wind/breath. It is Dawn Woman (Changing Woman) who, at the moment of conception, determines the nature of the wind soul or breath each person will have at birth. Thought and behavior are expressions of wind soul.[4]

"*Nilch'i* meaning Wind, Air, or Atmosphere, as conceived by the Navajo, is endowed with the powers that are not acknowledged in Western culture. Suffusing all of Nature, Holy Wind gives life, thought, speech, and the power of motion to all living things, and serves as the means of communication between all elements of the living world. As such, it is central to Navajo philosophy and world view. …by this concept the Navajo Soul is linked to the immanent powers of the universe."[5]

First Wind has existed since the birth of the Universe and is endowed with the power to give life and movement to all beings. The Navajo Windway is an important component of Navajo ceremonialism. Dedicated to maintaining and restoring health and wholeness, it conveyed knowledge of the First Wind to the first holy people. In some versions of the Navajo earth creation myth, the cardinal directions are associated with different qualities of light. This light misted up from the four principal horizons to illuminate an otherwise dark Universe. These cardinal directions, the basic structures of physical orientation recognized by all Indian tribes, were also marked by four Earth Mounds (mountains), each one enclosing an inner form.

The four mists of light were considered the breath of the wind soul or inner form of each Earth Mound. The Navajo conceived of these mists of light and the cardinal directions as living breathing entities. The Navajo creation myth and numerous other Indigenous philosophies make the metaphysical connections among wind, light, inner or outer forms, and cardinal orientations. This connection forms the basis for a sophisticated epistemology related to the nature and action of spirit as understood and expressed in Indigenous societies.

For the Navajo, the "wind standing within" guides their traditional learning about orientations, relationships, and responsibilities to spiritual dimensions in quest for living the "harmony way." "Wind standing within" is a traditional concept originating in the guiding myth and vision of themselves as Dine, the People. In the following dimensions of Navajo thought, Wind is conceived as a source of life and spiritual light, as a source of thought and wisdom, serving as inner forms of language and means of knowing things, and as a source of guidance and creation. The spiritual foundations of Indigenous education are exemplified in an extraordinary way.

Wind As A Source of Life and Spiritual Light

In Navajo mythology, wind in the form of Supreme Sacred Wind created the First Holy Beings. These were First Man and First Woman, Black God, Talking God, Coyote, Calling God, and others. Supreme Sacred Wind, guided by Dawn Woman, illuminated and animated all beings of the Universe as indicated in the following passages.

"While they were waiting for strength, they saw a Cloud of Light which kept rising and falling. …while they watched, it turned black, and from the blackness they saw the Black Wind coming. Then the Cloud of Light turned blue, and they saw the Blue Wind coming to them; then it turned yellow and the Yellow Wind appeared; then it turned white and the White Wind came. Finally the light showed all colors and the Many Colored Wind came…. This Cloud of Light also created the Rainbow of the Earth, and as the light changes, it creates *hayolkaal* the White Early Dawn; *Nahodeetl'izh*, the Blue Sky of noon and also the blue that comes after the dawn; *nahootsoi*, the Yellow of Sunset; and *chahalheel*, the Dark of Night. These were also made for the people of the Earth, and each of these is a holy time of the day from which comes certain powers.

"When the Winds appeared and entered Life they passed through the bodies of men and creatures and made the lines on the fingers, toes, and heads of human beings, and on the bodies of the different animals. The Wind has given men and creatures strength ever since, for at the beginning they were shrunken and flabby until it inflated them; and the Wind was creation's first food, and put motion and change into nature, giving life to everything, even to the mountains and water."[6]

Light is illumination and wind is that which moves. The Navajo combine them to represent the founding characteristics of what is called Spirit in Western tradition. Spirit denotes qualities of Being that we associate with the highest level of thinking, acting, and being human. The Navajo use the "mists of light" and the "holy winds" as metaphors to think about, explain, orient, and teach each other the qualities of spirit as they perceive it. At the beginning of time, it is said that Wind and the Light of Dawn lay upon one another, giving birth to Changing Woman and life. They were one and the same. Then they separated to light the way and to move all things with the different breaths of Wind.

Wind As A Source of Thought and Wisdom

Thinking is a process animated by wind in Navajo tradition. Wind provided a way to breathe and be alive in addition to offering guidance and protection for the first beings in their underworld domain. Wind did this by advising people, guiding their behavior, and informing them about events through the corners of their ears. Wind provided this important service to the first beings before their emergence to the present world. Before Wind, the People moved here and there without any sense of direction, without any thought. The People had no sense of where they would go; they were in chaos. In the underworld, before emergence, Wind appeared as a person who shared wisdom and knowledge and led the People in proper behavior.

"The various people went around aimlessly like sheep, lacking language and without plans until they came upon Wind in the form of a person who knew all and who told them that henceforth he would speak to them (through the corner of their ears). Wind then gave leadership to them and the words by which they would exercise this, the knowledge and means to lead themselves. Even then, however, Wind gave them a restricted governance over their lives so that a leader would not be able to do anything that he wanted to, 'just according to one's mind'. Rather, Wind made available the means of speaking particular words, including the threatening words needed by a leader."[7]

Through the "corner of the ear which could not be seen," Wind advised those first beings, those first leaders wisely, giving them directions, helping them plan their creations, and guiding their behavior in right ways. And so the Navajo Holy men and women of today, in their teaching, their advising, and their leadership, reflect that quality of wind to guide their thoughts and provide context for their wisdom.

Wind As A Source of Language and A Means of Knowing

Among the Navajo and other Tribal groups, language is sacred because it is an expression of the Holy Wind that exists as the breath of life in each person. Changing Woman placed the winds in the cardinal directions to provide orientation and to help the first people learn how to lead themselves in their new world. In one account of the Navajo creation myth it is said:

> Winds lying on one another from within the Earth, by which she spoke to the people, were placed on the Earth surface for the Earth Surface People. The first one placed in the East is very holy, is female,

and it gives direction to Life. Word two is male and lies in the South. Another female word was added in the West and another male word in the North. . . .

"These four Words which were put up in the four directions are conceived to be the Winds by which man is given direction of his Life, movement, thinking and action to carry out plans. These are the same as 'the wind standing within us' which 'enters in the process of reproduction'. . . .

"While these Winds placed in the Cardinal directions enter within people as 'the one standing within us', other Winds formed on Earth's surface which could influence human life and behavior: Two Winds emerged from the Earth, two came from the water, and another two came from the clouds: when these met, six Winds were formed above and six below. We live between these, and they all affect us and some of which cause difficulties and sickness. . . .[8]

Education is largely based on language and oral communication. For the Navajo, language and its oral transmission are the foundations of the sacred traditions that bind them, through breath, to each other, other living things, their Holy Ones, and the world in all its immensity and beauty. Language is a form of Wind that informs, expresses, and orients the "wind standing within". Orientation is a way of learning and understanding where you are, your place, and your relative level of development. The use of language and symbolic words carry a responsibility because they cause things to happen. They evoke; they instruct. In Navajo tradition, their use must be learned and applied with great respect for they are connected to the inner forms in the mountains at the cardinal directions. These inner forms of the mountains each have words, songs, and a language by virtue of their unique Wind; they also have the plants and animals associated with their form. This is why they influence humans who live in their shadows.

Wind, in all its forms, provides a means of knowing and communicating with the inner forms that guide the four cardinal winds. Wind also interacts with all life bounded by the four sacred mountains of the Navajo Universe. According to the Navajo, a thought always has a certain type of Wind as its source. Wind represents the spirit behind the thoughts, actions, or words. Thoughts are the result of Winds acting on the individual and his or her "wind standing within".

We are influenced by a multitude of winds from birth to death. Some winds are good; others are bad, but most are neutral, bringing us information and knowledge as necessary. These neutral winds are called "messenger winds" and are often sent from benevolent spirits to guide our behavior and decisions. Some of the most powerful messenger winds are sent by the inner forms within the mountains at the four cardinal directions, the abode of the Holy Ones. These winds are like guardian spirits because they protect and advise us. For this reason, the Navajo refer to them as "the wind which stands beside". This Wind tells us about distant events, the intentions of others, the activities of plants, animals, and natural phenomena — such as the lightning and rainbow associated with the cardinal mountains.

Wind As A Source of Guidance and Creation

In Navajo belief, the Holy Ones send different Winds to the unborn while they are in the mother's womb. A particular wind combines with the Wind of the Mother and Father to make the unique "wind which stands within" characteristic of each person. This is the creative quality of the Winds coming together. When the child is born it is this unique "wind which stands within" that enables the child to breathe and be alive. If the combination of winds before birth has been lucky and of the proper nature, the child will be strong and well made. The child's unique combination of winds will determine his life, personality, and fortune. As the child grows, he or she will be exposed to many winds, from other people, as well as from the natural and supernatural worlds. These will have an effect in accordance with the nature and relative strength of the "wind standing within". It is each child's unique wind that will have the greatest effect on behavior and way of life. This is a person's first wind; it is the wind that learns, relates, and creates. The nature of this wind must be understood and respected as the foundation for seeking and finding one's pathway in life.

Wind's child exists everywhere. The same Wind's Child exists within us in our tissues. We live by it; we think by it. Wind standing alongside warns us of danger or the repercussions of our actions. If we do not listen then Bad Luck befalls us![9]

There is a twin to the "wind which stands within" that the Navajo refer to as the "wind which stands beside". This is the wind that represents intuition and acts as a guide and conscience in each individual. It is the Wind that receives and sends messenger winds. It protects, guides, and communicates through dreams. These winds that form and motivate our behavior represent the dual nature of the human spirit.

The Concept of Pathway

The concept of Pathway, revealed in numerous ways in Indigenous education, is associated with mountains, winds, and orientation. Learning involves a transformation that unfolds through time and space. Pathway, a structural metaphor, combines with the process of journeying to form an active context for learning about spirit. Pathway is an appropriate metaphor since, in every learning process, we metaphorically travel an internal, and many times external, landscape. In traveling a Pathway, we make stops, encounter and overcome obstacles, recognize and interpret signs, seek answers, and follow the tracks of those entities that have something to teach us. We create ourselves anew. Path denotes a structure; *Way* implies a process.

Many structures of Indigenous spiritual traditions are referred to as "ways." The Navajo Chantways are one example of specific Pathways for gaining spiritual knowledge. There are multiple expressions of similar ways in other tribes. These Pathways related to spiritual learning and teaching provide a view of the questing and vision-seeking that transforms the spirit and consciousness. Such constancy reflects the essence of all spiritual teaching and can provide a foundation for structuring contemporary educational experiences.

The Pathways for learning about the spirit have been traveled before. Those who have traveled them before lead those who travel these Pathways now. We follow the tracks of ancestors in our individual and collective journeys to spirit. To exemplify Pathway, I present the process of Indigenous tracking to see the ways of a path. As an example of the mythic dimension of Pathways, I present the Indigenous ideal of the Hunter of Good Heart. As an example of the spiritual journey through which a vision is received and shared, I present the visionary hero, Scar Face of the Blackfoot. Finally, I will present "Tracking the Story," an educational process model that exemplifies how a contemporary Indigenous Pathway of education might unfold.

Indigenous Tracking

The practical art of tracking animals evolved during the history of humans as Tribal hunter/gatherers. It was a highly evolved survival skill based on direct and personal experience with Nature. The animals, plants, geography, and the spirits of Nature taught the Indigenous people the meaning of their lives in relationship to the natural world. As hunter/gatherers, Tribal people naturally used their physical environments as the ground for their teaching, learning, and spiritual tempering. For them, the earth was a great book of life cycles and constant change, and presented a story of the flow of spirit through everything, including themselves.

Everything leaves a track, and in the track is the story: the state of being of each thing in its interaction with everything else. Indigenous people considered animals and plants the first teachers and participants with human beings in the evolution of life on the Earth. Based on this perspective, Indigenous people included the realm of spirit in their experience with animals, plants, and other entities and qualities of Nature. In the eyes of Tribal people, Nature and spirit are the same. The natural and the supernatural are dimensions of the same spirit moving.

Indigenous tracking presents a simple yet profound way to understand the connection between direct experience with Nature and the development of the spiritual traditions of Tribal people. As a learning process, tracking seems deceptively mundane, yet all the complex cognitive and intuitive abilities of humans, including the higher levels of spiritual consciousness, come into play. Metaphorically, tracking is intimately involved in the process of seeking wisdom, vision, and coming to the source of spirit. Following such a path, learning to read the "tracks left by the ancestors in the Dream Time"—as Australian Aborigines relate—reveals the interrelationship of all things through the direct observation of Nature.

In the process of tracking, actions and relationships are reflected in concentric circles. This pattern of activity and relationship reoccurs constantly in all of Nature. Concentric circles of action are the primary structures of Nature's creative process. In Nature, concentric circles of action connect to form a path revealing, through tracks and signs, the story of "the animals moving through their lives". Tracks, and the concentric circles of living they represent, are the manuscript of existence in a place and through time.

Scientists study the tracks of subatomic particles that exist only a millionth of a second. They find the human observer influences the energy relationships and even the nature of existence of these subatomic particles. Humans do participate with everything else even at this level of natural reality. Indigenous people understood this relationship of human activity as concentric rings that extend into the spirit realm. Burnam Burnam of the Australian Wurundjeri tribe explains an aboriginal perspective of this relationship in the following way:

> The most profound and essential aspect of our root culture is called *Tjukurpa*. The words "dreaming" or "dreamtime" are inadequate translations of the word. Tjukurpa does not refer to dreaming in the conventional Western sense of things imagined in sleep. Nor is it a collection of enchanting stories, like Aesop's fables or Grimm's fairy tales. It does not refer to a past long gone. Tjukurpa is existence itself, in the past, present, and the future. It is also the explanation of

existence, and it is the law that governs behavior.

"Tjukurpa is expressed in two facts of existence. It is the land, creeks, hills, clay-pans, rock-holes, soaks, mountains and other natural features. And it is people and their actions of hunting, marrying, ceremony and daily life. The Tjukurpa has always been . . . it is still unfolding along present events, and it is being recreated and celebrated by certain Aboriginal people today.

"We say that our country was made during the Tjukurpa, ... This was the time when beings traveled across the land in the form of humans, plants, animals, performing remarkable feats of creation and destruction . . . . The Tjukurpa creatures are travelers. Aboriginal people recount their journeys in stories, songs and dances. Their paths pass over, under and upon the land; sites along these paths are often named and treated as especially important . . . .

"The traveling stories link sites, to place, to people across the continent. By living on the land and learning the Tjukurpa, we experience an identity between people, places and the Tjukurpa . . . . For a person to become a socially responsible human being, he or she must learn the named tracks or "song lines" of his or her Tjukurpa . . . . The knowledge of the songs and paths tells us where we are going, without maps or compasses . . . .

"The link between the time of the Tjukurpa and daily life remains even at death, for it is then that we become part of the Tjukurpa itself, part of our own creation.[10]

Burnam Burnam's description of Aboriginal orientations to the mythic and spiritual paths of those first ancestors illustrates the teaching process inherent in the art of tracking. Tracking, from the Aboriginal perspective, connects people to their own spirits, the spirits of their land, the animals, plants, and other entities. Their Tjukurpa is founded upon learning about their spirit and understanding its meaning in relationship to their contemporary life and to other spirits of place. Essentially, it is learning how to live a complete life that honors all levels of their reality.

The Hunter of Good Heart

In North American hunting cultures, the hunter of good heart is a metaphoric ideal that reveals the nature of journeying toward completeness. This goal is reached through a direct relationship with animals and through hunting a path to our innermost spirit. The hunter is an archetypal form that resides in each of us, man or woman. The hunter is that part of us who searches for the completion that each of us, in our own way, strives to find. The Huichol Indians follow the tracks of the five pointed deer, their elder brother and the spirit of their sacred peyote. They say the act of hunting is about trying to find our life. Hunting from this perspective becomes a sacred act tied to our primal beginnings as hunter/gatherers. This is the perspective of becoming the animals we hunted, when humans and animals spoke to each other, and when humans began learning to be human, to be People.

Humans have always hunted to satisfy their hunger. It is one of the most basic of all human activities. It is the most basic reciprocal activity of all living things, that is, to eat and be eaten. Hunting, and all it involves, is a primal foundation of human learning and teaching. All the physical, emotional, and cognitive abilities of humans are applied in the act of hunting. Hunting is a complete and completing human act. It touches the heart of the drama of being born, living, and dying. Hunting characterizes our species to such an extent that, even in modern society, men and women far removed from hunting animals for sustenance still metaphorically "hunt" to be filled, to be satisfied, to be complete. Hunting involves coming to terms with elemental relationships at the physical, social, and spiritual levels. Hunting, in its most spiritual sense, is based on following the path of one's own spirit, manifested in the physical form of what you are hunting. In modern society, people are no longer hunting an animal, but something they have come to yearn for, the soul our ancestors were able to touch through their hunting and ritual; "that place Indians talk about." So it is in our times that we continue to hunt for ourselves, in our families, in our communities, in our careers, in our schools, in our institutions, and our relationships.

Mimbres Hunter of Good Heart

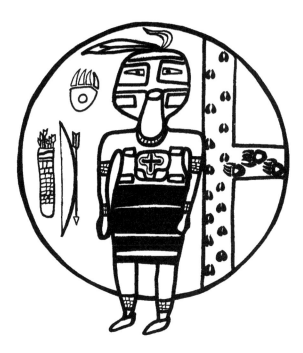

The Hunter of Good Heart is an ancient metaphor of one path of human meaning. It is a path of spiritual ecology with various descriptions in all ancient cultures. Before there were warriors, there were hunters, and if war was waged in that world of the first people, it more than likely was waged for advantage in hunting. The Indigenous art of war has its roots firmly planted in the strategies and single-minded focus of hunting. They are both spiritual acts, matters of life, death, and learning about spirit.

The Hunter of Good Heart is a state of completeness reached through an educational process involving the hunter's whole being. The culmination is the hunter's initiation into a communion of his spirit with the animals and the world. This process gives life to the hunter and his people. The good hunt is a responsibility undertaken not only by the individual, but by the community as well. The hunter hunts to perpetuate the life of family, clan, and community. The hunter represents the community to the world of animals and spirits; therefore, the community as well as the hunter is judged through his behavior. Wife, children, parents, relatives, the whole community participates with the hunter in a cycle of life and spirit involving prayer, hunting technique, ritual, art, sacrifice, and celebration. It is, as Plains Indian people say, "a medicine circle."

The act of hunting in the context of a medicine circle is a mythical act based on the central foundation of life and the taking of life to have life. Life feeds on life, continually transforming the physical substance of life and spirit through the never-ending cycle of living, dying, and being reborn. Like the predator revealing its most primal characteristic during the moment of predation, so humans awaken when they hunt with full consciousness of their actions. This higher context of hunting allows full awareness, understanding, and reverence for the spiritual meaning of hunting. Hunters participate in the "great dance of life"—a dance of holy communion that has been joined since the dawn of human history. The hunter/shaman paintings of Tres Frieres, Altimira, and Lascaux, the Eland dance of the Bushmen, and other Indigenous art forms around the world attest to the hunter's special covenant with the life of animals and the life of a community. It is a communion merging inner and outer, with the hunter coming to know his own spirit through the spirit of that which he hunts. In this seemingly paradoxical union, a window appears into the reality of spirit where the most elusive prey resides—one's true and complete self.

Hunting is a path to a spiritual reality where each participant gains a set of universal understandings; deep relationship, abiding respect, fulfillment, and love for life meld into one. It becomes a spiritual foundation for teaching and learning ecological relationship. The foundational qualities that the hunter internalizes include: complete attentiveness to the moment, integration of action, being, and thinking, a sense for concentric rings of relationship, and humility.

Indigenous stories of Hunters reflect in the most eloquent way the nature of this path and way of spiritual learning. The following story from the Navajo Deer Hunting Way provides advice to all Hunters of Good Heart. It is presented here with deep respect for the "Diné" way of Indigenous being.

The Navajo Deer Hunting Way

The basis of Navajo ceremonialism is establishing and maintaining a harmonious balance with all that surrounds them. The Deer Hunting Way is one of the Pathways that form ceremonial structures. These ceremonies establish the harmony and balance the Navajo deemed essential for being prosperous. As is true of all tribes in whose territory deer lived, the Navajo venerated deer as a source of food and life. Deer were considered spirit beings who had to be respected and properly treated. Deer were teachers of a source of life and knowledge of spirit that originated with the First People, the Holy Ones. But they had to be hunted. For his own well-being and success, the hunter had to possess, not only the technical skills for hunting them, but the necessary spiritual preparations as well. The hunter had to know the origin of the deer. He needed to know how to behave and be successful in taking their life, for his own life and that of his family and clan. With respect and honor, the story goes this way:

There was a hunter who waited in ambush. Wind had told him, 'This is where the tracks are. The deer will come marching through in single file.' The hunter had four arrows: one was made from sheet lightning, one from zigzag lightning, one of sunlight roots, and one of rainbow.

"Then the first deer, a large buck with many antlers, came. The hunter got ready to shoot the buck. His arrow was already in place. But just as he was ready to shoot, the deer transformed himself into a mountain mahogany bush, tse esdaazii. After a while, a mature man stood up from behind the bush. He stood up and said, 'Do not shoot! We are your neighbors. These are the things that will be in the future, when human beings come into existence. This is the way you will eat us.' And he told the hunter how to kill and eat the deer. So the hunter let the mature Deerman go for the price of his information. And the Deerman left.

"Then the large doe, a shy doe, appeared behind the one who had left. The hunter was ready again to shoot the doe in the heart. But the doe turned into a cliffrose bush, *aweets aal*. A while later a young woman stood up from the bush. The woman said, 'Do not shoot! We are your neighbors. In the future, when man has been created, men will live because of us. Men will use us to live on.' So then, for the price of her information the hunter let the Doewoman go. And she left.

"Then a young buck, a two pointer, came along. And the hunter got ready to shoot. But the deer transformed itself into a dead tree, tsin bisga. After a while, a young boy stood up from behind the dead tree and said, 'In the future, after man has been created, if you talk about us in the wrong way we will cause trouble for you when you urinate, and we will trouble your eyes. We will also trouble your ears if we do not approve of what you say about us.' And for the price of his information, the hunter let the young Deerman go.

"Then the little fawn appeared. The hunter was ready to shoot the fawn, but she turned into a lichen-spotted rock, tse dlaad. After a while, a young girl stood up from the rock and spoke: 'In the future all this will happen if we approve, and whatever we shall disapprove shall be up to me. I am in charge of the other Deer People. If you talk badly about us, and if we disapprove of what you say, I am the one who will respond with killing you with what I am. If you hear the cry of my voice, you will know that trouble is in store for you. If you do not make use of us properly, even in times when we are numerous, you will not see us anymore. We are the four deer who have transformed themselves into different kinds of things. Into these four kinds of things we can transform ourselves. Moreover, we can assume the forms of all different kinds of plants. Then when you look you will not see us. In the future only those of whom we approve shall eat the mighty deer. If when you hunt, you come across four deer, you will not kill all of them. You may kill three and leave one. But if you kill all of us, it is not good.

"'These are the things that will bring you happiness. When you kill a deer, you will lay him with the head toward your house. You will cover the earth with plants or with branches of trees lengthwise, with the growing tips of the plants pointing the direction of the deer's head, toward your house. Then you will take us to your house and eat of us. You will place our bones under any of the things whose form we can assume. At these places you may put our bones. You will sprinkle the place with yellow pollen. Once, Twice. Then you lay the bones. And then you sprinkle yellow pollen on top of the bones. This is for protection of the game animals. In this manner they will live on; their bones can live again and live a lasting life.'"[11]

In the story Fawn, speaking on behalf of the Deer people, gives advice to First Hunter about how to respect the spirit of the deer. Fawn also refers to Talking God as the holy being who decides when and how the Deer People will give their life to sustain humans. The proper relationship of hunters to Deer People is thus determined in the realm of spirit. It is then passed on through ritual practice and understanding rooted in the guiding myths of the Navajo. The story presents a foundation for developing a spiritual orientation to the act of hunting. The first step in this hunting way is the development of the hunter's heart in preparation for the hunter's journey. This is an education through the spirits and landscape of Nature. It is an education founded on a deep level of ecological understanding and responsibility. When it takes hold, this education transforms the hunter and firmly establishes his journey toward becoming complete. Thus, a Pathway to self is found through deeper understanding and responsibility.

Teaching spiritual ecology in Indigenous settings is really teaching personal power. The gaining of Personal Medicine, as Plains Indian traditions relate, is the real goal of a Pathway of learning. Gaining personal power begins with establishing a context of respect. Personal power and a deep sense of respect are what "empowerment" really means!

The Indigenous hunter not only learned how to attract his prey, but in the process of development as a hunter, he also learned how to obtain luck by gaining the attention of the spirits of Nature. The power gained reflected and transformed the hunter at physical, psychological, social, and spiritual levels.

Indigenous complexes of hunting found throughout the world followed a pattern that, while finding a diversity of expressions, included the following basic component processes. The first stage of Indigenous hunting began with setting one's intention through prayerful asking; this was followed by a process of purification. These preparations were meant to set the tone of respect and proper relationship. The second stage included intense questing and application of skill and attractive behavior toward the goal of a successful hunt. The third stage included the community process of respectful treatment of the prey, celebration, and thanksgiving. In all these processes, comprising the circle of Indigenous hunting, the connecting thread is reverence for a giving Earth and the spirit relationships to the animals. In this traditional context of hunting, the Hunter and the Hunted joined in a kinship, a conscious and respectful sharing of the flow of life. The lesson for the hunter lies in gaining a deeper understanding of spiritual relationship and transformation. He and the community he represented reinforced their understanding of the deep ecological meaning of mutual reciprocity. The Hunter and his community entered a spiritual exchange, a creative process of learning and teaching that has formed the foundation of human meaning since the dawn of history.

While these relationships with animals have undergone significant transformations since earlier times, they are still there in spirit if not in reality. The crisis of our times beckons us to retrace the tracks of our ancestors and the animals they knew. We must understand the meaning of our lives in relationship with the natural world. The Hunter of Good Heart shows us spirituality and ourselves as spiritual beings. It is an aspect of our humanity that we must reclaim if we are to find our life. The compacts made by those first hunters were covenants of spirit and were for life. They were based on an abiding relationship of respect.

Modern perceptions regarding animals are infused with representations of attitudes about the other. Moderns no longer experience a daily and direct relationship with animals. They are informed by a media that skews the images of animals. This has led to a host of reactions ranging from fear to romanticization to outright inhumanity. Modern society's biased orientation to animals mirrors contemporary misunderstanding about other races, especially those who have become few in number, such as American Indians. To truly understand animals, is also to truly understand the other.

The Journey of Scar Face

The Blackfoot legend of Scar Face presents an archetypal hero's journey of spirit. The story of Scar Face is a teaching story that reflects the courage of an individual in overcoming obstacles of cosmic proportions. It illustrates the nature of the way Indigenous people viewed relationships with all things, people, animals, the earth, and the sky. The story is about "face," that is, the spiritual nature of character and learning how to develop our true selves. The story is also about journeying to the center, to "that place that Indian people talk about." This is a place of spirit within ourselves and in the world as a whole. It is in "that place" that knowledge and gifts of spirit can be obtained. It is a place of vision where one must learn how to seek. Its inherent message is found in the landscape of our souls and our wondrous universe.

With deep respect and honor for the Blackfoot way of "Indigenous" being, the following version of the story of Scar Face is presented. Scar Face lived with his grandmother because his mother and father had died shortly after his birth. His face had a birthmark that set him aside from all others and became the source of ridicule and shame. Because he was different, he was taunted by the children and whispered about by others in the tribe. As Scar Face grew older he withdrew and spent much of his time alone in the forest befriending and learning the ways of the animals he encountered. It is said that he learned to speak with them. And through them he learned how to be related with all things.

As Scar Face grew older he experienced all the things of life with humility and great reverence. He even fell in love, as young boys do, when they come of that age and express that facet of their face. The focus of Scar Face's affection was a young woman, Singing Rain, the chief's daughter. Singing Rain was also a special person, kind and with a gift of insight. Although all the other young men competed for her affection, it was Scar Face who she came to respect and love because of his honesty and good heart. However, when Scar Face asked for her to marry, she revealed her sacred vow to the Sun never to marry. This was her pledge of spiritual piety in the way of the Blackfoot. The only way she could marry was if the Sun were to release her from her pledge. On hearing this, Scar Face determined to undertake a journey to the place where the Sun dwells to ask the Sun to release Singing Rain from her pledge. And so, it is said that Scar Face began his visionary journey to the land of the Star People.

Scar Face did not know where the Star People lived, only that they must live in the direction the Sun set every evening, beyond the Great Water in the West. So Scar Face prepared himself with help from his grandmother, and when he was ready he set forth on his journey, a journey to the land of spirit. He first traveled familiar territory, but then began to enter into lands that neither he nor other members of his tribe had ever seen.

As the snow of Winter began to fall a hundred paths became open to him, and he became confused; he did not know which way to go. He met a wolf on one path, and with great humility asked for help and direction. Knowing the goodness of his heart, the wolf spoke to him and guided him to the right path. He traveled that path for a great distance until he came to another series of paths, and again he became confused. He stopped, set his camp and prayed. Soon a mother Bear and her cubs appeared on the path in front of him. Again, with great humility he asked for guidance from the mother Bear. The Bear spoke with great kindness and pointed out to him the right path. Scar Face followed the bear's path for many days until the path ended. Now there were no longer any paths in front of him to follow, only the vast expanse of the great forest. As he stood and pondered in front of the forest, a wolverine approached him. He called out, "good wolverine, my friend, I need your help." Again, he asked for direction and help from this friend. Knowing his heart and the nobility of his quest, wolverine responded with great kindness and guided him through the forest to the edge of the Great Water, where, exhausted, he made camp. He thanked the wolverine, and he thanked each of the animals that had helped him by offering them a gift of song and tobacco. He could see a twinkling of lights across the Great Water, and he knew that was the land of the Star People.

Scar Face did not know how to cross the water to "that place that his people talked about." But he was determined to find a way. Then two snow geese swam by and offered to take him across the Great Water. When they arrived on the other side, he thanked the geese and their relative for their kindness and great service to him. He made camp and then fasted and prayed for three days and nights. On the fourth day, a path of sunlight began to form in front of him leading toward "that place". He leaped onto the path and followed it as it took him higher and higher into the sky. When he reached the end of this path of sunlight, he came to a beautiful forest and another path, a path of great width as if made by thousands of people traveling on it for a long, long time. As he followed the path he came upon a richly decorated quiver of arrows leaning against a tree. He wondered who they must belong to, so he waited to see. Soon, on the path coming from the other direction was an extraordinary looking Warrior dressed in richly decorated white buckskin. As the Warrior approached, Scar Face could see that this man was an image of perfection. He asked Scar Face if he had seen a quiver of arrows. In response, Scar Face showed him where the arrows were. Grateful and curious, the stranger introduced himself, "I am Morning Star." Then he asked Scar Face his name and where he was going. "I am called Scar Face, and I seek the lodge of the Sun." "Then come with me, Sun is my father and I live with my mother Moon in his lodge."

When Scar Face arrived at the Lodge of the Sun, he saw that the walls were painted with the history of all people of the world. Morning Star introduced Scar Face to his mother the Moon. As his father the Sun entered the lodge, a great light entered with him. Morning Star introduced Scar Face to his father Sun, the greatest chief. Scar Face was so impressed that he could not bring himself to reveal his reasons for coming to the land of the Star People. Sun and Moon treated Scar Face with great hospitality and asked Scar Face to stay with them as long as he wished. Over the next few days, Morning Star showed Scar Face the many paths in the beautiful land of the Star People. There was one path to a distant mountain that Sun had warned Morning Star and Scar Face never to go near. It was a mountain on the top of which lived a flock of seven giant birds that the Star People greatly feared.

One morning, Scar Face woke to find Morning Star gone. Scar Face arose and quietly left the Lodge of the Sun to take a walk and decide how he might ask Sun to release Singing Rain from her vow. He thought he might meet Morning Star and ask him for advice. As he walked, he began to feel that something was wrong, and the nearer he came to the mountain where the Giant Birds lived the greater his feeling became. He knew that there was some reason Morning Star had gone to the forbidden mountain.

Scar Face set out in search of Morning Star. As he climbed to the top of the mountain of the Giant Birds, he found Morning Star engaged in a ferocious battle with the birds. These birds were indeed savage and extremely large. They were about to overcome Morning Star when Scar Face joined the battle. Scar Face fought valiantly and soon turned the tide of battle. One by one, Scar Face and Morning Star began to kill the Giant Birds until all seven were slain and their tail feathers taken by the two warriors.

Tired, yet proud of their accomplishment, Scar Face and Morning Star descended the mountain and returned to the Sun Lodge to inform Sun and Moon of the defeat of the Star People's most feared enemies. Sun and Moon were very impressed by the courage shown by both young men and were especially grateful to Scar Face for saving the life of Morning Star. In honor of the courage of Scar Face, Sun offered to fulfill any desire he would request. Yet, Scar Face could not speak his greatest desire. He remained silent until Moon, knowing his heart, spoke of Scar Face's love for Singing Rain and her vow to the Sun that prevented them from being together. Sun immediately responded by saying to Scar Face that he would release her from her vow. Sun touched the cheek of Scar Face, and the scar he had borne all his life disappeared. Morning Star in turn gave him special personal gifts and revealed to him that he was his spirit father, confirming the feeling that Scar Face had all along. Then Sun and Moon began to sing songs in praise of Scar Face and Morning Star. Sun and Moon then gave Scar Face many gifts, rich clothes, and a special shirt. In addition, Sun renamed Scar Face "Mistaken Morning Star" because now without the scar on his face he looked like Morning Star. Sun taught Mistaken Morning Star his own special dance, the Sun Dance. He said that if Earth People wished to honor him and bring health and well-being to their tribe, they should dance the Sun Dance each year when he had reached the highest place in the sky. Then Morning Star led his Earth son to the path called the Wolf's Trail (the Milky Way) and placed a wreath of juniper on his head. In an instant, Mistaken Morning Star was back on Earth and on a path leading to his own village.

Singing Rain was the first to meet Mistaken Morning Star as he approached the village. He told her that Sun had released her from her vow, and she knew in her heart from seeing and feeling the magnificence of him that they could now be together always. Mistaken Morning Star called the people together and taught them the rituals of the Sun Dance. He showed the women how to build the Sun Dance Lodge, and he taught the men how to conduct the sweat lodge ceremony and raise the Sun Dance pole. He taught them about the sanctity of their individual spirit and the nature of sacred visioning. He taught them from "that place that the Indians talk about."[12]

There are profound lessons to be learned from stories like Scar Face. The traditional versions of the tale told in the Native language have a richness and depth of meaning that are difficult to translate. Such richness and depth are true of similar tales among Indigenous people around the world. They are like the mythical spirit deer: they leave tracks beckoning us, if we would but follow.

Tracking A Story, A Metaphoric Path For Vision and Education

The journey and quest of Scar Face represent a mythic archetype of the spiritual Pathway of learning. It is learning about the deepest dimensions of human life. The term "lifeway" may be more appropriate for the deep learning metaphorically represented by this story. The story of Scar Face also represents an Indigenous ideal for process and development that has implications for contemporary education. The metaphors and processes of tracking, hunting, questing, pilgrimage, visioning, orienting, and pathway are used in the mythic stories of all cultures. They reflect a basic way that humans process and structure their learning. Current research in the cognitive process is just beginning to investigate the metaphoric structures and inherent processes in stories and storytelling. The research is to find clues about the way the brain contexts reality in preparation for learning.

Humans are one and all storytelling animals. Through story we explain and come to understand ourselves. Story — in creative combination with encounters, experiences, image making, ritual, play, imagination, dream, and modeling — forms the basic foundation of all human learning and teaching. Learning and teaching unfold through time, space, and place forming a path through life. It is a simple fact, basic to human nature yet, elegantly complicated in its expression. The educational challenge of the twenty-first century is to move forward to basics. Indigenous education provides the clues and the tracks that we need to follow. The only limitation is the extent of our collective vision.

The perspectives inherent in the lifeways of Indigenous education imply tremendously creative possibilities for contemporary education. Indigenous perspectives can form foundations for exploring the universals of what it is to be educated. The key is empowering ourselves to make creative leaps of thinking and acting. We must revitalize ourselves and engender the courage and consciousness required to confront the monumental challenges human kind faces.

We have to facilitate our children and ourselves in that ancient journey to find our face (to understand and appreciate our true character), to find our heart (to understand and appreciate the passions that move and energize our life), to find a foundation (work that allows us to fully express our potential and our greatest fulfillment), and to become a complete man or woman (to find our Life and appreciate the spirit that moves us).

We must again create the kind of education that creates great human beings. To Indianize the education of Indian people constitutes a major revolution. To Indigenize contemporary Western education would require a global transformation of proportions we have never seen. Such a gargantuan vision evolves from millions of smaller visions that we individually and collectively consummate. We move mountains by first moving ourselves, and the way we educate makes all the difference in the world. The choice is ours. We make the difference. It is we who decide to live, or not live, our visions. We are the creators of the world and realities we live in. We are the ones who must choose the path of our own learning.

In this chapter, I have presented a number of stories that characterize the spiritual ecology of Indian people. For Indian people, traditional learning begins and ends with the spirit. It is an old maxim that puts in context what Indigenous people view as education. The perspective incorporates the metaphors of Pathway, orientation, hunting, and seeking life and completeness into a system and a symbolic language for education. These metaphors have been expressed and translated in countless ways among American Indians and other Indigenous groups of the world. They have provided models and continue to provide an essential frame of reference for learning. They are already contemporary because contemporary Indigenous groups continue to apply them for the survival of the People. The key to allowing them greater viability is to translate their values, their meaning, and their process into modern education while supporting their revitalization in their original Tribal contexts. This is taking a creative leap in imaging and applying the lessons of Indigenous education into another cultural context.

The following is a translation of Indigenous thought into modern educational curriculum modeling. Curriculum modeling is the first step in the systematic process of designing a learning experience based on a philosophical perspective. It is but one of many creative possibilities.

A Contemporary Pathway For Ecological Vision

In many Plains Indian and Aboriginal Tribal traditions, learning the pathway of vision embodies a process that unfolds through a variety of dimensions. As mentioned earlier, in traditional Native American perspectives, learning begins and ends with spirit. This learning path begins with appropriate orientation, acknowledging relationships, setting intentions, seeking, creating, understanding, sharing, and then celebrating one's vision with reference to a place of centering. Imagine an aboriginal sandpainting composed of seven variously colored concentric rings connected to each other and to a seventh concentric ring through a pathway. The eighth ring is the centering place and the place of beginning and of completion, "that place that Indian People talk about." Each of the rings has its own center and contains the colored rings of the others. The pathway between each concentric ring is white bordered by black. The field in which the sandpainting is set is half red and half blue. This imaginary sandpainting symbolizes a structure, a process, and a field for learning about the creative stages and the inherent nature of visioning. (See Diagram)

The Centering Place is where the soul and intention of the vision are formed. This is the place where the "soul of the dream is honored". The intention is energized and guided by one's innermost conscious and unconscious thoughts and feelings. In whatever we learn, and by whatever means we learn, we are always true to our inherent nature and personality. This is why, in all that we endeavor to learn, we always learn something about ourselves.

Asking is prayer, and is the first ring of the path. Every journey involving one's whole being begins with asking for illumination. Asking names the quest and sets forth its essential goal. This goal focuses intention for seeking something one's inner being truly desires. True learning results from deep motivation, the desire to obtain something for which one cares deeply, down to the bones, with one's whole heart and soul. Such desire sets into motion the process of making ready and preparing the ground. Physical, mental, and psychological preparations are basic tasks of this concentric ring. Exploring the relationships and accomplishing the tasks of this ring may take hours, days, months, or even years. What one learns in this first ring is all relative to the vision one is seeking. What matters is how much the individual desires their goal. Motivation is central to human learning and is the foundation for all systems of education. Knowing how to ask and prepare for knowledge is a special kind of orientation. Learning necessary skills, discipline, focus, and how to walk a path are all a part of learning about one's own character, one's face.

Asking is the initiation of a creative flow of thought. It is the place of first insights, intuitions, encounters, and experiences. The activities of Asking are like tilling the soil, planting the seed, and then saying to the spirits of the world, "I have planted my most precious seed, help it grow, give it life." They are tasks that are simple yet complex, hard yet liquid, inward in feeling yet outward in expression—all rolled into one. They are all tasks that are essential for gaining a sense of direction, for orienting to one's center. It is asking for life and being awakened to the life of our own soul.

The Connected Rings of Indigenous Visioning

In every process of visioning there are side events which influence the process of a particular connected ring.

Seeking is the second ring of the path. Seeking is the actual process of questing. It is looking for what we mysteriously yearn for, that part of ourselves that we need, and it is missing. We may not know what that something is; it may be a gift, a special song, an animal, a plant, a person, a place, a feeling, a wisdom, a dream. These are all expressions of vision, that innately human calling to search for higher levels of meaning. To find that special thing, we have to explore the boundaries of our world and beyond. We have to expand our consciousness and paradoxically go outside ourselves to find that special something inside ourselves. We all become Scar Face when we take the hero's/heroine's journey and seek what we most desire. In this concentric ring we test ourselves against the limits of our courage and endurance, deal with a myriad of conflicting demands, and overcome obstacles. In our seeking we begin with what we know, but we come to realize it isn't very much. Then we begin to wander, to go here, to go there; we learn how to let go, open up and deal with uncertainty. We experiment; we learn again how to listen, how to observe, how to be humble, and how to find and ask for help. Seeking is always about searching for the authentic, the basics, the meanings of life. In the process of seeking we learn to search not only for ourselves, but for all people. We learn the lessons of care, self-sacrifice, and humility.

Making is the next connected ring. Making involves the act of creating something new as a result of one's visioning. The Making is a work, or series of works, of deep significance that symbolically include what one has learned about the self, the world. Through the visioning process we contact the universal center of creativity, and we create our lives anew.

Making is the connected ring where we learn that we can create who we want to be and create the life that we truly wish to live. With our gift of creativity, empowered by our vision, what we create has the power to affect the lives and thoughts of others. The song, dance, artifact, model, or anything we create from our vision changes not only our lives, but those of others as well. This is the ripple effect that characterizes the action of connected rings of relationship.

Making is also a stage where — through the act of creating something — we fine tune and elaborate on what we have learned. This leads to further discovery and understanding.

Having is the next connected ring. We learn what our vision and our creation mean, and what our inherent responsibilities are in relationship to them. This dimension of understanding essentially begins from the first ring, but it comes into clearer focus after we have made something from our vision. We learn to accept and honor a part of ourselves we have learned about in our visioning. We identify more closely with our own soul. We come to a higher level of self-acceptance and maturity in understanding the difference between being created by circumstance and creating our own circumstances. In the process of Making from our vision, we come to be mature and conscious participants in creating our world. We develop the courage to accept the responsibility of becoming co-creators with the world.

Throughout the process of visioning, we learn to recognize and manifest our unique potential. We find how to apply our personal power and, in every sense, empower ourselves through what we make from our vision. The Having stage honors being with our vision and our creations. It is a time of reflection, a time of decision, and a time of incubating strategies for implementing our vision in our own reality.

Sharing is the connected ring through which our vision becomes a part of the life and spirit of the community. We share the life we have sought and found with others. Sharing may involve a diversity of forms and dimensions. Sharing, in this stage, is essentially teaching others what we have learned, just as Scar Face shared the knowledge of the Sun Dance with his people. We are all teachers; it is a primary characteristic of being human. We do it all the time, whether we are conscious of it or not. The forms that teaching took in earlier times may have included songs, dances, stories, rituals, or sacred art. Today they include this and much more. Teaching and sharing are part of the process of becoming more whole and spiritually mature.

Celebrating is a natural outcome of spiritual sharing, and it too can take a diversity of forms. It is an individual and communal process that celebrates the mystery of life and the journey that each of us takes. Celebration is a way of spreading the light around.

Being is the seventh ring of the visioning process. Being joyous, thankful, reflective of the gifts of life and vision are important states of mind. They open us to the illumination of the Centering place, the place where our soul and spirit reside, "that place that the Indians talk about."

This chapter has outlined a perspective of Indigenous education inherent in Native American spirituality. Native American traditionalists would contend that all learning is related to the spirit. Native American progressives would agree that this may be so, but it is also essential that Indian people be trained to compete and exist in a modern world. Many people are uncomfortable with spirituality in any aspect of modern education because of the instances of misunderstanding and misapplication of spirituality in modern society. As with everything in human affairs, it becomes a matter of perspective and consciousness.

My intent has been to present a point of view based on my own visioning and tempered by my experience as an American Indian, image maker, and professional educator. There are many paths to the Center. There are infinite ways to talk about and image that Center, "that place the Indians talk about." We walk infinite paths and talk in infinite ways about getting to the Center every day of our lives. This has been going on in every generation of every culture of mankind since the first words were spoken and the first images were constructed. It is a very, very, long human quest!

SINGING WATERS

THE ENVIRONMENTAL FOUNDATION OF INDIGENOUS EDUCATION

Overview

NATURE IS A SACRED REALITY FOR AMERICAN INDIANS. Relationships to the natural world formed the basis for their expression of traditional education. Historically, a direct and abiding understanding of the special significance of Nature's cycles — life, death, struggle, and survival — was integral to the survival of Indian people. Given this reality, environmental education among American Indians took many forms, and it was here they established their most profound and intimate expressions of culture.

Environmental understanding and education were directly tied to the cosmologies of Tribal life. Tribal cosmology reflected the sacred and elemental expressions of life on earth and in the cosmos. The key questions that each cosmology addressed included: how the Tribal community might ecologically integrate into the place they lived; and how a direct relationship among the individual, the community, and the natural world could be established and maintained.

Indian people, in every place they lived, addressed these questions of survival and sustainability in diverse, yet harmonious ways. They thought of their environments richly and of themselves as truly alive and related to their world..

"We are all related," is a metaphor used by the Lakota in their prayers. It is a metaphor whose meaning is shared by all other Indian people. It is a guiding principle of Indian spiritual ecology reflected by every tribe in their perception of Nature. It is a deeply spiritual, ecological, and epistemological principle of profound significance.

Guided by this metaphysical principle, Indian people acknowledged that all living and non-living entities of Nature have important inherent meanings within the context of human life. Based on this understanding, American Indians symbolically recognized their relationship to plants, animals, stones, trees, mountains, rivers, lakes, streams, and a host of other living entities. Through seeking, making, sharing, and celebrating these natural relationships, they came to perceive themselves as living in a sea of relationships. In each of the places they lived, they learned the subtle, but all important, language of natural relationship. With this awareness, tempered by intimate relationships with various environments over a thousand or more generations, Indian people accumulated and applied their ecological knowledge.

In contrast to the relatively one-dimensional reductionist Newtonian-Cartesian view of Nature, Indians perceived multiple realities in Nature—that experienced by our five senses was only one of many possibilities. In such a perceived "multiverse," knowledge could be received directly from animals, plants, and other living and non-living entities. They perceived that animals and plants have ritual ways of behavior that interact with one another. All life and Nature have a "personhood," a sense of purpose and inherent meaning that is expressed in many ways and at all times.

Over the past 500 years, the changes to the environment of America have been dramatic; at one time America may have been the most pristine and rich natural environment on earth. The first Europeans saw America as wilderness, an obstacle to overcome through settlement and the use of resources, living and non-living. They looked upon the land primarily as a material object, a commodity they could gain from economically. For the most part they viewed the Indians they encountered as one of those resources, which they would either use or abuse according to their agenda for material gain.[1]

Yet, to Indian people, the land and the place they lived were in a perfect state. For them, the real test of living was to establish a harmonious relationship with that perfect state that was Nature—to understand it, to see it as the source of one's life and livelihood, and the source of one's essential well-being.

In the minds of many Europeans, Indians were the other—seen either as savage, as heathen, as noble, as good or as bad. They were never understood for what they were and are: a people who, in a variety of ways and with all their heart and being, tried to establish a direct relationship with the essence of natural life. They understood Nature as the essence of the Great Mystery, which guides and breathes life into all things. For Indian people, the land was full of spirit, full of life energy. Everything—a rock, a tree, a plant, a mountain, an animal, a bird, an insect—had its unique expression of life and way of Spirit. Indigenous people coded this understanding into their process of education. This nature-centered orientation helped individuals come to terms with the environment where they lived in a holistic way.[2]

Oren Lyons reflects this understanding in terms of the contemporary voices of Native American ecological thought. He states:

> And each generation was to raise its chiefs and to look out for the welfare of the seventh generation to come. We were to understand the principles of living together. We were to protect the life that sur-

rounds us, and we were to give what we had to the elders and to the children. The men were to provide, and the women were to care for the family and be the center, the heart of the home. And so our nation was built on the spiritual family, and we were given clans... the Turtle, the Eagle, the Beaver, the Wolf, the Bear, the Snipe, the Hawk, all of whom were symbols of freedom. Our brothers the Bears, the Wolves, and the Eagles are Indians; they are natives, as we are. We went to Geneva, the six nations, the great Lakota nation, as representatives of indigenous people of the western hemisphere, and what was the message that we gave? 'There is a hue and a cry for human rights,' they said, 'for all people,' and the indigenous people said, 'What of the rights of the natural world? Where is the seat for the Buffalo or the Eagle? Who is representing them here in this forum? Who is speaking for the waters of the earth? Who is speaking for the trees and the forests? Who is speaking for the Fish, for the Whales, for the Beavers, for our children? We are indigenous people to this land. We are like a conscience; we are small, but we are not a minority; we are the landholders, we are the land keepers; we are not a minority, for our brothers are all the natural world, and for we are by far the majority. It is no time to be afraid. There is no time for fear. It is only time to be strong, only a time to think of the future and to challenge the destruction of your grandchildren.'[3]

Oren Lyons gets to the heart of what has characterized Indigenous understanding of the natural world; a mindset derived from an ecological sensibility that has continued to evolve traditional contexts for Indian communities. Ecological education, wherever found, revolves around the issues that are essentially ethical, religious, and sacred. Ecological education provides the foundation that enables human beings to resonate individual and communal "inscapes" with the natural landscape. This is in direct opposition to the orientation permeating modern education; an orientation that emphasizes extreme profaneness and materialism. This leads to conditioning that engenders a radical destructiveness at the individual, spiritual, communal, and environmental levels of being.

In contrast, Indigenous education traditionally cultivated ecological piety, based on letting the other be, and appreciating other entities for their unique being.

Native American people, through their ecological educational processes, evolved a natural response to the other—that other being, the natural world—

and allowed the other to define itself to them, rather than imposing preconceived intellectual meanings. As a result, Indian people lived with as little impact on the natural state of the land as possible. They allowed the land to be, taking from it only the resources necessary for their survival, but always remembering that it was given to them as a gift.

It is important to reflect on the changes that Native American people have had to accommodate in their relationship to their natural environment. It is the educational processes that allowed them to establish that essential relationship.

The arrival of Europeans ushered in a prolonged period of warfare, persecution, social, cultural and individual oppression and deprivation that is echoed to this day in spirit, if not in actuality, in Indian/White relationships. Today the bulk of our traditional system of governance has been replaced with a federally prescribed structure. The primary purpose has been to establish, within the context of American Indian societies, a system with which the federal government can administratively communicate. This prescribed governmental structure significantly diminished the power of the Indigenous forms of govern-ment — to govern within the ecological framework of relationship with the natural environment as their contextual frame of reference.

Traditional expressions of educating have been all but eliminated in favor of institutions founded on the psychological premise of behavior modification, of command and control. These institutions continue to adhere to a Eurocentric orientation to life and resist any attempts to integrate the understandings that come through cultural diversity. To survive, most Native Americans have been forced to give up their traditional livelihoods in favor of working in the technocratic system of economics. The vestiges of their social structures are rapidly disappearing with each generation. Extended families are being replaced by nuclear or single parent families, resulting in all the modern abuses and dilemmas of fragmented families.

Along with the disappearance of the extended family and the communal system of clans, the ravages of alienation — expressed through alcoholism, drug and child abuse, and a host of other abuses — are becoming all too apparent in Indian communities today. Every area of traditional Native American thought and spirit has suffered grievously. In spite of a dire history and the highly visible effects in Native American communities today, Native American thought continues to reflect an ecological orientation that presents a model for a new kind of society. Such thought presents the deep ecological philosophy and under-standing of relationships to the natural world that we need to balance a homogenizing, technosocial paradigm.

This paradigm is founded on the Western mechanistic philosophy of control of Nature and the idea that homogenization allows greater freedom. It is based upon a body of accepted theory that underpins modern society's assumptions of reality. It considers that reality to be the only reality. This is the "real world", the foundation of the only firm answers. This is what the hidden curriculum of modern education communicates. This paradigm so guides the consciousness of American mainstream education, that it forms the nature of thought, research and education. It motivates the views, methods and solutions that are a result of that education. This conditioned orientation has resulted in a colonization of perception with repercussions of a magnitude almost beyond description. One can begin to understand such colonization by realizing that there are alternative cultural realities and by honoring their presence. Mechanistic knowledge is not the only legitimate knowledge. Such an orientation can block us from realizing the kind of relationship that must be established if we are to survive the ecological crises beginning to unfold.

Indigenous People and Their Environmental Knowledge

The accumulated knowledge of the remaining Indigenous groups around the world represents a body of ancient thought, experience and action that must be honored and preserved as a vital storehouse of environmental wisdom. This environmental understanding can form the basis for evolving the cosmological reorientation so desperately needed. Modern societies must recapture the ecologically sustainable orientation that has long been absent from its psychological, social, and spiritual consciousness.

Indigenous people have preserved ways of ecologically based living that have evolved over 40,000 years of continuous relationship with special environments. Their understanding and application of relating to their land represents models for the *art of relationship* that must be re-taught through modern education. Modern understanding and reapplication of Indigenous relationship to the land are keys to creating social and economic structures that may mean the survival of modern societies.

Yet, Indigenous cultures are in peril in the midst of modern realizations regarding their importance to the vitality of global human ecology. Indigenous Tribal societies are being devastated by the effects of civilization and the pressures of Western-style economic development. As a result, many Indigenous cultures are no longer viable and many will literally cease to exist in the next generation. Their irreplaceable Tribal knowledge and collective ecological wisdom are disappearing at an enormously accelerated rate.[4]

Cultural diversity parallels species diversity in the realm of human ecology. This is especially true of primal cultures who have co-evolved with distinct natural environments. Every time one of these primal cultures is dispossessed, forced from their land in the name of progress, the viability of humans living in that environment is directly affected. Supplanting Indigenous knowledge and care of a particular ecotone with Western-based technological approaches rarely succeeds. This is because Western methodologies consistently fail to respect the intimate and profoundly important relationships established by Indigenous people with their environments. More often than not, a human and ecological wasteland is left in the wake of Western economic and resource development schemes.[5]

The approaches developed by Indigenous people around the world tax the imagination. Indigenous knowledge bases evolved over thousands of years and hundreds of generations. With the loss of that knowledge, one loses access to the approaches and techniques that may become life-saving as we move into the next century. These modes will become essential as we try to deal with the megalithic environmental, social, and cultural problems—the result of the mindset that modern people have evolved within the last century, particularly their disregard for establishing a viable relationship to the natural world.[6]

The knowledge of Indigenous people about their environment is a testimonial to the ingenuity, creativity, resourcefulness, and ability of people to learn and to teach a harmonious way of existence with Nature. From methods of navigation, to application of medicinal properties of plants and animals, to traditional techniques of agriculture, to understanding the properties of specific ecologies, Indigenous people have demonstrated a way of knowing and relating that must be regained and adapted to a contemporary setting—not only for the benefit of those cultures themselves, but for all humankind. Indigenous cultures around the world that have survived the onslaught of natural time and a variety of natural challenges, have little defense against Westernization. Only a few of the existing Indigenous tribes around the world, including American Indian groups, have any real chance to escape cultural annihilation. Ways must be found through the process of education to reclaim and reintegrate traditional knowledge into a context that will allow survival in these trying times. This is especially true if we are collectively to develop a framework for addressing the monumental environmental challenges facing our globally interlocked society.[7]

Two factors may give those Indigenous people who still have some of their Tribal culture a fighting chance. For those who have lost elders and knowledge, but still retain a willingness to revitalize their Tribal ways, the following factors offer hope to recover some of their former life and integrity. The first factor deals with the reintroduction of Indigenous education within the context of their communities and understanding the socio-economic potential inherent in the traditional lifeways of these people. This would require a radical shift from the destructive schemes of cultural assimilation through Western-style economic development. It would require a shift towards direct empowerment of Indigenous communities through understanding and honoring their knowledge and relationship to their environments. This would also require a realistic appreciation of Indigenous cultures that attempt to repair the arrogance of Western contempt for Tribal people, lifeways, and knowledge. This can happen through a new kind of education, which honors the foundations of Indigenous teaching, while incorporating what we know about how humans and their environments interrelate.

The second factor is an honest reassessment of how Indigenous people are viewed by everyone—not only by those who would exploit them and the resources of their lands, or those who would harvest their souls for Christianity, or those who would "develop them for their own good," forgetting that Indigenous people have their own sense of personhood and need to survive in their own ways and on their own terms. Only after restoring and cultivating an abiding respect for the humanity of Indigenous people and their lifeways, can we express in our relationships the reality that the Lakota phrase so poetically announces, "We are all related." Plants, animals, the earth, and all those forces of Nature that surround us are part of us. Only through understanding those forces can we truly be human, because humans not only live in relationship to the natural world; we are the natural world.

Contemporary educational systems, ways of living, ways of relating to other people and other cultures have evolved from a paradigm that does not serve life, but modern technology. In many ways, we are bound to those technological tools that create our environment. These tools do not allow us to establish a sustainable and direct relation to the earth or realize our primal relationship to it because they have largely been created with reference to the old Newtonian-Cartesian paradigm.

Cultural diversity is as important to human ecology as bio-diversity. It is the diversity of the human solutions to every terrestrial environment that has been the foundation of our success as a species. Without this cultural diversity—and the cultures that have evolved unique, ingenious, and creative ways to survive within the natural world—the modern global economic world order, with its standardized solutions, bottom-line mentality, lack of relationship to the life of the earth, assures its eventual extinction. Its overspecialization, its inability to act at the communal level, and its menacing evolution of artificial environments ensures modern society's continued alienation from Nature and its life-sustaining processes.

A final factor relates to Indian people themselves and revolves around a central question of Indian education. The question is how Indian people will revitalize their ecological relationships, their spiritual forces and attitudes toward their environment through a contemporary form of Indigenous education? This is an essential and difficult question that poses one of the most important creative challenges in the evolution of Indian Education in the twenty-first century. We must make a place for this important dimension of the human experience in a world that has not yet learned to value the essential message of Indigenous education: We are all related, and that includes the natural world.

To understand the breadth of this problem, we must address its corollary issues: What was the nature and context of Indigenous education, and what was its relationship to the psychology of place among American Indian people? How is this environmental foundation of traditional Indigenous education reflected in the art, the stories, the prayers, the ritual, and the self-identity of Indian people? How is the environmental foundation reflected in the theology and nature of ethics Native American people have practiced? These are the basic questions that underlie this exploration of the environmental foundation of Indigenous education. Our exploration begins with "that place that the Indians talk about."

That Place The Indians Talk About

In the face of the rapid transformation of the Earth by science and technology, and the ecological crisis that has begun to unfold, leading thinkers are exploring alternative cosmologies, paradigms and philosophies. They are searching for models that may sustain Nature rather than destroy it. Many of these thinkers have found that Indian cosmologies offer profound insights for cultivating a sustainable relationship to place, and a spiritually integrated perception of Nature. These are needed to address what has become a global crisis of ecological relationship.

American Indian people's inherent identification with their Place presents one of the most viable alternative paradigms for practicing the art of relationship to the natural world. American Indians have consistently attempted to maintain a harmonious relationship with their lands in the face of tremendous pressures to assimilate. Traditionally, Indian people have expressed in multiple ways that their land and the maintenance of its ecological integrity are key to their physical and cultural survival. The importance American Indians traditionally place on connecting with their place is not a romantic notion out of step with the times. It is rather the quintessential ecological mandate of our time!

In spite of the importance of connecting to the natural world and the Indigenous models available for doing this, much of what Indian people have to offer has been ignored or trivialized. Western culture, through its unique play of history, disconnected itself from the natural world in order to conquer it. In doing so, Western culture also disconnected from the wellspring of the unconscious and ancient primal orientations to spiritual ecology and a deeply internalized sense of place. The symbolic unity of the inner and outer dimensions of the human psyche had to be denied in order for the rationalistic Newtonian-Cartesian paradigm of science to take hold. Through such a denial, the natural world was objectified so that it might be controlled and subsequently exploited for economic gain and for the greater glory of the Western ego. During the Age of Enlightenment, Western culture broke with the ancient human "participation mystique" as the basis for its relationship with Nature. It substituted a relationship based on objective scientific/rationalist thought that viewed the universe from a purely materialistic standpoint. Nature became a mass of dead matter ripe for manipulation and material gain. Animals became dumb, and Indigenous people became savage primitives. All had to be controlled and developed for their own good, and that of Western society.[8]

Modern governments, businesses, mass media, institutions and organizations are still driven in greatest measure by this mechanistic Newtonian-Cartesian paradigm with its emphasis on profit, economic development, standardization, command and control. Many of these entities continue to operate from a perspective in which other living things, natural resources, land, and even Indigenous people matter only in proportion to their material worth and their political clout. Indigenous people have become as endangered as indigenous places. Nonetheless, harmonizing with their place remains a matter of spiritual, psychological, and cultural survival for Indigenous people. This is why they struggle so tenaciously to hold onto or regain their ancestral lands.

Harmonizing involves the integration of mind, body, and spirit through a dynamic and complex set of activities. For Indians, living in a harmonious and sustainable relationship with the land was a sacred responsibility. It was a perspective tempered with the realization that neglect of this responsibility would bring dire results and retribution from the Earth. The perpetuation of this sacred and survival-oriented responsibility from one generation to the next was accomplished through myth, ritual, art, traditional education, and honoring the psychology of place.

The Psychology of Place

Indian people expressed relationships to the natural world that can only be called "ensoulment". The ensoulment of Nature is one of the most ancient foundations of human psychology. This projection of the human sense of soul and the archetypes contained therein has been called "participation mystique."[9]

Participation mystique for Indian people represented the deepest level of psychological involvement with their land and in a sense reflected a map of their soul. The psychology and spiritual quality of Indian behavior with its reflections in symbolism were thoroughly "in-formed" by the depth and power of their participation mystique and their perception of the Earth as a living soul. It was from this orientation that Indian people believed they had responsibilities to the land and all living things. These responsibilities were similar to those they had to each other. In the Indian mind, spirit and matter are not separate; they are one and the same.

Indian people projected the archetypes they perceived in themselves onto the entities, phenomena, and places that were a part of the natural environment. Indian people traditionally understood the human psyche and the roots of human meaning as grounded in the same order that they perceived in Nature. They experienced Nature as a part of themselves and themselves as a part of it. They understood themselves literally as born of the Earth of their Place. That children are bestowed to a mother and her community through the direct participation of earth spirits, and that children came from springs, lakes, mountains, or caves embedded in the Earth where they existed as spirits before birth, were widespread Indian perceptions. This is the ultimate identification of being Indigenous to a place and forms the basis for a fully internalized bonding with that place. This perception is found in one variation or another among the traditions of Indigenous people throughout the world, including the archaic folk traditions of Europe.

The archetypes—being born from the earth of a place, and the participation of earth spirits in human conception—are universal among Indigenous people. This perception is reflected throughout the myth, ritual, art, and spiritual traditions of Indigenous people because, in reality, our development is predicated on our interaction with the soil, the air, the climate, the plants, and the animals of the places in which we live. This projection of inner archetypes onto a Place formed the spiritually based ecological mindset that was focused upon establishing and maintaining a correct and sustainable relationship. This orientation was reinforced by a physical mimicry and reflection of a "geopsyche" that often takes place when a group of people lives in a particular place for a long time. There is an interaction between the people's inner and outer realities that comes into play as we live in a place for an extended time. Our physical make-up and the nature of our psyche are formed in direct ways by the distinct climate, soil, geography, and living things of a place. Over a few generations of human adaptation to place, certain physical and psychological traits begin to self-select. The development of mountain people as distinct from desert people and as distinct from plains people begins to unfold. Though it is not as apparent now as it was in the past, American Indians of the Northwest, Southwest, Plains, Great Lakes, and Southeast reflect unique physical and psychological characteristics that are the result of generations of interaction with the geographies and ecologies of their respective regions.

But people make a place as much as a place makes them. Indian people interacted with the places in which they lived for such a long time that their landscape became a reflection of their very soul. So phrases such as, Land of the Hopi, or Land of the Sioux, or Land of the Iroquois, etc., have a literal dimension because there was a co-creative relationship between Indian people and their lands. Many Indian groups managed their territories in ecologically viable ways. Through long-term experience with the ecology of their lands and the practical knowledge that such experience brings, they interceded in the creation of habitat and the perpetuation of plant and animal life toward optimum levels of bio-diversity and biological vitality.

The Indian groups in northern California have long practiced a kind of "environmental bonsai" through their centuries-long hunting and gathering activities. California Indian practices of selective gathering in their prescribed ancestral territories actually formed the flora and fauna of their region. Their harvesting of wild potatoes, acorns, pine nuts, buckeyes, bunch grass, and other wild staples perpetuated these species and ensured their availability, not only for people, but for other animals as well.[10]

Ultimately, there is no separation between humans and the environment. Humans affect the environment and the environment affects humans. Indigenous practices were founded on this undeniable reality and sought to perpetuate a sustainable and mutually reciprocal relationship.

What Indian people practiced was a "highly sophisticated, very competent land stewardship that was universal and very indigenous to this hemisphere."[11]

The pre-contact landscapes of America were as much an expression of Indian cultures as their arts and ceremonies. Today, the artifacts of Indian cultures are legally protected; yet the wellsprings from which such cultural expressions came — the land, the plants, the animals, and the waters — are viewed, by mainstream society, as being outside the realm of cultural preservation.

"When Indians talk about restoring or preserving their cultures they talk about restoring their lands in the same breath."[12]

The relationship between Indians and their environment was so deep that separation from their home territory by forced relocation in the last century constituted, literally, a loss of part of the soul of that whole generation. Indian people were joined with their land in such intensity that many of those who were forced to live on reservations suffered a form of soul death. The major consequence was the loss of a sense of home and the expression of profound homesickness with all its accompanying psychological and physical maladies. They withered like mountain flowers pulled from their mother soil.

Traditionally, the connection of Indian people to their land was a symbol of their connection to the spirit of life itself. The loss of such a foundational symbol for Indian tribes led to a tremendous loss of meaning and identity that, only with the most recent generations, has begun to be revitalized. Indian loss of their homelands took such a toll because inner kinship with the world is an ancient and natural extension of the human psyche. The disconnection of that kinship can lead to a deep split in the inner and outer consciousness of the individual and the group. It also brings with it a whole set of social and psychological problems that can only be healed through re-establishing the meaningful ties to the land that has been lost. Revitalizing ancestral connections with Nature and its inherent meaning is an essential healing and transformational process for Indian people.

A Sacred Covenant Revisited

The American Indian sense of place, and the importance of being in harmony is embodied in all cultural traditions. Our collective experience with the land, integrated by myth and ritual, expressed through social structures and arts, combined with a practiced system of environmental ethics and spiritual ecology to create a true connection with places and a full expression of ecological consciousness. American Indians have an important legacy of traditional environmental education that must be revitalized for ourselves and for the generations that are to come. We have been entrusted with an important package of memory, feeling, and relationship to the land that forms a sacred covenant. Our sacred covenant with the land bids us to learn about our traditional forms of environmentally based education. Our covenant bids us to reclaim our heritage of living in a harmonious and sustainable relationship and, thereby, fulfill a sacred trust to the land that is an ancient part of this covenant.

Today fewer and fewer Indian people have the opportunity to engage the land, its plants and animals, in the way that our ancestors once did. Yet, experience with the land was the cornerstone of traditional education. It truly was both the medium and the message of Indian education. Environmental education from the perspective of Indian people must again become one of the collective priorities of modern Indian education. Indian people must take a leading role in environmental education as Western society begins to realize that it needs to forge an ecologically based cosmology, complete with new myths and new applications of science and technology. Western society must become Nature centered if it is to make the life-serving, ecologically sustainable transformations required in the next decades. Indian people have historically expressed the ecologically sustainable models that could form the basis for evolving the educational models needed. But, it is we, as Indian people, who must reassert our sacred covenant with the land. America is an extension of our collective Tribal minds. It is this place that holds our collective memory. It is this place with its unique natural spirit, that provides us with meaning and defines us as distinct People of Place.

Traditional Education Through A Theology of Nature

An ecological sense of relationship encompassed every aspect of traditional American Indian life. American Indians understood that an intimate relationship between them and their environment was the essence of survival and identification as People. American Indians lived in every place the Europeans called the New World, and in every place they established a direct and enduring relationship with their natural environment. They transmitted this understanding of relationship through the learning and teaching processes that they evolved in many unique ways. Their understanding of ecological relationship was reflected in every aspect of their lives, their language, art, music, dance, social organization, ceremony, and their identity as human beings.

Traditional education for Indigenous people has always been an ecological education. Ecologically based thoughts, sentiments, and action became one and the same. Tribes adapted to specific environments in unique ways, which gave rise to a diversity of expressive cultures. Yet, though there was such diversity, there was adherence to a common set of life principles. They understood that the natural universe was imbued with life and with sacredness.

Adaptations to place among Indigenous groups in America took many forms. Living in the forests of the Northeast, Indians venerated the trees and integrated that reality of their environment into every aspect of their lives. Living in the Plains, Indians followed the buffalo and made themselves portable in the way of nomadic hunters around the world. They understood and expressed themselves in relationship to the land and the animals upon which they depended for their survival. In the desert Southwest, Pueblo Indians became dry-land farmers and venerated the cycles of water, earth, wind, and fire, all environmental elements essential to life and continuance as a people in their place. The fisher and forest people of the Pacific Northwest established intimate relationships with the salmon upon which they depended for life, the sea mammals that they encountered and the great rain forests that characterized their environment. In similar fashion, relationships to a place were established by all other people, such as the Paiute in the Great Basin, the Seminole in the Everglades, and the Inuit groups throughout the Far North.

In each place, Native Americans actively engaged their respective environments, and in this engagement became participants with everything in their place. They affected their places and understood that their effect had to be accomplished with humility, understanding, and respect for the sacredness of their place and all living things of that place. They expressed a *Theology of Nature* that, while focusing specifically on their place, included all of Nature. The environments may have been different, but the basis of the theology was the same. The word "Indigenous" is derived from the Latin root *indu* or *endo* that is related to the Greek word, *endina* meaning 'entrails'. Indigenous means being so completely identified with a place that you reflect its very entrails, its soul.[13]

For Indigenous people around the world, education in Nature is life. For Native people throughout the Americas, the paradigm of thinking, acting, and working evolved *through* their established relationships to Nature. The foundation, expression, and context of Indigenous education were environmental. Through art, community, myth, or any aspect of human, social or Tribal expression, the theology of Nature reverberated. All were inspired through an integrated relationship of living in the reality of their physical environments.

The environment was not something separate from their lives, but was the context, the set of relationships, that connected everything. An understanding of ecology was not something apart from themselves or outside their intellectual reality, but the center and generator of self-understanding. As a center, that environmental process of education became the guiding mechanism for the ways they expressed themselves and their sense of sacredness.

In all tribes, environmental understanding, environmental conservation, expressions of religion, and economic enterprise were fully integrated. Every step was a prayer, every waking moment was spent in communion with fellow humans; the natural world was a sacred pathway of knowledge, of learning and teaching the nature of being truly human, truly alive. It was a continuing process of developing one's capacity, one's potential, one's humanness, with the goal of reaching completion. Through striving for completion, each person gained an understanding of true relationship and purpose in life. When one views the world as a sacred place, a place that reflects a living process and way of being that goes beyond the human sense of experience, one deals with Nature in a very different way. It becomes a life- and breath-charged experience.

The expression of life in relationship to environment and to one's relatives, tribe and community, is expressed most directly by the term "lifeway". Lifeways are those activities that people do in communion with each other and with the natural world. They address the key issues of what it is to be alive, to live in a harmonious and complete way in one's relationships. Lifeways provide a Nature centered frame of reference that directly reflects an abiding respect for the natural world. Lifeways help people understand that human beings are indeed a part of the natural world and not separate from it. Human beings interpenetrate, not only with one another, but also with the life around them — the breath and lifeways of trees, grass, earth, water, rocks, animals, and natural phenomena. Honoring and understanding this interpenetration of living things provides profound lessons of how one can live in proper relationship in a community of human beings, animals, and plants, which share the same breath of life. A true sense of ecological piety is gained when one sees how lifeways are interrelated and how they affect one another in specific ways. The Sioux say, "We are all related; we are all related," — because this *is* the ground of Indian experience with the natural world!

In the expressions of Indigenous education among American Indians, the active focus on maintaining or striving for a harmony between one's self and one's natural environment was the most essential principle for applying knowledge. As a result of this orientation, Indian people determined that there were right purposes, right acts, right ways of approaching and understanding the natural world. These codes of behavior were consistent with the way that Indian people conducted themselves in a reciprocal relationship to the natural world. When something was taken from the natural world or animals were killed, ceremonies and symbolic ritual acts were performed to ensure the perpetuation of this right balance and attitude toward relationships.

Mutual reciprocity was engendered in all the acts that Native American people joined and effected within the context of their natural environment. Ceremony and ritual were social and spiritual mechanisms that maintained or re-established harmony with natural processes. They were also ways of learning how to maintain one's relationship to the natural sources of life that Indian people recognized within their place. Offering tobacco after taking the life of an animal, such as the deer or antelope or buffalo, was a reflection of this understanding, this environmentally educated sense of being that Indian people practiced in their everyday lives.

For Indian people, the Earth was alive and had its own sense and expression of consciousness and being. The natural environment was a spiritual reality and the earth entities, living creatures, were not used haphazardly or without great respect. A sense of spiritual ecology, founded on a deep spiritual resonance with the natural world, characterized the process and reflection of environmental education among Indigenous people.

This sense of relatedness to the natural world came from a much deeper source than intellectual understanding. It came from a spiritual orientation and responsibility for maintaining a conscious relationship with those things human life depended on for survival. This sense of relationship unfolded through the perpetuation of "natural community", which reflected a spiritual ecology connecting the People to their Place, and to each other. Since everything was mutually dependent, nothing in Nature could be viewed as purely self-sufficient, especially human beings. The idea of a community that included not only the human species, but all species, became an integral foundation and context for expressing Indigenous environmental education. The understanding of a natural community led to the social organizational concept of "natural democracy." Within this context of natural democracy, there is the idea that plants, animals, and other entities in the natural world, have rights of their own and must be given respect, as would any member of a human tribe.

Today, natural democracy may be considered a revolutionary concept, yet it was the foremost principle guiding the process of Indian people in their interaction with their physical environments. Conservation and preservation of natural communities were integrally reflected in the practices of Indian people. This basic environmental ethic was predicated on the perception that life should be preserved for life's sake. This ethic espoused that it was the responsibility of human beings to ensure that all life, because it was sacred — a direct reflection of the same breath as human breath — had to be respected and preserved, if the web of life, upon which all human beings depended, was to be maintained.

At the root of the *Theology of Nature*, was the concept that the life energy of the world had to be understood to maintain the right relationship to the world. The way that life energy could be understood was through direct observation. Observing energy as it reflected the natural life process was fundamental to Indian environmental understanding. So the sense of the ecological, or resonance with natural energies, which constituted the earth and all of its life processes, became for American Indians the context of religious expression. The natural world was the American Indian church. The life processes of those things that ensured that life continued within a natural context, became the focus of veneration and attempts towards understanding. This was a kind of metaphysics, an ecological philosophy for understanding the spirit that moved through Nature and human beings.

Through the observation of Nature, Indian people perceived two complementary forces that constituted the creative process of life as it unfolded on a moment-to-moment basis. These perceptions of natural principles were symbolized in entities such as the Corn Mothers, recognized by Pueblo people as participants in the creation of the world and representatives of the earth's natural feminine related creative process. The Zunis perceive these forces as manifestations of the Great He/She Spirit, which is both male and female and gives definition to the nature of all expressions of life. Through observing the natural world, Indians reflected on life's complexities, its paradoxes, and Nature's great wisdom in orchestrating the dynamic and mysterious expressions of life. Myths became the primary oral vehicle for expressing, in metaphoric and instructional ways, principles of life and Nature. Rituals became the process for applying the most important principles to human life.

The Hero Twins, the Coyote/Trickster myths, and many others presented profound ecological lessons based on experiences of generations of Indian people relating to their environments. Traditional arts, for instance, used natural materials taken from the environment to create something with aesthetic quality, while reflecting the understanding of relationship to the natural world. Each traditional art form created by a Tribal group of people expressed their participation with their natural environment. The plants and natural materials used for paint, the natural clays for pottery, the types of wood used for carving entities, the hides and other animal products used for the creation of art were all a direct expression of Tribal people connecting to spirits and energies of the natural world. Through the extensive use of oral tradition, ritual, and ceremony, Indian people established and maintained a dynamic participation with the natural world that deeply informed the meanings and understandings they had about themselves as a particular kind of people. These relationships became bound together within the context of the environmental expression of traditional education. All education that Indigenous people reflected was integrated with this centering place, this central and most primal expression of human education, human learning, and human teaching.

The common phrase used by many Indians at the conclusion of an important ceremony, when translated into English means, 'We do this for Life's Sake!' This phrase reflects the constant attempt by Indigenous people to maintain their relationship to the natural world and to life as a whole through their conduct in community and the natural world. They do this with regard to their purest sense of self. In this way they also reflect a *Theology of Nature*, which represents one of the most profound attempts of man to understand life, relationship, and Nature.

Journeying Through A Sacred Landscape

At the core of American Indian traditional foundations is the reality of vision and visioning. That vision, variously expressed by all American Indian tribes, is: "We are of this land, and this land is us."

Journeying through a sacred landscape has been a central metaphor and foundation for traditional Indian education. In the body of myth of all Indians there are stories of the travels and migrations of the People through time and place. In each Place that a tribe stopped to live, they established an abiding relationship with the land and all things therein. These stops of the People established an ecological connection and learning relationship that was commemorated through story, song, and ceremony. In each stop of their migrations through the landscape, they learned something about themselves and the essential principles of environmental relationship. In this sense, the landscape is like a textbook of ecological understanding, interpreted through the traditional stories and activities of tribes.

The long journey of Indian people through the Americas has formed a common frame of reference that can be experienced through the myths that underlie their guiding ethos. While Tribal guiding myths are diverse and unique, each mythic complex reflects similar principles and foundations for understanding environmental relationship. These common threads include the understandings that: Nature is sacred, humans share the breath of life with other living things, we exist within and are affected by the mutually reciprocal web of interrelationships in a natural community, plants, animals, and other natural phenomena and entities are imbued with power, the natural world creates through the interplay of opposite yet complementary primal energies, and there exists a guiding creative force in Nature that affects everything. Many metaphors, structures, symbols and stories have been used by tribes to convey these basic understandings. The following exemplify these understandings.

Look to the mountain is a metaphor that capsulizes one aspect of the ecological vision of Indigenous education. Metaphoric images such as Mountain are ecological symbols carried from the first visions of Indigenous man. *Look to the mountain* is an invocation that focuses on the journey to a higher place, a place that allows one to see where one has been, is, and may wish to go. As the Tewa say, *pin peyé obe*... "toward the mountain look." In every place where mountains occur, they have been venerated as the place of vision and orientation. For many Tribal people, mountains have been the homes of the highest earth spirits and the boundaries of the sacred cosmos. The mountain, as ecological metaphor and symbol of higher thought and attainment, is often integrated with the metaphors of pathway, pilgrimage, and cardinal orientations forming the boundaries of a sacred space. The Navajo, like other Indian tribes, symbolize the founding of sacred space in the primal structure that they call the *hogan*.

"The first hogan was made of the four sacred mountains and the space between them. Having made their way to the top of a hollow reed to escape the flood that was devouring the previous world, First Man and First Woman looked around and determined to mark their hopes of remaining here in the Fifth World by embellishing the land for generations to come. First Man took the bundle of mountain soils he brought from the Four Worlds below and proceeded to create the mountains that are the foundation of Navajo culture and consciousness.

"To be Diné (Navajo) is to be supremely conscious of one's relationship to the ultimate reality that is the place between those four sacred mountains. Navajo, and holy people who embody the inner forms of all the natural features in this place, are jointly engaged in perpetuating the welfare of the earth. To go to the sacred mountains in prayer, song or ceremony is to acquire the means of activating harmony and the earth."[14]

The "way" to the mountain is embodied in the experience and the process of Indigenous education. Climbing these metaphoric mountains of orientation to gain the unique perspective afforded by each embodies the age-old process of Indigenous education. It is a way of developing the ecological understandings and relationships that ensure the attainment of life's needs. Journeying to that sacred mountain top, one can begin to envision a sense of relationship, not only to one's self and one's community, but also to the natural world. This was the guiding sensibility that allowed Tribal people in the Americas to establish an abiding resonance with the places, plants, animals, and other natural entities with which they related and through which they came to know themselves as The People. From the vantage point of that visionary mountain top, we have the opportunity to envision, regardless of cultural orientation, our most basic sense of identity to our environments.

As Tribal people moved from that primal mountain top to settle in the valleys, along the lakes, streams, rivers and those beautiful lands that make up the wondrous landscape of the Americas, they came to know themselves as creators, as participants in the greater order of the natural world.

The White Mountain Apache venerate mountain spirits that were sent by the Giver of Life to teach them how to care for themselves and all living beings. The Apache call these spirits of the mountains "Gaan". The Gaan taught the Apache how to hunt, plant, heal the sick, govern, and live together harmoniously. They were teachers of Nature, relationship, and spirit. While they lived among the Apache, in that time in the deep past, the Gaan instilled in the Apache an abiding sense of respect for the life-sustaining qualities and nature of the mountains. After a time, the Gaan returned to the sacred caves in the mountains where they continue to live to this day.[15]

The Mountain Spirit Dance of the White Mountain Apache reenacts the teachings and revitalizes the gifts brought by the Gaan from their mountain homes. For the Apache, as with many other Indian tribes, the metaphor, "Look to the Mountain," is a way of remembering to remember one of their most essential ecological relationships.

In the Southwest there is a metaphoric figure often represented in the petroglyphs found throughout New Mexico, Arizona, Utah, and into Mexico. The figure has many names; in some places it is called the Kokopeli. It is a mythical figure who represents the creative process, the human instinct for learning, and the procreative energies and powers within ourselves and within the natural world; it affords a symbol that allows us to expand our thinking as it relates to developing and maintaining the proper relationship to ourselves and our environments. As is true with all Native American mythic figures, the Kokopeli is an ecological symbol. Kokopeli, sometimes called the Antman or Humpbacked Flute Player, was a mythical figure who journeyed from village to village in the Pueblo Southwest with his peaceful music and engaging tales that taught people about relationship.

Kokopeli represents an enduring visual symbol of the procreative, life giving, and nourishing power of Nature. The symbol of Kokopeli probably originated in Mexico as a representation of one of the fertility spirits recognized since ancient times by tribes throughout Mexico, Central, and South America. Various stories and representations of Kokopeli appear as far north as California and Oregon and as far south as Peru.

There is evidence that Kokopeli is a reflection of a caste of merchants who traveled far and wide carrying news, trading seeds and other goods from village to village. His characteristic hunched back may have been a real physical affliction, but more likely represented a back pack in which he carried his goods. His flute may have served to notify villagers of peaceful intentions. Modern counterparts of Kokopeli, know as "Cobaneros" still travel mountain trails from village to village in Belize and Guatemala plying their trade and playing flutes. The ancient Kokopeli were also healers, teachers, magicians, and storytellers.[16]

In both their mythical and historical realities, the Kokopeli facilitated communication, learning, the spread of ideas and stories, as well as fertility, sacred seeds, and the creative spirit embodied in a myriad of expressions of Nature. This is why Kokopeli captures contemporary imagination. Kokopeli represents a universal reality of transformation and creative learning that reflects the processes of Nature and the activities of humans as they interact with their environment and with each other.

Kokopeli is a symbol of creative exploration that guides us as we journey through the times and places of Native Americans and begin to explore how Indian relationships to those lands and places evolved through time. Kokopeli is a metaphoric guide in the story of environmental knowledge of Indian America.

Our Relatives, The Animals

There is an extended history of Tribal hunters in America following the deer, the bison, and the mastodon. Indian elders say that we have always been here. The relationship to the animals they hunted engendered the first thoughts that today we call ecology and ecological philosophy. The first hunters developed such an intimate relationship with the animals they hunted that they became resonant with the spirit and essence of the life of animals. Early hunting cultures depicted their relationships to these animals in the megalithic cave paintings of Spain and France. They enacted a variety of initiatory rites in the deepest reaches of earth's womb — caves like those found at Tres Fries in France. Inside these caves they created the symbols of their relationship and their understanding of their life in Nature. They created shrines to the animals they depended on for their life and well-being. They sculpted the figures that they considered the most important, entities who allowed the game to exist. These were the game mothers, who in their archetypal fashion, represented the Earth Mothers, those first mothers that represented the essence of the Earth's procreative power.

In an attempt to develop and maintain a balance and harmony with the relationships they felt essential between themselves, the animals they hunted and the environment in which they lived, these ancient hunters created roles that today are called "shaman," the first teacher, first artist, first doctor, first priest, first psychologist. All the roles reflected by the archetypal figure of the shaman came into full application during the times of the hunting cultures. The first shamans laid down the basic frameworks for establishing and maintaining a direct relationship between human beings and the animals and plants that inhabited their environments.

This spiritual journey through relationship was the beginning of the first religions of man. Those first religions were wholly Nature centered. They evolved through an abiding respect for natural entities, the understanding that all natural entities had a spirit and shared breath with human beings. Art was a tool to express the nonverbal, the innermost reflections of the dream, the understanding of relationship to the natural world that those first shamans and first hunters experienced. The origins of art among the first shamans document the original attempts by hunting men to express their relationship to their natural world. As communities became more sedentary, this tradition of art and this way of relating to the natural world expanded to form the expressions of sacred art we find worldwide today.

Those first tribes learned how to build shelters from the natural materials in their environment. They learned to understand the habits of animals. They learned how to use, through trial and error, all the things that were part of their environment and apply them to the betterment of their lives. They had an abiding understanding that everything in Nature was interrelated and that they were indeed a part of the earth and the earth a part of them. And so they created, as in the Southwest, shelters made from mud, stone, wood. They created clothing from the animals they hunted. They developed strains of corn and other foods, squash, pumpkins, beans, etc., that became a dependable source of life for them and their families. They created art forms from the natural materials around them including baskets, pottery and textiles that they decorated with natural plant substances and paints. Through this process, the ceremony that characterized the Nature centered Tribal arts of Native America came into full effect. These Tribal arts remain today as powerful expressions of interdependence on their natural community and understanding their responsibility to other life and the earth.

As time went by, and societies became more complex, the people lived in communities of increasingly greater density. They built towns and cities and evolved more complex societies, but they did not forget that everything came from Nature and that Nature was indeed the field of their being. As American Indian societies became more complex, so did their ritual, their conceptual frameworks, and their applications of appropriate technologies. The metaphysical concept that guided the development of these natural communities focused on the idea of natural orientation. Natural orientation began with a symbolic center and radiated out to include the entire cosmos, all plants and animals, the mountains, rivers, streams, lakes, all of those natural entities that made up the reality of a community. The concept of orientation was interpreted and expressed in the art forms they developed. It was reflected in the pottery, basketry, the ways that utilitarian tools were made (such as the birch bark canoe or the large cedar dugout canoes used by the Indians of the Northwest), in totem poles, jewelry, and architecture.

Every tribe incorporated into their traditional art forms a sense of the sacredness of Nature. They reflected their understanding of that sacredness in the symbols they used to represent that relationship. Among the earliest symbols was the Hunter of Good Heart, a metaphoric symbol containing a complex of principles, ways of relating to and understanding animals that evolved from the primal relationship of hunters to the animals that they hunted. The Hunter of Good Heart is probably one of the oldest educational metaphors in existence and can be found in hunting cultures around the world. Among the Pueblo people of the Southwest, the Hunter of Good Heart represented a way of living, a way of relating, a way of ethics and proper behavior. This was the foundation for teaching and learning about relationships to the animals they depended on for life.

Some art forms, such as those produced by the Anasazi and Mimbres people of the Southwest, reflected an intimate integration of the human being with the animal in the various design motifs found in their pottery. They are also represented in the petroglyphs found throughout the Southwest. These petroglyphs incorporate and communicate relationships between the hunter and the animals hunted. They represent the forces, natural, spiritual and otherwise, that combine to teach and bring completeness to individuals who hunted and maintained the sacred relationship with the animals they hunted. The deer, for example, presents a metaphoric icon, as well as a living entity, around which Indian people expressed a variety of philosophical, environmental, and conservation ideas. The deer is represented in many forms in traditional Native American arts. Among the Huichol Indians, the five-pointed deer represents the mythical essence of the spiritual energy of Nature. It is an icon used in the traditional art form of yarn painting to represent the spiritual essence of their sacrament, peyote. In whatever habitat the deer was found, it was venerated for its spiritual qualities and as an important food source. The tracking of deer was also a metaphor for the hunter and his sense of self, for the deer represented a source of life and was a meaningful representation of life itself.

During the 40,000-year tradition of hunting among Indigenous tribes in America, there evolved songs, ceremonies, rituals, and art forms that focused on ensuring the success of the hunter and the survival of the communities and families they represented. Rituals evolved among hunters including special dances, songs, initiatory rites, and cultivation of a spiritual quality to the act of hunting. Such rituals were founded on an intimate understanding of the behavior of the animals hunted, an abiding respect for their life needs, and an awareness of how those animals should be used and properly treated. These thoroughly evolved understandings formed the basis for an ecological ethic of such a depth and intimacy that it continues to have a profound impact on contemporary Indigenous people today.

The Hunter of Good Heart, in a direct and literal way, represented oral tradition and Indigenous teaching at its best. It was the foundation of a complex and profound teaching process that began in childhood and extended into old age. As the successful Pueblo hunter gathered his extended family to tell the story of the hunt, he provided an instance for people to gather and listen to the stories that had been passed from generation to generation. These were also coded in the traditional art forms such as the hunter's canteen, created among the Pueblos from clay and decorated with a deer who has a spirit arrow going from its mouth into the heart. Through such symbolic art, Native American people focused on those principles that emanated from their guiding myth. These traditional symbols reflected the profound relationship and understanding of the animals and plants in their environment. The symbols offered a context to remember to remember what that relationship was.

Through ceremonial dance complexes such as the Deer Dance among Pueblo people, the deer are danced and the community gathers to witness, in ceremony and ritual, the story of the responsibility that all human beings have to respect the animals they hunt. The dancing of the deer happened not only in the Rio Grande Pueblos but also among the Indians of California, of the Northwest, the Southeast, and among other Indigenous groups around the world.

In every place that hunting occurred, and it occurred every place, it brought the individual and community in direct contact with the magical reality of animals and with the life of the natural environment. The lessons were similar in Native American hunting — whether the hunter was a Cheyenne coming home with a buck and sharing it with his grandparents, or the hunter was an Abenaki, hunting moose in the Maine forests and calling his extended family to share and help him carry his catch back to their village, or two Inuit hunters battling for their lives and those of their families with a mother polar bear. In every case, hunting brought people, tribes, and societies into direct contact with life and death, with the need to establish and maintain proper relationships in their environments for the sake of their survival and that of their communities.

All teaching based on hunting was predicated on the principle of abiding respect and relationship with the animals hunted. Every tribe observed careful rules of conduct and embellished these rules with prayers, songs, and offerings to the animals, the animal spirits, the game spirits, or the game mothers and fathers from whom the animal spirits derived their being. Hunting rituals and the act of hunting prepared individuals for the important matters of life. They taught individuals the nature of courage and sacrifice, the importance of sharing, and the special power gained through vision and spiritual questing. Individuals learned that we have within us an animal spirit, and understanding that spirit through hunting was one of the most important lessons of self-knowledge. Hunters learned that preparing for the hunt was also preparing for life, a preparation most essential to body, mind, and spirit. It involved a spiritual ethic of conservation and ecologically sound approaches for maintaining the life of the animals hunted.

There was a widespread belief that each animal had a spirit village to which they returned and reported their treatment by humans. This report directly affected whether that species of animal would give its life for humans in the future. Such beliefs were part of the way American Indian people related to their environment and to the animals therein. Other ritual activities, such as making offerings and prayers of thanksgiving to the animals taken, were a part of a grand and well-evolved web of spiritual relationships gained primarily through the Indigenous process of education.

Indigenous hunting rituals reflected the perpetuation of a covenant between the hunter and hunted. This covenant was often symbolized through the ceremonial use of talismans that embodied the qualities of the animals hunted or other animals who were hunters, such as wolves, mountain lions, or killer whales. Among Aleut hunters, talisman amulets provided a spiritual connection between themselves and the animals that they hunted.

"For a successful hunt a man prepared himself both physically and spiritually. Included in his hunting equipment were amulets to attract the animals and appease their spirits. Their preparation and place of preservation are kept secret, otherwise amulets will lose their power. It is necessary to protect them from wetness; if an amulet becomes wet its owner will rot."[17]

Hunting rituals, and the act of hunting, empowered not only the individuals but also the communities from which they came. Ritual before, during, and after hunting provided the context for the appropriate use of technology and the tools that were the extension of human's abilities to hunt. Even the tools that were used—spears, the atl-atl, snares, traps, the bow and arrow—were sanctified in relationship to their use, so the technology that evolved regarding hunting had a sacred relationship with the interaction of humans to animals and the natural world.

The context of hunting itself spread far beyond the actual act of hunting or fishing and included the entire community in celebration, sharing, and commemoration of the life that animals had shared with the people. The rituals performed for hunting functioned to attract animals and to cultivate a proper attitude and respect, but also allowed human beings to reconnect with those mythic times when humans, animals, and plants shared a relationship with each other that was much more intimate and interactive. The atmosphere in which traditional Tribal communities educated its individuals evolved around a process of coming into being. Each step along that pathway of knowledge — relationship to animals, to self, community, and environment — formed the foundation for the concept of completeness. This ecological ethic, expressed through Indigenous education and in ritual and ceremony, have been preserved by various tribes. They continue to be practiced with reference to traditional tenets of ecological relationship and the ecological foundations of Indigenous education.

The process of hunting allowed the hunter to understand the nature of self-effacement and humility. It taught him why it was important to treat animals properly and honor the greater family of animals of which he was a part. Dancing, offering prayers of thanksgiving, asking for life for one's family and community all added to the development of the individual hunter as a complete expression of human nature.

In many Tribal contexts, there was such an identification with animals that hunters' personal names were derived from animal experiences or expressions. Also whole clans and societies traced their lineage and their essence of power and social place to animal totems. They recognized animals they hunted as being the personifiers of their sense of themselves as a particular group within the greater community of Nature. Therefore animals, and the way that Indigenous people viewed their relationship to them, formed an infrastructure for social organization.

This relationship to animals formed a context for the expression of conservation and ethical treatment of animals. All hunting tribes evolved a game management system predicated upon the eco/spiritual ethics of the community. Modern conservation principles, such as taking only one kind of game during a particular season and leaving others alone — the single-prey principle — was in widespread use among Indian hunters. The maintenance of a hunting territory, a sacred and practical method of allowing a group of people to maintain a particular area for their use and survival, became another basic principle widely applied in Indian hunting. In some cases hunting within a territory was strictly controlled by a particular society within a tribe. The Cheyenne Dog Society, for instance, played the role of policing the community; they also maintained and ensured that all Tribal members adhere to the proper practices and respect a hunting area and the animals therein.

At every turn Indian hunters sought to establish a direct and intimate resonance with the animals hunted. They focused on special animals whom they considered important for their survival. These animals embodied a special spiritual quality and provided a model for human behavior by their habits, character, and lifeways. Animals such as the bear, the dog, salmon, the deer, coyote, wolf, mountain lion, turtle, the great eagles, the raven, the hare, the fox, the badger, the hummingbird, the elk, the moose, and a host of smaller animals and birds were recognized for their ability to teach through their behavior and what they represented in the overall fabric of an environment.

These expressions of relationship to the animal world provided a rich multiverse of experience and learning processes that Indigenous people under-stood in both practical and philosophical ways. They effectively applied these understandings in a direct process of helping each individual become fully human and move toward being a complete man or woman.

Hunting formed an elaborate context for Indigenous education. It was integrated with other experience in the natural environment that could provide models for Indian teaching. For instance, animals provided the creative inspira-tion and design motifs for a huge portion of traditional Native American art forms. Animals played roles within the Indian mythologies that were used as orientation to the animal kingdom. The vibrancy that one finds in traditional art forms and traditional stories is in part due to the rich metaphoric application of understanding and reflection on human relationship to the animal world.

The concept of transformation occurs throughout Indigenous ritual, myth, dance, and performance. It reflects that rich interaction in relationship to the animal world. Stories abound in which humans become certain beings or vice versa, interacting with each other in an intimate way. For instance, the idea of animals with a powerful spirit-nature is reflected in the shamanistic practices that permeate the northern latitudes of North America and Siberia. When a reso-nance between humans and the animals existed, there was an expression of spiritual ecology that was truly bonding.

These animal relationships were expressed through the ceremonial rituals that focused on their connection and their ability to connect humans with the universal order. The world and animal renewal ceremonies, practiced by all tribes, expressed the human responsibility to preserve, protect, and perpetuate all life. In the Northwest, the salmon ceremonies reflect this responsibility:

"The salmon ceremony was observed everywhere along the Northwest coast. For the Yurok and others its symbolized a renewal of the world's creation. Many groups also held ceremonies for the first fish taken or other species—the first deer, the first berries, or even the first acorn in the southern regions.

"The salmon (or first four salmon) received the most elaborate rites, though this varied from place to place. Usually the salmon were laid with their heads pointing upstream on a newly woven mat or cedar board, often under a special shelter and sprinkled with down feathers of birds. A formal speech or prayer of welcome was intoned as in this particular example:

> Old friends, thank you that we meet alive. We have lived until this time when you came this year. Now we pray you, supernatural ones, to protect us from danger, that nothing evil may happen to us when we eat you, supernatural ones, for that is the reason why you have come here, that we may catch you for food. We know that only your bodies are dead here, but your souls come to watch over us when we are going to eat what you have given us to eat now.'

"The salmon were offered fresh water symbolically after their long journey through the salt sea. The first salmon were then cooked and divided in small pieces among all the people present at a communion. The celebration, often seven days in length, included feasting, gift-giving, torch-bearing processions, dancing and singing. During all the ceremonial of welcome, countless salmon were allowed to pass upstream to the spawning grounds, and thus the ritual actually helped to assure the continuation of the salmon runs."[18]

The concepts of sharing, connecting, and relating one's life to animals formed a basic premise of Indigenous education. However, the animal world was not the only focus of thought and reverence within the natural environments inhabited by Native Americans. Plants, stars, and the celestial bodies of the cosmos provided other focus and expression for Native American environmental education. Indian people observed plants in their environment as keenly as they observed animals. They sought to establish with plants (as they had done with animals), a relationship, a resonance, and a deeper understanding.

Plants, The Hair of The Earth Mother

There is a perception among some Indian herbalists that plants are the "hairs" of Mother Earth. Every time you pull a plant from the earth, she feels that pull, and you must always make the proper offering of tobacco and prayers. This ensures that the pulling of one of Earth Mother's hairs does not hurt her too much. She must understand that you comprehend your relationship to her, and you know what she is giving you is one of the parts of her body. In honoring and understanding that, you also honor and understand your reciprocal relationship to all of life and Nature.

Plants have always played an intimate role in the life and survival of Indigenous people around the world. Indeed, major forms of human society came about as a direct result of evolution to agriculturists from the earlier hunter/gatherer lifestyles. Plants provided food, medicine, fiber for clothing, paint for decoration, a material source for shelter, and fire to keep oneself warm during the winter's cold. As was true with the respect accorded animals, plants were treated within a context of ritual and ceremony. As one Navajo elder has stated:

> You must ask permission of the plant or the medicine will not work. Plants are alive; you must give them a good talk.[19]

The world of plants had its spirit keepers. These might be the major kinds of trees in a particular environment, or they could be certain medicinal plants deemed important to a tribe. Indians understood that plants, like animals, shared a quality of spirit that could be used to ensure the survival of a tribe. Therefore, ceremonies performed by Indian tribes throughout North America incorporated symbolic representatives of plants and plant kingdoms. Ritual plants such as cornmeal, tobacco, and sweetgrass, were used as offerings to the spirit world and provided the material substance for both food and medicine. Plant symbols reflecting the sacred procreative power of Earth also abound in American Indian philosophies.

The Tree of Life as a metaphor for the foundation of the cosmic order was expressed in numerous ways in the ceremony and philosophy of tribes throughout North America. Among the Pueblo people of the Southwest, for example, the Evergreen, which in most cases is the Fir or Spruce, is a symbol of everlasting life and the connection of all life to the Earth Mother. Therefore, as a symbol of this magnitude, it is used in every ceremony that Pueblo people perform. The Evergreen represents the universal Tree of Life, and the sentient being of plant life as a whole. It was well understood that plants were the first living things and that both humans and animals depended on plant life for their existence. As the first living things, plants provided the most primal connection to the teeming life that is the direct expression of Earth Mother's being.

The dependence on certain plants for the survival and maintenance of a people expressed itself in many ways. Among the Pueblo, corn, squash, pumpkin, and beans became the primary staple foods that gave rise to social and community expressions of Pueblo societies. The relationship of the Pueblo farmer to corn is especially noteworthy. To Pueblo people, corn is a sacrament, a representation, an embodiment of the essence of the Earth Mother's life. Corn provided not only food, but also a symbolic entity that cradled the entire psyche and spiritual orientation of Pueblo people. Pueblo farmers developed an intimate understanding of the life of corn and through that understanding, developed techniques, technologies, and strains of corn adapted to various growing conditions in Southwestern environments. They developed a practical technology and understanding of basic genetics, plant behavior, and communities based on their special relationship with corn. This helped them understand the nature of evolution and natural selection among plants.

Hopi farmers, through long experience and comprehension of the growth and life of corn, evolved a variety of strains that grew well in different soils and environmental circumstances. Through understanding the life and breath of corn, they established an elemental spiritual connection between themselves and this sacramental plant. That relationship extended not only into the technology of growing corn, but also into communal, artistic, and philosophical expressions reflecting the abiding relationship between humans and the plant kingdom.

Indigenous people evolved ritual and ceremony expressing their partnership with those plants and animals they depended on for life. Among the Pueblos, the varieties of Corn Dances performed during the growing cycle reflect such communal expression. The community comes together with all its entities — old and young, male and female — to celebrate and remember to remember the connections that the community and individuals have with such a sacramental plant.

This basic spiritual ecology provided different occasions in which the relationship between themselves and the natural world could be expressed. These expressions included the grand ceremonial representations of the plant and animal worlds. They were also reflected in engineering and other forms of practical technology connected with Southwestern Indian agriculture. The great canals built in the valley of Tucson by the Hohokam provide one example. Numerous other examples — of this integration of technology with the practicality of maintaining a lifeway revolving around key plants — occurred among the Anasazi in southern Colorado. Each instance (the grand ceremony or the communal work associated with corn) occasioned an experience of people coming together to celebrate and learn the nature of being in community and depending on one another for survival.

This communal interaction with Nature reflects a natural community of human beings as active participants, with other entities and energies in an environment, in a dynamic expression of their lives and the life of the Earth. This sense of natural community is expressed in the design motifs of traditional art forms that relate to natural elements essential to the growth of plants. The Zia Pueblo Sun, which appears commonly in traditional Zia pottery designs; or the terraced cloud designs on traditional black Santa Clara pottery; or the reflection of wind, rain, lightning, or representations of creatures such as the frog, water bird, dragonfly, tadpole, and butterfly illustrate the connection that Pueblo people felt with their environment and their lives as agriculturists. Such design motifs, inspired by natural entities, formed the basis of Pueblo artistic expressions and aesthetics. The commonly used motif of Corn Mother and her Corn Children (represented by two perfect ears of corn, each a different color yet related through the common ancestry of the Corn Mother), is another example of the way the connections of plant, human, animal, and all life is portrayed through Pueblo pottery.

The Indigenous educational process of each Pueblo community demonstrates, through its pottery, the essential perspective of Pueblo ecology. It reflects the attempt of Indian people to understand their relationship to, and place within, their natural community through ceremony, thought, expression, and making traditional art forms. The making of a traditional art embodies, both in form and process, the understanding of the basic resonance of relationship and the importance of establishing, reaffirming, and continuing it. Plants and animals are food that nourishes and perpetuates human life. Therefore, there is a symbolic connection between pottery making and making life from Nature.

Traditionally for Pueblos, making pottery is a ceremonial act; it is an act of faith, an act of understanding the significance of relationship. The relationship is to what is being formed as a result of digging into the earth: the clays that are the building material for pottery. It is also a metaphor of a learning process to establish and reaffirm those basic connections that every human has to the earth. The making, designing, and using of Pueblo pottery reflects the understanding that all things made, in whatever form they appear—ultimately have their beginnings in the natural materials provided by the world and by Earth Mother.

This sentiment extends to the collection, preparation, and eating of foodstuffs from one's natural environment. The food of humans is also the food of life, and understanding the nature of those things that give you life provides the context for what Indigenous people have termed "right relationship". For Pueblo people, collecting clay, making pottery from that clay, the design motifs used to decorate these pots of clay, all symbolize that those things that give us life—in this case the pottery to hold food or water—are a way of understanding right relationship.

Therefore, what goes on or in the Pueblo pot reflects the realization that the food we eat must be appreciated; it is sacred and symbolic of that which gives us life. It is a metaphor of our relationship with, and dependence on, the natural world.

The Ecological Foundations of Indigenous Health and Wholeness

For Indigenous people around the world, the food they depended on for life was also their medicine. The two were so intimately intertwined that many plants were used in one instance as food, while in others, under the proper supervision and application by a medicine person, were used as components of a system of healing. Food was always a component of ceremony and ritual in Indigenous communities. Food was the most basic symbolic representation of how humans depended on other living and natural things for their lifeway. Indian relationships to food, combined with their physical lifestyle and spiritual orientation, formed an interactive triad that created the cornerstone of Indian health. In short, it is food that best symbolizes the ecology of Indian health.

American Indians used food in a number of ways, and since all food that Indigenous people traditionally ate came from the land or animals, it had a symbolic relationship to the way they viewed themselves vis-a-vis Nature. Food's place in the ceremonies of groups in the Americas reflected a spiritual ecology that integrated the life experiences of Indian people. For instance, Indian people of the Great Lakes domesticated wild plants such as the pond lily, rice, and other marsh-growing plants. These plants provided them not only with food but also a frame of reference for defining and refining their existence and relationship to their place. Their knowledge and utilization of marsh environments embodied their relationship to plants and food.

As was true in the Great Lakes, the Paiute Indians of the Great Basin evolved numerous uses for naturally occurring food sources such as the pine nut. In the Northeast, the Algonquin people evolved a technology of how to use maple sap in a variety of ways. This provided them not only with food but also a source of reflection and understanding of their dependence on the trees that dominated their natural environment.

Indigenous people in America learned how to use the food plants in their environment in the most productive, effective, and ecologically sound ways. Through long experience, they began to understand the relationship between the plants that they took as food and the healing properties for which these plants might be most appropriately used.

Thus the knowledge of how to use plants for food evolved into the use of plants for healing. This knowledge, which ensures survival within a given environment, was an essential foundation of the first aspects of Indigenous education. It was a knowledge passed on to children through mythology, ritual, experience, and observation. They learned through helping to make traditional art forms or preparing foods and in a host of other ways. It was an integral part of the early life experience and learning of all Indian children. As with all knowledge, how to use plants and animals for medicine evolved along a continuum that addressed each stage of life and each age of an individual in an appropriate way. Young people were given their first experience in how to use plants through simple observation, through the use of story, and through the actual demonstration of how plants could be used. This kind of teaching occurred primarily within the context of their extended family, clan group, and tribe.

This learning continuum evolved in a number of ways and incorporated the full body of traditional philosophy of the human place within the greater natural world. Among all tribes, illness was directly associated with a disharmony of the individual, family, clan or tribe, with regard to some key element of the natural environment. Much of the healing ritual and ceremony of Indian tribes involved re-establishing the harmony between the individual, family, or clan group and their immediate environment. Harmony and resonance were sought with those environmental energies, principles, and entities that formed the foundation for the expression of the group's lifeway.

The mediators for the transference of this knowledge, and re-establishment of these basic foundations of balance, were primarily the healers or medicine people. Medicine people, depending on tribe and location, could fulfill a variety of roles within the context of their communities. The herbalists, a primary group of healers, were predominantly women whose work in many tribes was to gather wild foods. Through their experience and understanding of plant communities came an understanding of the kinds of plants that could be used for medicine. The next group of individuals had a greater knowledge that included knowledge of the human body and muscular structure. They were adept at massaging and fixing bones. The next group were individuals who had access to special knowledge related to certain plants or animals as a result of their position or as a direct result of clan initiation or societal membership. Through ceremonies these individuals were empowered to address certain illnesses that they learned to treat effectively.

The most pronounced role was that of the shaman. The shaman's role embodied the integration and nature of relationship between humans and the natural entities around them. These teachers provided a centering point for a teaching process that incorporated all aspects of Indigenous education toward the goal of establishing and maintaining balance between the individual community and the forces that acted upon them. Whether one was a Singer in the context of Navajo tradition, a Tribal midwife, or a keeper of the specific songs, dances, and chants of a clan healing ceremony among the Tlinget of the Northwest—the role of the shaman was similar. As First Doctor, First Visionary, First Dreamer, First Psychologist, First Teacher, and First Artist the shaman's focus was on the spiritual ecology of the group in relation to their environment.

In the philosophy of Indigenous systems of healing, illness and disease were often caused by improper relationship to the natural world, to the spiritual world, to the community, and/or to one's own spirit and soul. Therefore illness, as defined by Indigenous groups, was an environmental imbalance. In one form or another, the environment provided the context for illness, health, and healing.

Within all systems of Indigenous healing, the breath of each human was seen as being connected to the breath and the spirit of the earth itself. We breathe the same air that the plants breathe; we breathe the same air as animals; we depend on the same kinds of invisible elements as plants and animals. We share a life of co-creation and coexistence in an integrated web of relationship. Natural elements such as sun, fire, water, air, wind, snow, rain, mountains, lakes, rivers, trees, volcanoes, and others played a role symbolically and physically in the expression of healing developed by Indigenous people.

There could be many causes of illness. The most important were: improper behavior toward particular kinds of animals or plants, disrespect toward natural elements such as fire, wind, water, or insults to natural entities such as rivers, lakes, or mountains. These relational misdeeds could have dire effects on the well-being of individuals who were involved. Improper relationship and disrespect toward one's body or other individuals could also have dismal effects and cause illness. Misunderstanding, naive use of, or attraction to, the malevolent forces of Nature (those forces of chaos and darkness that lived and operated alongside the positive aspects), could also have direct and dire effects, not only on one's self, but also on one's family and community. The violation of taboo, misconduct in the execution of an important ritual also could have dismal effects on one's well-being. Strong emotions such as love, hate, fear, or anger were seen as being not only symptoms of disharmony, but also emotions that could bring about a disharmony leading to illness.[20]

Understanding the nature of illness and health had its basic frame of reference with regard to the natural environment. Among Indigenous people, this understanding was inclusive of all aspects of one's world and in no way overlooked the interrelated threads of the fabric of health. This is why Indian people honored their heritage of knowledge and understanding of their environment. They deeply appreciated that balance and harmony with the natural environment had to be maintained or it would result in a cataclysm of dysfunction and disease.

Communal ceremonies related the people's guiding myth to their self-understanding with the greater cosmos. Ceremonies were choreographed so they helped both individual and community come to terms with the sense of relatedness considered an essential foundation of wisdom. The Great Corn Dances of the Pueblos are performed in relation to the growing and maturating cycle of sacramental corn. The Great World Renewal ceremonies performed by the Indians of the Northwest and California, or the Sun Dance performed by Plains people, are performed to maintain right relationship with all Nature. They re-establish that relationship for the benefit of the individual, the community, and the natural world as a whole.

There are hundreds of examples in which Indian people have represented their understanding of health and wholeness in metaphoric, symbolic, and ceremonial ways. The realm of healing and renewal at the communal level by Indian societies presents a window to view the relationship that Indigenous people established in the places where they lived.

Plants and The "Ecology" of Healing

The use of plants for healing by Indigenous people presents a practical and visible foundation for viewing themselves as participants in a natural community. As such, the use of plants and animals by North American tribes presents a diverse, yet universal, expression of the intimate bonding that occurred over many generations between a particular tribe and their place.

Traditional Indian beliefs about health reflect a similar orientation with a variety of expressions. These beliefs revolve around attempting to live in harmony with Nature while developing the ability to survive under exceedingly difficult circumstances. Intertwined with their belief is the individual and communal focus upon seeking life. In the context of Tribal practices and the use of herbs and animals for healing, the primal concept of complementary relationship forms a basis for understanding. Everything in Nature reflects a basic quality that can be viewed as male or female, light or heavy, positive or negative. The balance between these two creative energies is essential for maintaining a dynamic state of health and wholeness. This balancing of creative energies was primarily accomplished through spiritual means; the medicinal use of plants always contained the application of a spiritual connotation as the primary field through which true healing and wholeness could be established and maintained.

The concept of two complementary forces was combined with the American Indian concept of "life path" or purpose. Illness was understood as having a role in each individual or community life process. Illness and health were mirror images of each other. Even though one may have been seen as positive and one negative, both played a role in the expression and reflection of the life process. Just as one would need male and female within a family to create the dynamic of life through children, the health and development of a tribe occurred within the context of those complementary forces interacting in the community. Illness played a distinct role in the perpetuation of the idea that life was a process of creation and destruction. In order for life to exist, there had to be death and illness; for us to grow and evolve as humans and community, there had to be situations that caused dissension or illness. These had to be addressed through restoring harmony.

Seeking life metaphorically represents this interplay of philosophy with practical medical knowledge and application. It is a metaphor that provides a way of viewing and understanding life processes at the individual and the communal level. Illness, and its association with the coming of death, is reflected in the origin myths of all Indigenous people. These origin myths expressed the idea that illness and death were natural parts of the process of life. What was important, was to understand the role of these processes, to accept them, and to deal with them in traditional education. The understanding of this dynamic balance in the natural order was maintained on a regular basis through ceremony, through the proper execution of prayer, and through care of oneself and one's community. As mentioned earlier, this dynamic balance was emphasized at the communal level through ceremonial cycles that renewed a tribe's quest of seeking life, from year to year and generation to generation.

Tribal origin myths contained the precedent for developing ceremonies and rituals that restored individual and collective harmony within the expression of a particular Tribal way of life. The use of herbs, because they are natural entities, provided a metaphor and practical physical example for understanding the human relationship to the order of things in the natural world. Plants were viewed as the hairs of the Earth Mother; they were considered to have their own spirit, their own life. They lived in communities and they provided food and nourishment for human and animal life. They provided the fibers for clothing and colors for paints, and they provided beauty. They lived a life in community with one another and established certain ways of living which were noticed, studied, and observed by Indigenous people.

Along with animals, plants formed one of the first ways human beings defined themselves in relation to the natural world. By observing plants, Indigenous people began to understand that there were differences in their needs regarding how and where they would grow. These observations began to resonate with the needs and perspectives that Indigenous people developed about themselves. Plants were the basis of life, and because they held a particular power or medicine, Indigenous people began to view them as playing an essential role, not only for healing, but also as bridges to the spiritual world of Nature. Plants such as tobacco, corn, datura, peyote, and a number of other medicinal plants, played a role as intermediaries between humans and the spirit world of Nature. Through the burning of sage or tobacco, and other symbolic plants, Indian people established a ceremonial dialogue with the natural world.

According to Donald Sandner, scholar of Navajo healing, the categories of disease recognized by the Navajo included: displeasing the spirit entities, annoying the primordial elements of Nature, disturbing or disrespecting animal or plant life, neglectful or disrespectful behavior to the celestial bodies, misuse or misconduct in a sacred ceremony, and finally the category of diseases that reside primarily within the human heart, which included jealousy, envy, hatred, and being in service to the ego without regard for one's actions or their effects on others.[21]

Each of these categories has much to reveal about how plants formed a focal point and a way of understanding this elaborate process of human interaction with the healing process. For instance among the Navajo, displeasing the holy ones could include a whole variety of transgressions. Those holy ones were representatives of certain elements and dimensions within the natural world that required reflection, understanding, and proper behavior. Displeasure of the holy ones was a reflection of misconduct in relationship to oneself, one's community, or to the natural world. The displeasure of the holy ones or spirits of Nature could take many forms—a particular stomach ailment, a particular skin rash, sores and boils or even a non-distinct psychological spiritual illness. These could be understood in relationship to the natural entity or spirit that may have underlaid that particular disease.[22]

The next category included the primordial elements of Nature such as wind, fire, water, and air. These elements were the foundation of life on earth. They were primary medicines, but overexposure to, or misuse of them could cause an illness that could be treated through an understanding of how these elements worked within the human body. A more direct transgression would include disturbing or disrespecting animal or plant life. Each in their own way represented the spirit world of both plant and animal life and were in direct contact with all the forces of the natural world. Therefore, disrespect of an animal carcass after taking it during the hunt would, in Indian perspective, bring retribution from that animal's spirit or spirit village. With plants, misuse or misconduct in picking or applying them could have dire consequences leading to illness.

The neglect or disrespect of certain celestial bodies, such as the Sun, Moon, Pleiades, Venus or others, became another category of misrelationship, a disturbance in the dynamic balance and harmony between humans and the rest of the natural world. Finally, misapplication or misconduct during ceremonies, which were to restore health and harmony, was an element in the propagation of disease and disharmony.[23]

To counteract, restore, and maintain the balance once compromised, required a special educative process that involved an understanding of how to use plants for direct applications of these harmonies and for understanding, viewing, and living life. In most indigenous societies, this form of traditional education revolved around, and was applied through, a medicine person. This medicine person provided a direct model of the goal of becoming complete — finding the right vocation through which one could express most completely one's innate creative potential.

There were particular characteristics sought and exhibited by individuals — herbalists, shamans, other healers, and keepers of knowledge about plants and their uses for healing. These included: first, intellectual and intuitive intelligence, highly evolved to understand the dynamics of plants used in healing; second, a predisposition toward social service and a strong religious and pious orientation; third, love for one's people, culture, and tribe. Self-knowledge, achieved through the process of individuation, was also required. This did not mean that these individuals dealt solely with spiritual concerns; they were also keen observers of the natural world. They were naturalists, botanists, and ecologists.

Because of the nature of their roles, healers also became keepers of the cultural understandings, both material and social, related to using plants in the context of their sacred guiding myths. In addition, they were unique individuals who no doubt had peculiar qualities and characteristics setting them apart from other people. These included well-developed perceptual natures, acute skills of memory and observation, and a developed level of maturity and understanding that could be called natural wisdom.

In the communal context, there were ceremonies and training that initiates were regularly involved in. As is the case with all traditional art forms, healing integrated at a communal level the perspectives important to how a people saw themselves and how they related to the natural world.

The general steps in the Indigenous healing process moved through a group of phases which were themselves contexts of significant learning and teaching. Initially, there was a *diagnosis*. This began by tracking backward the individual's or community's steps to examine the symptoms, past and present.

There was also an examination of the ideas and actions preceding the symptoms, to find what could be the root of an illness. The emphasis in this healing phase is on the causative factors and understanding these factors in the way a tribe viewed itself in the natural world

The diagnosis could take many forms. It could be direct observation and questioning of the patient, including an examination and discussion of the individual's dream process, activities with regard to the categories such as ceremonial preparations, encounters with natural forces in hunting, etc., that might allow the healer to see some possible causes of the illness. Another aspect of diagnosis might include meditation. This focused the thought and the life energy of the healer toward finding the cause of an illness.[24]

In some cases, this *meditation* was assisted by a particular psychoactive agent such as peyote or other trance inducing plant. Some of the uses of plants among the Huichol, Aztec, Inca, and other tribes in North America are examples of such plant-induced meditations.

Diagnosis could include *divination* in which individuals, through self-hypnosis or other self-induced processes, became hypersensitive to signs, sights, and sounds that gave them clues to the nature of the their illness. An understanding of these methods of diagnosis needed to go beyond the description and into the comprehension of the human dynamic, human mind, human spirit. This had to be understood to a much greater degree by traditional healers than other members within the community.[25]

The *treatment* phase took many forms. For instance, the Sing among the Navajo represents a communal ritual involving a complex process. Chants, combined with the creation of sandpaintings, and the application of plants based on the illnesses reflect the guiding myth of the Navajo. The Sing represents one of the complex systems of healing that evolved from an acute awareness of relationship to the natural world. More common forms of treatment might include massage, heat treatment, sweat baths, other forms of physiotherapy, and psychological and spiritual counseling. Various treatments were combined in a system and refined over a number of generations. Through time certain systems were seen to succeed for certain illnesses or patterns of disharmony. These systems became the unique expression of a tribe's healing tradition.[26]

The whole realm of healing, the application of plants, and the understanding of the roles played by the healer, exemplifies an ecological dynamic. It revolves around establishing and maintaining relationship to one's own natural healing process as well as spiritual, communal, and environmental healing processes. Healing traditions provide a benchmark expression of the intimate relationship that Indigenous people established with their environments. Every cultural group establishes this relationship to its place over time. Whether that place is in a desert, a mountain valley, or along the seashore, it is in a context of natural community. Indigenous people came to understand themselves as part of a natural community, and through that understanding they established an educational process that was practical, ultimately ecological, and spiritual. In this way they sought and found their life.

Conclusion

To say that Native American ritual traditions are cultural artifacts, places them and the ecological understanding of Native American people, into a category that is at both highly constraining and ultimately misleading. Though much misunderstanding continues by some scholars who have studied Native American ritual traditions, a new perspective and respect for Native American knowledge are beginning to emerge. As a part of this new perspective and as a foundation for education, the art of ecological relationship established by Native American people represents a focus that can provide profound reflection and illumination. The Indigenous art of ecological relationship is like a seed pregnant with potential. The understandings and integrations now being sought concerning restructuring modern education toward an environmentally sustainable consciousness are only one dimension of what Indigenous people were able to develop in their traditional processes of education.

Natural community provides one of the metaphors that must be reintroduced and revitalized in the context of modern education. The understanding of natural community is a foundational aspect of the environmental education that must take place in the next century. Human beings must come to terms with the fact that we are a part of the natural community. It is through the educational process of ourselves and our children that we can internalize this basic understanding and reflect on the relationship we must establish with the natural world. Indigenous people around the world have been able, through experience and their direct relationship with the natural world, to establish this much-needed understanding of natural process and relationship. For them, this understanding was part of becoming complete within the context of traditional forms and systems of education.

It is important that we revisit these forms, understandings, and ways of expressing relationship within a natural community. It is important that we again give credence to the ways that primal people around the world have established their right relationship in their community and natural environments. Educators must again teach for "living the sky," "living the plain," "living the desert," "living the mountain." We must again "look to the mountain," climb it, and after that struggle and journey of understanding, complete the pilgrimage to our higher selves. We must look with new vision upon where we have been, where we are, and where we wish to go in the evolution of education as a process within natural community.

Indigenous communities around the world integrated within themselves, and within the expression of their traditional forms of education, innate human wisdom that connected to the natural world in such an intimate way that we are only beginning to understand its sophistication and the level of true understanding they had of natural environments. Within that natural community of being, relating, understanding, educating, teaching, and learning, we may once again find, in its most true form, a way of being fully human and fully alive.

The contemporary development of Indigenously based, environmental education curricula can take a myriad of forms. It is an area of curriculum development that offers tremendous possibilities for creative exploration and truly inspired teaching and learning experiences. There are, however, some key areas that a comprehensive curriculum process should address. These areas include: immersion in learning cultural and historical content that puts into context a particular Tribal way of knowing a Place, learning practical skills for living in specific environments, creating opportunities for spending extended time in a natural place to develop personal relationships with Nature, incorporating service related activities for students to enhance or restore a natural place, and creating activities that help re-enchant the students toward Nature thereby setting a foundation from which they may perceive the innate worth of perpetuating the environmental traditions of Indians in the contemporary framework of their lives.

Collectively, we must begin to address ways for revitalizing our innate and Indigenous perspectives, Indigenous sources, attitudes, and orientations to the environment. We must evolve a contemporary form of Indigenous environmental education if we are to address the monumental environmental crisis of our time. This is indeed a time to "look to the mountain!"

LIVING OUR MYTHS

THE MYTHIC FOUNDATION OF AMERICAN INDIAN EDUCATION

Tribal Myth As A Body of Knowledge

WHEN APPROPRIATELY ACCESSED, TRIBAL MYTHS contain tremendous potential for illuminating the education of both the individual and the community. Every body of Tribal myth contains a variety of stories that are culturally important to a tribe and reflect their uniqueness. Tribal myths are filled with metaphors, symbols, images, and creative linguistic and visual forms that are emotionally affective for members of a tribe. They present accounts of the world as experienced and interpreted through the history of the people of a tribe. As a whole, they are reflections of the role of people and entities that affect a tribe's world. They are a body of explanation that forms the Story of the People as they have perceived themselves through generations of relationship to their lands and to each other.

Every tribe created vehicles for accessing the psychological energy contained in their body of myth. Through the telling, performance, and artistic expression of myth, Tribal teachers actively brought their bodies of myth alive and made its lessons relevant to their audience's time and place. While keeping true to the core meanings of their myths, Tribal teachers continually improvised, reorganized, and recreated the particular elements of a myth to fit their audience, the situation, and their own personal expression. In reality, every myth is renewed with each time and in each place it is told. Myths live through each teller and through each audience that hears and actively engages them. Myths and their enactment in every form were the way a tribe remembered to remember their shared experience as a people.

There are as many ways to tell a myth as there are myth tellers, and there are many ways to view myth as well. Western academic schools of analysis have ranged in orientation from evolutionist, to symbolist, to psychoanalytic, to functionalist, to structuralist, to folklorist in their attempts to explain the human phenomena of myth. Yet, only recently have Western scholars turned to the "keepers of myth" for guidance. And, only recently have some Western scholars of myth begun to cultivate an appreciation for these keepers, and reverence for the *power* of myths in shaping human learning and experience.[1]

Humans are storytelling animals. Story is a primary structure through which humans think, relate, and communicate. We make stories, tell stories and live stories because it is such an integral part of being human. Myths, legends, and folk tales have been cornerstones of teaching in every culture. These forms of story teach us about the nature of human life in all its dimensions and manifestations. They teach us how to live fully through reflection on, or participation in, the uniquely human cultural expressions of community, art, religion, *and* adaptation to a natural environment. The myths we live by actively shape and integrate our life experience. They inform us, as well as form us, through our interaction with their symbols and images.

Myths explain what it means to live in community with one another. They explain human dependence on the natural world and essential relationships that must be maintained therein. They explore the life-and-death matters of human existence and relate such matters to basic origins, causes, or relationships. They reflect on the concerns that are basic *and* crucial to humans' understanding of themselves. Creation, survival, relationship, healing, wholeness, and death are the consistent themes of myth in every culture, place, and time. In short, myths are everything the people and community that create them are.

The function of myth is as diverse and complex as human life and cultures. The myths that we live by glue our communities together through shared metaphors of identity and purpose. Myths help to balance individual psychologies and connect them to the greater whole of the tribe, natural environment, and global community. Myths resound the spiritual essence of religion and ritual in life-related terms. Myths mirror the paradoxes of life and reflect the truth behind every paradox.

Myth, in its expressions through narrative and performance, is a communicative art form that integrates other art forms such as song, dance, and visual arts in its expression. Indeed, myth is a primary contextual field for artistic expression and may have led to the development of art in the early stages of human culture. Art is one of the languages of myth.[2]

Finally, myths live or die through people. Myths, as human creations, are messages — as well as a way of conscious reflection — that live through the people who share them by the breath of their thoughts, words, and actions.

Living through myth means using the primal images that myth presents in a creative process of learning and teaching that connects our past, present, and future. Living through myth also means learning to live a life of relationships to ourselves, other people, and the world based on appreciation, understanding, and guidance from our inner spirit and our wealth of ancestral and cultural traditions.

To seek such a life is a foundational metaphor of Indigenous education that invites the empowerment and cultivation of a creative life of learning. The images and symbols brought to life through myth at the personal and group levels provide impetus for this creative life of learning.

"Mythic images are...pictures that involve us both physiologically, in our bodily reactions to them, and spiritually, in our higher thoughts about them. When a person is aware of living mythically, he or she is experiencing life intensively and reflectively."[3]

Indigenous Education: Connecting Personal and Cultural Mythology

The connection between personal mythology, cultural mythology, and the educational process is complex and dynamic. Since our personal stories fuel our emotions and shape our beliefs, as we come to understand the principles by which our personal mythology operates, we will become more able to participate consciously in its development. This is equally true of one's personal educative process, since the two types of understanding are intimately intertwined. Integrating personal and cultural mythology through imagery is a primary component of the Indigenous education process.

Our individual personal mythology forms a dynamic *web* that *informs* the very essence of our lives. Awareness of the influence of our personal mythology on the unfolding process of our living is an essential part of self-knowledge. Such awareness begins by becoming more completely conscious of the way our personal myth interpenetrates that of the multicultural universe in which we live.

This awareness first becomes apparent through an in-depth exploration of our personal and cultural origins. Exploring cultural origins is inherently a holistic process of learning our connections and affirming our evolution as *interdependent* human beings. It is becoming aware that we all live a mythic life and that this life is guided every step of the way through our process of mythologizing. In understanding this process, we become conscious of our relationship to our family myth, our societies' conventional myths, and the universality of the human condition.

By being unconscious of these mythic relationships and our personal mythology, we doom ourselves to look through a distorted lens at other people, the world, and ourselves. A level of critical consciousness concerning our own and our culture's mythology is essential to a deeper learning and teaching situation. The Indigenous education process infuses itself with opportunities for exploring various levels of personal and cultural mythology.

The beginning of this personal mythic journey in the Indigenous educative process focuses on *mythic images*. It is through this focus that one begins the process of living a mythically literate life. That is: to live life with conscious reference to more than day-to-day concerns; to live a life with greater under-standing and appreciation for cultural and ancestral roots, and to live a life of cultivated relationship with significant people, practices, institutions, and the world, based on guidance from inner and creative sources. The mythic image at the personal and group level provides the visual language for the beginning of such a learning process.[4]

The structures, images, symbols, and emotional undertones that con-stitute the language of myth speak to our psyche in its own language. Human consciousness is a collage of deeply embedded mythological complexes that we shape by our life experiences and the mythos of the social environments in which we live. Our lives are expressions of the myths we live by and that live through us.

Myth presents a doorway through which human and natural energy moves in the expressions of human culture. A key to expressing Indigenous education in a contemporary sense includes attempting to influence the way Indian people construct their understanding of themselves and their place in a contemporary world. This understanding stems from their Indigenous mythic language (both personal and cultural) as it finds contemporary expression in ritual, dream, art, dance, music, social interaction, and learning. Tracking the way myth acts to motivate people and communities is an important first step in learning how to use myth effectively in the context of teaching.

Tracking A Myth: The Concentric Rings of Indigenous Education

The working of a metaphor is a creative way to explore the teaching processes using myth in Tribal societies. Such a process is a foundational dynamic of Indigenous teaching and learning. This working evolves around the symbols and metaphors in myth and *is a way of asking for knowledge*.

The metaphor of tracking and the symbol of concentric rings are examples of Tribal analogies that can be worked to present verbal and visual images as profound teachings. It is exactly this working in the context of myth that leads to profound and highly creative Tribal expressions of teaching and learning.

Tracking involves observation, common/natural sense, following an intuitive yet discernible direction, and developing intuition and visual thinking. Tracking in the literal sense involves observing the rings that are coming into you and quieting the rings that are going out from you. Tracks can be read at many different dimensions and from many perspectives.

Tracking strategy begins with scanning the rings of a landscape with a macro-vision. Such scanning eventually leads one through smaller concentric rings down to a micro-focus on a specific animal.[5]

The rings I refer to in this discussion are those that comprise observable interrelationships in Nature and social-psychological processes. Every process in Nature and society occurs in a context of concentric rings.

Concentric rings radiate from every thing and every process. The concentric ring provides a visual symbol of relationship; it is a way of visualizing how all processes radiate concentric rings, which in turn affect other rings of other processes. The symbol of concentric rings is useful in seeing how one thing affects another, how one thing leads to another, and how one thing is connected to another.

The concentric ring is also a basic symbol of wholeness. It allows for representation of wholeness as the interconnection of many concentric rings of relationship. The *mapping* of concentric rings of relationship is a major activity that occurs in primal people's mythology, ritual, and adaptation to their respective natural environments. In all these concentric rings of wholeness, there is the awareness of a particular aspect of Nature, reordering it, and then representing it in some form. This process is one of the universals of the creative act and as such is a primary dimension of science and art.

Tracking from this perspective is intimately involved with learning how to see connections between concentric rings. The analogy of tracking is useful to illustrate an essential process in Indigenous learning; that is, the process of seeing connections, being aware of concentric circles of interrelationship and following the tracks of a parable or mythic process. The process of tracking is itself comprised of a group of concentric rings beginning with the physical, followed by the psychological, then the social and metaphysical. These rings of tracking represent interrelated dimensions of process and field thinking.

Field thinking within the context of tracking simply means becoming aware of a particular field of relationships and being able to pick out specific possibilities within this field that directly relate to what one wants to find or to do.

Tracking at the first level usually requires the ability to *see* physical connections. For example, an Indian hunter of wide experience in a particular environment can tell a fox is coming when a blue jay begins to scold in a certain way. How does he know this? In all likelihood some time in the past the hunter *observed* and *heard* a blue jay scolding a fox in just this way. The old hunter fixed that image and that sound in his memory. He saw a specific connection within a field of possibilities. When he hears that particular blue jay scold again, the hunter remembers the sound and the image.

Tracking at the physical level requires developing the ability to discern patterns using our visual acuity, to discern differences in sound, feeling, smell, and even taste. It involves the ability to *know*, using these basic human perceptual abilities, how to track a particular problem or situation.

Tracking in the metaphysical sense is basically following the concentric rings of the physical, psychological, social, and spiritual to their origins. Mythology presents the primary example of this process.

Try to visualize tracking the trace of an animal through the eye of the hunter, then into the mouth of the hunter, then back through his hand, his body and his psyche in the forms of art, dance, song, and ritual. Through myth and its associated rings of expression, the hunter celebrates the animal to make more animals, to dance more animals, to increase the fertility and vitality of certain animal species, and in doing so, to keep the concentric rings rotating and interrelating in a positive way. This is the essence of the hunting mythology of early man.

Primal mythologies abound with examples of tracing and working the tracks of the ancestors through time and through a geographical landscape of mythology whose concentric rings radiate to the present time and place. A key to understanding mythological tracking of concentric rings is developing the ability to think upside-down. In mythological contexts, things are reversed and inside-out. For instance, the peyote hunt of the Huichol Indians of Mexico is characterized by tracing the steps of the Huichol ancestors to the mythological land of Peyote, which is called *Wirikuta*. This reverse tracking of the ancestors' steps occurs over a geographical and mythological landscape in which those Huichol seeking the peyote are led by a *Mara a kame* (Huichol Shaman) through concentric rings of relationship. Each of these rings is symbolized by its own state of mind, its own ritual, its own natural energy and geographical landmark. The geographical landscape from the Sierra Madre, where the Huichols now live, to the desert flats just outside San Luis Potessi, where the peyote cactus is to be found, represents the trail of the ancestors' tracks. Along the geographical landscape of this trail are natural landmarks that are representative of the concentric rings of important natural and life-sustaining energies of the earth. These are the archetypal energies of earth, wind, fire, water, plant, and animal. Each of these energies is represented in Huichol traditional yarn painting by mythological animals, beings, and entities. They are symbolic of the natural shaping energies of the earth's landscape.[6]

Tracking the ancestors' mythological steps takes the Huichol through different levels of knowing in reference to peyote, Huichol origins and myth, Huichol cultural philosophy, and the energies of the Huichol's natural habitat.

This metaphysical tracking through concentric rings of interrelationship illustrates how landscape, natural energies, plants and animals affect each other. Noting these relationships and their mutual effects is the beginning of primal science and the wellspring of Indigenous environmental knowledge.

Within the contexts of Native American mythologies, certain geographical features personify ties between natural processes. Generally, such features are looked upon as sacred places. These natural features may be specific formations, springs, lakes, rivers, mountains, or other natural places. All these features, physically, visually, and metaphysically represent concentric rings in Nature. Many are symbols of life sustainers such as corn, deer, buffalo, fish, rain clouds, and forests. An understanding of the relationships inherent in these ties is essential to survival. Therefore, much attention is given to ways of knowing and learning about important natural phenomena.

Myths present a way of mapping a particular geographical landscape. Relating the stories associated with a particular geographic place is a way to begin developing a cognitive map of that place and of its concentric rings of interrelationship. Migration myths, for instance, are tracking stories through a geographical landscape. In many Native American migration myths, it is implied that the ancestors left representations of themselves in natural forms or phenomena to remind people how to act and how to relate to the natural world.

Through the symbol of concentric rings, myth is able to give us a visual image of how one thing in reality is like something in myth and vice versa. Every myth has its concentric rings of meaning and is told and retold in this way. The telling of a myth begins with a simple version for children, then moves to a slightly more complicated version for adolescents, to a deeper version for initiates, and to a still deeper version for the fully mature.

The symbol of concentric circles, in its many manifestations throughout the cultures of the world, seems to connote a process event. The concentric ring, when it is used in primal myth, ritual or art, denotes that something happened here, or that something is happening here — it might be a waterhole, a ceremony, a distinct natural phenomenon, or an important life activity.

The concentric ring represents a major process symbol in the mythology, ritual, and art of the Australian aborigine. As represented in Aboriginal traditional art, the concentric ring is a place of an important event of sacred significance and great insight. The mandala and the medicine wheel are other symbolic exemplifications of significant process events. Since myth mirrors and analogizes natural processes, it is no wonder that one of the simplest symbols represents one of the most complex processes of both Nature and the human psyche — that of interrelationships.

The symbol of concentric rings images the fact that everything is unique and leaves its own signature track. Yet it also shows that all things share likenesses that are to be found in the overlap of rings.

Knowledge grows and develops outward in concentric rings. Concentric rings can also form the basis of learning how to track ideas and intuitions, how to observe fields of knowledge, and how to see patterns and connections in thought and natural reality.

Indigenous education in process is following tracks in a particular field or level of natural, social, or spiritual reality. This tracking at any given dimension requires opening one's mind to the possibilities within each of the many concentric circles in that dimension. Learning how to blend the mythological, aesthetic, intuitive, and visual perspectives of Nature with the scientific, rational, and verbal perspectives is an integral part of Indigenous education. Education, from this viewpoint, involves learning to see Nature holistically. This requires a continual shifting and interplay between the two complementary perspectives mentioned. Facilitating learning to orchestrate these two ways of viewing Nature toward the greatest effect must become a major activity of contemporary Indian education.

In this Indigenously modeled approach, a first track begins with a symbol. It is these symbols that are the keys to access the myth, the relationships of concentric circles, and knowledge and perceptions of natural realities. In teaching and learning a process discipline such as ecology, beginning with a mythological track and following that track — through its concentric circles from its abstraction to its reality and then back again — presents one of the most natural and potentially creative approaches. (See Diagram.) In such an instance, a person learns about the nature of spiritual ecology through focusing upon a mythic symbol — with the help of a mentor and through the creative dimensions of experience, reflection, and application of the understanding of what the symbol represents.

The previously discussed symbol of the humpbacked flute player, sometimes called "Kokopeli," or antman, provides a case in point. The Kokopeli is a mythological symbol that represents the bringer of seeds, fertility, sexuality, abundance, the spreading of art and culture. The Kokopeli is a natural process symbol that is pregnant with meaning.

As such, the symbol of Kokopeli is surrounded by many myths; these myths abound with metaphors representing various dimensions of the procreative processes of Nature. Each of these processes is encircled by a body of psychological, aesthetic, and cultural expressions. These expressions in turn are tied to realities that are observable and that form a basis for

Indigenous teaching through myth.

The Kokopeli is a mythical visual metaphor that acts as a kind of gatekeeper. Tracking its meaning through multiple levels of use and various appearances in myths, from Mexico to the Southwest United States, one reaches a foundational root of an Indigenous archetype and mythic tradition. Tribally specific gatekeepers exist for the Navajo, Sioux, Iroquois, Ojibway, Pima, Huichol, Inuit and every other tribe from Alaska to the tip of South America. The complex of Raven myths in the Northwest, the Coyote/Trickster myths of the West and Southwest, the Inapi (Old Man) myths of the Northern Plains, the Sedna myths of the Far North, the Abiding Stone — Inyan and White Buffalo Calf Woman myths of the Central Plains, the Tree of Peace and Great Turtle of the Northern Woodlands are a few of the other American Tribal mythic gatekeepers. Each of these contains numbers of gatekeeper symbols whose tracking leads to the roots of a Tribal tradition and mythic knowledge base.

Tracking selected Tribal gatekeepers through key myths, concepts, symbols or orientations that illustrate the process and content of teaching/learning (in each of the orienting foundations of Indigenous education) is an Indigenous method of interactive/integrated education.

This methodology is a form of creative analysis in which the logic for myth and its validation is internally consistent with the perspective of a tribe's understanding an essential message reflected through the myth.

Those gatekeeper symbols that are used in a particular region and have a wide breadth of meaning can be explored within the context of myths from the same region. A major Indigenous cultural and philosophical concept, they provide ideal vehicles for seeing, understanding, and relating what is considered important by a group of tribes in a region. (See Diagram)

Tracking Concentric Rings of Relationship

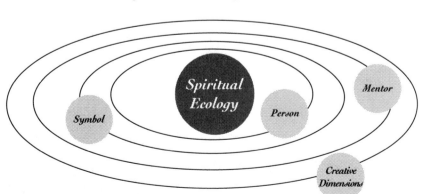

The Tanoan myth of Water Jar Boy is a story whose variations are still told in a few Pueblos around Santa Fe, New Mexico. Its roots begin in a mythic past that is ancient and reflective of the way the visual symbolic form of Kokopeli was employed in both the oral narrative and petroglyphic illustration of this Anasazi teaching story.[7]

On a petroglyph panel located near the ruin of La Cienega Pueblo, twelve miles south of Santa Fe, New Mexico, a series of Kokopeli figures herald the story of Water Jar Boy. Water Jar Boy is a story that originated from the now extinct Tanoan villages of La Cienega, San Marcos, and Galisteo. It is a teaching story, a story about why things are and the importance of coming to know the sources from which human life proceeds. (See Diagram.)

Water Jar Boy Myth Petroglyph At La Cienega

Diagram reprinted with permission of the author, Carol Patterson Rudolph.

Water Jar Boy

A young girl lived with her father and mother in a very old village near a place where the waters come together. The girl was very beautiful, kind, and good of heart. When she became of age many boys of the village tried to win her eye. But, she was very shy and did not pay attention to any of the boys of the village. She did not want to leave her father and mother since they were quite old and needed her help.

The girl liked to help her mother make pottery, especially the water jars, which her mother made so well. One day her mother asked her to help mix the pottery clay. She went to a spring near the village to get a special colored clay to decorate the pottery. While she was mixing the clay with her feet near the spring, she began to feel very strange in her stomach. The more she mixed the clay, the more clay covered her feet, and the stranger she felt. She stopped mixing the clay and went home. She told her mother how she felt mixing the clay, but her mother thought nothing of it and told her not to worry.

A few days passed, and she started to feel something moving in her belly. She did not want to tell her mother and father. But soon she became very ill, and when her mother felt her belly she knew that her daughter was with child. When the child was born she saw that it was not like any other child. It was a beautiful little water jar. Her father came in, and upon seeing the beautiful little jar said, "It is a special gift, and although we do not know how this has happened we must accept it." The girl's father became very fond of the little water jar, and when it began to move and grow he became happy. The water jar grew very fast, and in a few days it was able to talk and roll itself around following him inside the house. One day, the little water jar asked the grandfather to take it outside so that it could play with the other children. The grandfather was surprised at the little water jar's request, but he took it out, and soon the little jar was rolling around to the delight of the children in the village. The children became very fond of the little water jar and would wait each day for the grandfather to bring it out to play. The children named the little jar, Water Jar Boy.

One day the young men of the village were gathering to go rabbit hunting. Water Jar Boy announced, "Grandfather, I want to go hunting with the rest of the boys; please take me to where the rabbits are so I can hunt too." The grandfather was shocked at the request and told Water Jar Boy, "How can you hunt, you have no arms or legs; besides hunting is for real boys!" Water Jar Boy replied, "But Grandfather, I am a real boy!" Grandfather decided to take Water Jar Boy to where the rabbits were, and as they were leaving his mother began to cry fearing that Water Jar Boy would be hurt. Water Jar Boy told his mother not to worry; he would return with many rabbits!

Grandfather placed Water Jar Boy near a mesa where he knew many rabbits lived and told Water Jar Boy that he would return to pick him up before sunset. Grandfather then joined the other older men as they set out to gather the rabbits together. Water Jar Boy began to roll around as he saw rabbits pass by. As he was rolling he hit a large stone and broke. Out of the broken jar jumped a very handsome boy. The boy picked up a stick and ran after the rabbits killing some of them and letting others go. As the sun began to set he walked toward the mesa carrying many rabbits on his back to meet his grandfather. As he approached, his grandfather did not recognize him. His grandfather asked, "Have you seen a water jar rolling around?" Water Jar Boy laughed and said, "Grandfather, it is me Water Jar Boy, your grandson!" Grandfather looked in disbelief as Water Jar Boy told how, when rolling around he hit a stone, broke his clay skin, and came out of the jar. "I told you I was a real boy!"

When they came home, grandfather announced to his daughter and the grandmother, "This is my grandson, this is Water Jar Boy!" Then they told the story of how Water Jar Boy had jumped out of the broken water jar and how he had killed many rabbits. Everyone was happy, and they invited all their relatives for a special feast to meet the new Water Jar Boy. From then on Water Jar Boy stayed with the young men and participated in the life of the community.

As time went on, Water Jar Boy became curious about who his father was. One day he asked his mother, "Who is my father, where does he live?" She began crying and said that she did not know, and she could not tell him where he could go to find him. But, somehow, Water Jar Boy knew the answer to his own question. He announced to his mother, "I know where my father is, and tomorrow I will go and find him!" The next day he set out toward the west and walked for a long time. He saw a marsh and knew that there was a spring there. As he neared the spring he saw a man dressed in buckskin sitting on a stone. The man asked, "Where are you going?" Water Jar Boy replied, "I am going inside that spring there to find my father." "Who is your father?" asked the man. Water Jar Boy paused and looked at the man closely and then said, "I think that it is you that is my Father." To which the man replied, "Yes, I am your father, and I am happy that you have finally come to see me. I came from the inside of that spring; that is my home." Water Jar Boy's father took him inside the spring. There Water Jar Boy met all his relatives. Water Jar Boy stayed in the spring and lives there to this day.

The tale of Water Jar Boy is simple, yet profound, and extraordinarily deep in its metaphoric meanings. Water Jar Boy is created through a traditional art form, pottery, which reflects the role and magic of the creative process in traditional Tribal art. It evokes and relates the power of hunting and the use of hunting as a metaphor for searching, learning, and understanding. It reminds us that all is not as it may seem and that what appears as handicaps in children may indeed be a special talent, since Water Jar Boy can roll as fast as other little boys can run. Water Jar Boy's belief in his ability to be a successful hunter shows us how "children" transform themselves through the challenges that they face and overcome.

Water Jar Boy's journey to find his father, culminating in his entrance into the spring, where he finds, not only his spirit father but his relatives, is a reflection of the journey deep into ourselves that is required for deep understanding and true learning. In discovering not only his father but his relatives in the spring, Water Jar Boy reminds us that while true learning is always individual, its ultimate goal is not "the individual ego writ large" but rather communion with our deeper spiritual self and that of our relations. Learning and teaching are always about, and for, life through community and relationship.

Stone Boy, The Symbol of Inyan

Many Indian myths serve to illustrate the mythically symbolic journey toward completion, the orientation to home, and the transition from boyhood to manhood. The Lakota myth of Stone Boy is just such a myth. The story of Stone Boy contains many traits of the universal archetypal character of the Hero. It talks about the energies and the nature of relationships a people of place, such as the Lakota, have established within their extended families, with the entities that surround them, such as Inyan (the abiding stone), and with the buffalo. All of these are represented by gatekeeper symbols and linguistic metaphors whose concentric rings of meaning flow from the heart of the Lakota world view.

In addition, the story of Stone Boy describes the nature of the boundaries of the home place and the world outside. These boundaries include those inside and outside a family, the security of one's home territory, and even the boundaries between life and death. In a holistic sense, the tale of Stone Boy relates the safety of the homeland, the security afforded through the bonds within a family, and the foundation of the abiding stone. For stone, Inyan, among the Lakota, is the first being of creation and the reflection of a primordial foundation of life. Stone Boy is Inyan come to life on earth and acting for the benefit of the Lakota people. With deep respect for the Lakota way of being "Indigenous," I present the story of "Stone Boy."

Stone Boy

The story begins with four young men sitting in their tipi during the ancient time. The youngest brother, whose name is Hakela, hears someone outside the tipi and looks out to find a young woman, with a large leather pack and her forelock bound, standing at the entrance. Hakela's brothers told him to ask her to come in, saying that she may become their elder sister since they are all men and have no women to care for them.

The young woman enters and sits down near the fire, but does not eat the food that the brothers have offered her. Thinking that she is too shy to eat in their presence, they excuse themselves and leave the tipi to take a walk. Hakela walks only a short distance and then decides to stay behind and watch the young woman. He soon smells a strange aroma coming from the tipi. He turns himself into a bird and flies to the top of the tipi to investigate.

Hakela sees the woman roasting human heads that she has taken out from her pack! Hakela flies to where his brothers are, turns into a man, and tells them his horrible story. The brothers decide to return home and act as if they know nothing of the woman's secret. They give the woman a pack strap and ask her to gather more wood for their fire. When the woman leaves, Hakela takes the heads and a metal shield out of her pack and throws them into the fire. Just then, the woman returns and retrieves her trophies from the fire. By this time, the brothers have started to flee. Enraged, the woman chases after them and soon catches up to them. One by one the brothers shoot arrows at her, but she carries the metal shield and deflects all their arrows. She catches the brothers and cuts off their heads, until only Hakela remains. As she is chasing Hakela, a bird flies over his head and tells him to shoot his arrow at her forelock. Hakela shoots right at the center of the woman's head where her forelock hangs and kills her.

Hakela then finds the bodies of his slain brothers, builds a sweatlodge and places them within it. He gathers stones and builds a fire and places the hot stones within the lodge. As he prays and pours water over the stones, his brothers begin to come to life and soon are talking to him. They return happily once again to their tipi.

Soon, another young woman is standing at the entrance to their tipi. She also has a pack, but this young woman's forelock is not bound. And so the eldest brother tells Hakela to invite her in to sit at their fire, saying that they will have her as their sister. As she sits at their fire she says that she is happy to be their sister. She eats the food that they offer her and then takes buckskin from her pack and makes fine moccasins for each of them. The brothers are very pleased.

One day the brothers decide to go hunting, and they leave the young woman alone in the tipi. The young woman becomes very sad and lonely as she waits for their return on a hill by the tipi. As night comes, she places a stone in her mouth and then falls fast asleep. In her sleep she swallows the stone, and she becomes pregnant. Soon a boy child is born. She called the child Stone Boy.

Stone Boy grows rapidly and learns about all the customs of his family's tipi. Soon he asks about his mother's four brothers. She tells him that they went to hunt buffalo and have never returned. Then he asks his mother to make him strong arrows. He tells her that he has decided to look for his uncles.

On his journey he encounters three old women who call him grandson. He tells them that he is going to a ball game and they lend him their powers. The first old woman gives him a yellow ball club with a yellow eagle plume. The second old woman gives him a kingfisher feather and the third gives him a turtle. Soon he comes to the land of the buffalo and they invite him to play ball.

He plays with an old woman buffalo and uses each of the gifts he has been given by the old women to defeat the old buffalo. When he has won four times the old woman buffalo tells him to shoot his arrow into her. When he does this he finds the bones of his uncles lodged in her neck. He gathers all the bones up, builds a sweatlodge and places the bones into it. Soon his uncles come back to life. He also wins four young buffalo women that he gives to his uncles. As they travel back to their homeland, Stone Boy returns the gifts he borrowed to each of the three old women. When they reach their tipi, they are greeted by Stone Boy's mother, and they celebrate the reunion of their family.

There is a time when Stone Boy undertakes another journey and meets four young buffalo women who have a sled. Stone Boy transforms himself into a little boy and slides with the buffalo girls. When they least expect it, he turns into a boulder and rolls down the hill, killing all four buffalo and taking their tongues. Then Stone Boy meets the Grandfather of the buffalo girls sharpening his horns, getting ready to avenge the deaths of his grandchildren. He kills the grandfather buffalo and four others, then returns home with their tongues. Expecting the other buffalo to attack in revenge for their slain relatives, he tells his uncles to make four special arrows and four wooden enclosures. Soon buffalo from all over surround the enclosures. Four buffalo chiefs in succession try to break through the enclosures but each is slain by Stone Boy. Then all the buffalo attack Stone Boy's enclosures, but they are driven off by Stone Boy and his uncles. They killed all the buffalo they needed and prospered.[8]

The story of Stone Boy illustrates the magical nature of hunting and the relationship of the Lakota hunters to their most-prized animal relative, the buffalo. The perception that buffalo have tribes, chiefs, and act like people, forms a foundation for the establishment of this deep and abiding relationship. And it is Stone Boy, as a living representation of Inyan, the abiding stone, that guides the Lakota in their relationship with the source, and symbol, of life that is the buffalo.

The Mythopoetic Foundation of Education

The tremendous influence of these mythopoetic traditions on the development of education becomes apparent when one tracks to their ancient sources the rich array of oral forms used by traditional societies. These traditions depended on the spoken word for communication rather than the visual word that dominates modern education today. Traditional people, through their use of mythopoetic communication, applied strategies and orientations to learning that are important to revive and nourish in today's education. Modern people, for the most part, are *mythopoetically blind* and suffer all the consequences stemming from such a handicap because their natural poetic sensibility has been largely schooled out of them. Yet, thinking and communicating poetically through the structures of myth is a natural expression of human learning that has been evolving for the last 40,000 years.

Mythopoetic orientations are apparent in most children before they learn how to read. Indeed, children at this illiterate stage of their lives show amazing metaphoric thinking and storying skills reflecting their poetic nature. In modern education's mad dash to make children—and for that matter Indigenous people—literate, it fails to recognize or honor a powerful dimension of human knowing and understanding. The hidden message is, "Stop being children and stop being Indigenous." It is ironic that today so many modern people lament the loss of this primal human sensibility and strive to recapture it through participation in some "thing" creative, Indigenous, and mythological.

Literacy and the written story are very recent developments in human history, even in the history of Western societies. They undeniably evolved from illiterate mythopoetic roots in spite of the negative connotation that Western civilized cultures have promoted regarding illiteracy as a sign of being uneducated, uncivilized, and primitive. The study and honoring of oral traditions and orality in children offer essential insights into natural learning. The human oral orientation to education offers techniques as well as windows into the world of Indigenous education. A better understanding of orally based learning revitalizes old yet highly effective techniques while opening up new dimensions that have been forgotten or have become dormant with the development of literacy. What then was the nature of the mythopoetic tradition, and why must it again become an important element of contemporary Indian education?

Mythic poems were performed, sung, or recited using a particular system of rhythmic structure that required the application of a different set of thinking processes and developed different learning capacities than today's modern schooling. The Aztec tradition of "flower and song" is one example of a mythopoetic tradition of education in which teaching, learning, and reflection were founded upon chanted stories, poems, or prayers. The Aztec poet, philosopher/priest, would compose poetic storied chants or teach the divine songs, the mythic tales, and poetic verse that embodied the essential thoughts and contents of Nahuatl religion and philosophy. He would then chant these stories and poems to students who would reflect on or internalize the essential messages that they contained. Later, as they became experienced in this oral system, students would compose poetic chants of their own to present to each other and their tlamatinime, their poet-teacher. In essence, the flower was the thought, the feeling, the insight, the bit of wisdom and knowledge that was considered of importance as a teaching. The song was the vehicle that transported and transformed the flower of knowledge and made it live through the breath of the chanter and in the hearts of the listeners.[9]

Indigenous mythopoetic traditions are essentially educational. Indian mythopoetic perspectives were founded upon an awe for the Great Mystery; the development of a strong, wise, and pure heart; an abiding respect for one's tribe, traditions and law; and a deep sense for the relationships and connections between all things. Indian myths transferred these basic teachings through enlivened images and metaphors that embodied an expansive view of people in relationship with each other and a multiverse full of potential.

Indian myths encompassed every thing within a context that was spiritual yet irreverent, serious yet humorous, logical yet illogical. The messages conveyed through these stories had the power to heal and bring resolution to conflicts because at its core, poetry illuminates, transforms, and mirrors the heart and soul of both the individual and a People. The presentation of these messages went beyond words to include sound, dance, music, games, gesture, symbol, art, and dream. In this way, thoughts, teachings, and emotions were amplified. Every word, every act, had meaning and energy. This allowed Tribal myth and poetry to become part of a larger context of situation and human expression, thereby, making the presentation of myth and poetry a true expression of the sacred breath within humans and all living things. How did this characteristic of Indian mythopoetic traditions educate its participants, and what does it have to teach us about the oral nature of human learning?[10]

The mythopoetic realm of teaching and learning is not a relic of the past as might be construed from the designation of the arts and theater in the curricula of so many American schools. Rather, it is an educational necessity for enabling the new imagination so desperately needed in today's sterilized and homogenized approach to public education. Modern educators must admit that non-European traditional cultures around the world exhibit a level of complexity and sophistication that equals and many times surpasses modern perceptions of what it means to educate. Many ingrained biases about the primitive that have been conveyed and conditioned through the hidden curriculum of modern education must be examined. This is especially true of the mythopoetic traditions of Indian America. The negative connotations associated with the word primitive must give way to a more enlightened understanding of the complexity and richness of primal traditions of myth, poetry, and storytelling.

In contrast to the usual conditioned modern perceptions of the primitive, oral traditions and Tribal art forms are as individually oriented as they are collectively determined. It is a fallacy that traditional cultures and their oral traditions do not change, or that creative self-reflection is not a part of the traditional formula. It is naive to think that orality alone defines Indigenous thinking. Indigenous oral traditions have always been integrated with drawing, the arts, and practical education. It is the perpetuation of injustice to think that Indigenous people have not attained as sophisticated an understanding of the nature of language, myth, art, culture, aesthetics, ethics, and philosophy as Western scholars. If anything, the mythopoetic traditions of Indigenous people reflect that there is no such thing as *primitive* in the way Western education has traditionally conditioned people to perceive it. The tendency of Western education to divide myth and poetry from music, dance, relationship to Nature, community, spirituality, history, and even politics reflects an illusion of Western thinking.

Indigenous mythopoetic traditions are highly integrated expressions of thought, reflection, and participation. They are connected to the living expressions and continuity of Tribal life, past, present and future. Primitive means complex! Among Indigenous people myth, poem, teaching and learning were all one movement. There is the creation of a unity within a diversity of expressions that establishes an extraordinary field for creative learning and teaching.[11]

In all Indigenous mythopoetic traditions, including those of the ancient Greeks during the time of Homer, complex processes of oral structure, image making, and presentation were developed. These processes were very complex in that they used a minimum number of words to create a maximum amount of meaning, affect, and involvement. These processes in turn engaged the fullest participation of both the giver and receiver in reflecting upon the message of the work. In this sharing of the poetic experience, both giver and receiver become involved in a dance of meaning in which complex images, symbols, and meanings are explored in direct and personal ways.

Nothing in contemporary modern educational experience comes close to affecting and engaging individuals as deeply and multidimensionally. Through the mobilization of an infinite array of vehicles to convey a message and engender a response, Indigenous mythopoetic traditions represent the most developed and continuously affective forms of education. In every case, mind, body, breath, and spirit of all participants were engaged in reflecting on the message of the story or poem. What is it then to think mythopoetically? How did it work in earlier times?

"The techniques of oral poetry developed in Indigenous societies over countless generations are designed to discourage critical reflection on the stories and their contents, and instead 'enchant' the hearers and draw them into the story. This process of enthralling the audience, of impressing upon them the reality of the story, is a central feature of education in oral cultures. Their social institutions are sustained in large part by sound, by what the spoken or sung word can do to commit individuals to particular beliefs, expectations, roles and behaviors. Thus the techniques of fixing crucial patterns of belief in memory, rhyme, rhythm, formula, story, and so on, are vitally important.

"Education in oral cultures is largely a matter of constantly immersing the young in enchanting patterns of sound until their minds resonate to them, until they become in tune with the institutions of their culture."[12]

"The Homeric poems were called the educators of pre-Classical Greeks because they performed this social function. Poems were not listened to solely because of their aesthetic value; that was incidental to their value as a massive repository of useful knowledge, a sort of encyclopedia of ethics, politics, history, and technology that the effective citizen was required to learn as the core of his educational equipment."[13]

Mythopoetic learning among Indigenous people can best be described as an integration of verbal with musical learning, which at times is complemented by kinesthetic and spatial learning. Indigenous learning does indeed involve a different orientation to learning than modern education. This different orientation in turn engenders an expression of understanding. It is an orientation that modern education has never really understood or valued. Yet, it engenders a cadre of valuable learning skills and supports other kinds of learning that many students sorely lack.

The Mythologically-Instructed Community

Culture and mythology are mental constructs whose evolution is based on the development of groups and individuals through the long history of Tribal societies. Within Tribal groups, the evolution of a cultural/social mythology closely parallels the evolution of the personal mythology of individuals. There is a mutual and synergistic relationship between the individual and his/her primary group. The individual, or group of individuals, whose personal mythology most strongly reflects the forces of change, impacts their group as change agents, and it is this dynamic that most directly influences the consciousness of the formal and informal educative process.

The evolution of human consciousness has generally been marked by transformations of the guiding myths that a society holds. In a sense, mythic stories trace the journey of a people through different stages of their consciousness as well as through the times and places in which they have lived.

Ken Wilber in his book *Up From Eden* describes four basic stages of human consciousness. The first of these stages begins with a pre-mythological state of consciousness in which the human sense of self is essentially identified with the physical needs of the body and the primordial forces of Nature. In this Eden stage of consciousness, humans reflected an almost complete communion with Nature, using only simple tools, organized in extended family groups, and engaged in a sense of self that was only slightly differentiated from that of their Place.[14]

Wilber describes the second epoch of human consciousness as the true beginning of myth-making. During this stage, consciousness was characterized by an integration between the mythical structuring of reality based on physical needs with the projection of magical relationships to entities in the outside world as well.

In the third epoch, language had evolved to a stage where it allowed more complete development of the verbal mind. Verbal symbols were developed to understand and codify information about the natural world to a greater extent. This allowed for the accumulation and transmission of knowledge through oral tradition, which in turn set the stage for large communities to evolve. More complex and sophisticated mythologies were developed through mythic story and ritual. All of these steps formed a foundation for what we call Education. During this third epoch people's consciousness was primarily identified with the cultural myths of their group and was engendered through group identification.[15]

As the fourth epoch began to unfold, an individualistic mindset gradually evolved with the development of the capacity for self-observation and reflection. This development seems to occur at an especially accelerated rate in Western cultures. With the development and associated repercussions of Western science and Individualist ideologies, the uniquely personal mythology of self-determining individuals began to characterize social, economic, political, religious, and philosophical consciousness.[16]

The "individual ego writ large" became the ordering paradigm of the culture and mythology of Western society. It affected everything, and Western science and technology became both the tools and the icons of the Western individualist. In essence, the Hero myth became the ordering paradigm of consciousness in the West.[17]

Today, a new paradigm and new era of myth are beginning to unfold. This paradigm is reflecting a new stage of human consciousness as it wrestles with an evolving global community, the unfolding environmental crises, and progressive democratization. The new paradigm and emerging myths are reflecting a mutualism and interconnection of all aspects of the earth. These new myths, by necessity of human survival, must be Earth centered mythologies. The concomitant education must reflect the teaching/learning process and content appropriate for such new myth making.

"The cost of having placed the individualism of the heroic journey above the values of caring and connectedness continue to mount. A new vision of democracy is urgently needed that can support the individual and at the same time promote a greater sense of community and more harmonious international relationship."[18]

Indigenous education and its expression in various cultures around the world reflect all the mythic stages of human consciousness. They form frames of reference for perceiving the whole evolution of human consciousness. In studying Indigenous education, every modern cultural group may explore the reality of the mythic thinking process through its manifestations. This introduces a mythological literacy to modern education, which is devoid of such explorations except in the highly specialized domain of the mythologist.

The re-emphasis on a mythologically instructed community presents a missing dimension of contemporary Indian education. This concept is desperately needed by Indian people and communities as they wrestle with the forces of change and deculturalization in an American society that is still guided by a mythology of the "Ego Writ Large". For American Indian people the frames of reference from historic/traditional American cultures are extensive.

Beyond addressing the acute educational needs of Indian communities, modern educators must realize that they urgently need to integrate and interconnect in a mutualistic way with the educational perspectives of other cultures. In this respect, Indigenous education and its inherent emphasis on the mythological perspective has much to offer to the evolution of modern education. However, Indigenous people must take the responsibility for leading themselves and stimulating the consciousness of their counterparts in Western society toward such basic realizations.

The insights presented by American Indian mythology (as a body of content and a process of thought and psychological exploration) have always presented a significant and readily accessible foundation for developing an Indigenously inspired education process. The evolution of a contemporary Indigenous philosophy of education also offers an authentic tool for countering deculturalization and alienation. It does this by offering a way to resynthesize foundational Native American myths into a contemporary context of meaning.

Each person evolves their own personal mythology and perceives and acts through the lens of that myth of self-creation. In the process of learning and education, one's personal myth intertwines with a group myth that has been elaborated to preserve that group's way of life.

If one's personal myth is wholesome and able to integrate well with the group's myth (as espoused through its educative process), then there is resonance with that group's world view. Education and the learning that results are compatible with the norms and expectations of that group, and there is little dissonance.

On the other hand, if one's personal myth has another cultural frame of reference or is significantly different from the educational myth of the group doing the schooling, the potential for conflict and resistance is great.

Alienation is the result of such a dilemma, and a search for alternatives becomes a natural response. Mirrored in such alienation are dysfunctional personal/mythic perspectives. This is exactly the dilemma of many American Indians, both young and old. The creative solution is to construct an educational process that resonates with a functional cultural/mythic perspective that is healthy and fits contemporary life.

American Indians are a homogeneous, yet heterogeneous, people. Though this statement sounds paradoxical, it is valid from a mythological perspective. Indigenous people of the Americas share elementary ideas and cultural values whose symbolic meanings and archetypes are similarly interpreted from tribe to tribe. In spite of anthropological and archeological statements that American Indians are as different from one another culturally as Germans and Chinese, Indian people from the tip of South America to Alaska recognize their innate relatedness. As a whole, Indian people share guiding thoughts, elemental ideas, symbols, and metaphors that cannot be denied. One such shared body of elemental ideas and archetypes occurs in the area of educational process. Thus the foundation for various expressions of educational philosophy in a Tribal context.

The differences of American Indians lie in the way each Tribal/cultural/ social group has expressed this shared cultural mythological paradigm of education. The variations are a result of the circumstance of adaptation to a geographical environment, the evolution of their world view, and the Tribal group's unique history. While a tribe is unique in terms of language, adaptation experience, and expression of cultural traits—Tribal groups employ similar conceptual-symbolic frameworks constructed around mythical life symbols. These represent the seeds from which cultural and mythic knowledge and process may grow and bear new fruits. It is possible to evolve learning and teaching models that build on shared ideas while honoring unique differences. This is especially true regarding the myths a tribe has preserved through its oral tradition. Indigenous teaching is essentially rooted in the structure and process of storying. Story has been a primary Way for connecting each generation of Indian people to each other. Story is the way that we remember to remember who we are, where we have come from, and where we can go as we enter the twenty-first century.

Indigenous Teaching as Story

The telling of story is such a universal part of human communication and learning that it may be that story is one of the most basic ways the human brain structures and relates experience. Everything that humans do and experience revolves around some kind of story. The predominance of television and the other mass media in modern life is largely because they are vehicles for storytelling, i.e., the transfer of information to relate a message or convey a meaning. Story is the way humans put information and experience in context to make it meaningful. Even in modern times we are one and all storied and storying beings. At almost every moment of our lives, from birth to death and even in sleep, we are engaged with stories of every form and variation.

Stories were the first ways humans stored information; they were the basis of the oral traditions of all Tribal people. Since the beginning of human history, Tribal cultures have ordered the understanding and meaning of human existence through their remembrance and enactment of stories in ritual, song, dance, and art. Stories have deep roots stemming not only from the physiology and contexting process of the brain, but also from the very heart of the human psyche. Stories mirror the way the human mind works, and they map the geography of the human soul. Yet, stories go beyond education and the recitation of words. Indigenous stories related the experience of life lived in time and place. They were not only a description but an echo of a truth lived and remembered. They remain the most human of human forms of communication.

It may be that we are all born with a sense of story. A basic wisdom of educating is to provide a context in which this natural human sense may be nourished. Indigenous education imparted an awareness of story that provided a context through which imagination and the unconscious could develop at all stages of life. Indeed, Indigenous storytelling engaged all levels of higher order creative thinking and imaging capacities. Indigenous storytelling developed a fluency of metaphoric thinking and mythic sensibility that served Indigenous people in their understanding of their own psychology and maintenance of their spiritual ecology.

The legacy and the innate learning potential of Indigenous storying must be recaptured and made an integral part of contemporary Indian education at every level. The basis of traditional Indian education is embodied in the structures of myth and oral expression. The development of four basic disciplines of thinking related to the creative process were engendered as a part Indigenous storying. These disciplines were attention, creative imagination, flexibility, and fluency of thinking. Each of these disciplines was exercised within the context of telling, enacting, singing, creating, or dancing a story that personified Indigenous life and meaning. These contexts of Indigenous story are as viable today as they were in the past. They must become more than just extracurricular activities reserved for free time and elementary grades. In the research regarding the educational dimensions of mythological thinking, Indian story making and telling should become as important to Indian educators as the latest "perpetual message" on the state of Indian education issued from Washington.[19]

In reality, what are called "modern educational disciplines" are bodies of stories. These stories explain and describe knowledge accumulated through the application of specific methodologies characteristic to each discipline. So science is a body of stories and has its unique oral tradition. The same is true of modern art, psychology, sociology, history, and anthropology. Each of these divisions of Western knowledge has subdisciplines that have their own stories and traditions. The difference between the transfer of knowledge in modern Western education and that of Indigenous education is that in Western education information has been separated from the stories and presented as data, description, theory, and formula. Modern students are left to re-context the information within a story. The problem is that most students have not been conditioned by modern culture or education to re-context this information. Their natural sense for story has been schooled out of them. They do not know how to mobilize their imagination to interact with the content that they are presented—they have lost their innate awareness of story.

"The Cree believe that a three-way symbiotic relationship unfolds between storyteller, story, and listener. Ultimately, if people nourish a story properly, it tells them useful things about life."[20]

Each teacher and student involved in Indian education must relearn and practice contexting information in culturally sensitive and holistic ways. Making story the basis of teaching and learning provides one of the best ways to accomplish this contexting and enhancing of meaning in all areas of content. It is possible to teach all content from the basis of story. We can again allow teachers to truly become storytellers and storymakers, and allow students to become active listeners. Teaching is essentially a communicative art form based on the ancient Tribal craft of storying. We must once again nourish our stories properly!

A curriculum founded on American Indian myths in science might revolve around stories of human relationships to plants, animals, natural phenomena, and the places in which Indian people live. This could also include stories of technological achievements of Indian people in such areas as plant medicine, architecture, astronomy, and agriculture as well as actual experimentation with Tribal technologies. Traditional American Indian art forms, since they are expressions of American Indian Nature based technologies, could be used in a variety of ways to explore American Indian themes and orientations to science. American Indian myths and art forms can be used strategically and creatively in the introduction of Western science to American Indians.[21]

Creating a classroom environment in which the Indigenous foundation of storytelling and storymaking again flourish is a creative challenge whose potential benefit far outweighs the effort required to bring it into being. Storying is a natural part of all learning. What is required is learning how to facilitate and guide its development in students. Indigenous education has always been characterized by a process of co-creation between teachers and students. The enablement of storytelling within the classroom is indeed a co-creation in which teachers and students learn the discipline of storytelling through constantly finding, or making, stories and telling them. Empowering the creative process of storying in both teachers and students requires nothing more than becoming conditioned for it. Just as distance runners condition themselves for running by increasing their distance a bit each month, maintaining a proper diet and a balanced schedule of work and recreation, teachers and students can condition themselves for ever greater capacities for storying. The following groups of activities are possible ways to bring the creative conditioning for Indigenous storying back into being.

First, creating opportunities to be in Nature and partake directly from the natural sources of life and creativity; gaining a perspective of past, present, and future through selected stories of one's tribe and place; and, recognizing and honoring our teachers that are in ourselves, in our relationships with others, and in the natural world. This triad represents the development of orientations that facilitate the deeper and more creative exploration of story.

Second, freeing our vision of preconceived notions and attitudes that are obstacles to our creative process of storying; exercising our imagination through creating and discussing all kinds of stories; and learning to envision a story from all sides to gain an understanding of all its dimensions and to practice the skill of thinking comprehensively. This triad represents the preparations needed to enhance the ability to comprehend a story with greater levels of clarity.

Third, learning to apply the lessons that come from storying to other life experiences; learning the techniques of Indigenous story making, story giving and story getting, all of which are centered in the social and interpersonal realm of community; and learning the communicative art of performing story in a variety of forms and settings, the foundation of the participatory and celebratory experience of story. This triad forms the foundation for applying stories in an integrated experience of learning and teaching that includes other forms of art and educational content.

Collectively, Indian people must address the inherent challenge of finding ways to live their guiding myths through contemporary life and educational contexts. The challenge is difficult, but the myths we live by define us as Tribal people, and when these defining myths cease to live through us, we become truly image without substance. Alienated from the roots of our primal stories, we become adrift in the vast ocean of contemporary mass society, continually trying to define ourselves through pre-packaged images and distorted stories that are not our own. Living our myths through a contemporary form of Indigenous storying ensures that we remain connected to the guiding stories that have given us life and "that place that the Indians talk about."

"Whenever men have looked for something solid on which to found their lives, they have chosen not the facts in which the world abounds, but the myths of an immemorial imagination."[22]

❋ VI ❋

SEEING THE VOICES OF OUR HEART

THE VISIONARY AND ARTISTIC FOUNDATIONS OF TRIBAL EDUCATION

Overview

IN THE UNFOLDING OF INDIGENOUS TRIBAL EDUCATION, the visionary and artistic contexts share a mutually reciprocal relationship. Indeed, they interpenetrate one another in their sharing and elaboration of dream, image, and creative response. Their forms of expression may differ, but their meanings stem from the same sources—the spiritual and mythic roots of a tribe. Both contexts reflect and honor an inner alchemy of the visionary/artist whose task becomes that of representing, sharing, and celebrating these roots. It is the divine dream, and the representation of its essence through symbolic images, that transforms both visionary/artist and user in some significant way and communicates some significant meaning. Vision and Art structure and bring to completion a transformative process of learning and development. Vision and Art reflect the reality of humans as imaginative and fully creative beings.

The tracks of Vision and Art can be traced back to the realm of dream and myth, which are the origin and motivation for creative expression. The first visionary, the first artist, was none other than the First Shaman, who sanctified and legitimized his/her vision through dream and myth.

"The Blackfoot Indians tell us that it was Old Man who showed them how to make everything they needed. 'Always at bottom there is a divine revelation, a divine act, and man has only the bright idea of copying it'... The first god-begotten hero-king of all nations and races—like Osiris in Egypt and Quetzalcoatl in Mexico, was the one who taught the arts and showed people how to make tools."[1]

Indeed, it is to the First Shaman that the guiding visions, the sacred arts, the knowledge of medicine, hunting, building, learning, and living in one's environment are usually ascribed. The shaman was the first dreamkeeper, the first artist, the first poet, the first hunter, the first doctor, the first dancer, singer, and teacher. While the shaman personified the archetypal visionary and artist, these are potentials that abide in each and every one of us, every man, every woman, and every child. Tribal people understood and honored this potential, this calling as an integral part of learning, being, and becoming complete.

Through encouragement, through ritual, through training and practice, Tribal people formed and guided this reflection of the divine in each other.

This chapter follows the tracks of the visionary and artist of Indigenous America. The *first track* reveals the nature of dream and vision as viewed through the eyes and words of American Indian visionaries and artists, both past and present. The *second track* explores the central role of vision in the context of Tribal educative endeavors. The *third track* reflects on the alchemy of the creative process from the perspective of transformation and orientation. The *fourth track* enters the realm of the Ceremony of Art as both a process and a context for deep learning and understanding among Indigenous people.

From each of the aforementioned tracks radiate concentric rings that overlap, not only the other tracks, but the previous foundation of myth. The triad of myth, vision, and art resonates with the other foundations of the environment, affective and communal. The integrated whole of Indigenous education becomes more apparent as we explore this dimension of "that place Indian people talk about."

Creating Through Dream and Vision In Native America

Dream and Vision are an integral dimension of artistic creation. For Indigenous people, there exists a huge body of belief regarding the nature of dreams and visioning. This body of belief is itself very ancient, with its roots first being reflected thousands of years ago during the creative explosion of the upper Paleolithic. This is when both Neanderthals and Cro-Magnons first began imaging their dreams on cave walls and in clay, wood, and stone. Of this diverse and extensive body of belief, the understanding that dreams represent the life of our spirit is the most commonly held and represented. A foundation of Lakota spiritual belief is that seeking a vision through the execution of proper rituals, fasting, and sacrifice brings one into contact with the dream world and the spiritual energy contained therein.

Among the Lakota, the elders tell that everything consists of four unique, yet wholly integrated, spiritual counterparts. These counterparts are similar to what Western theologians call "souls". The first of these souls is called "Niya" (life breath) and is the essence that animates all beings and entities. The second counterpart is called the "Nagi" and is similar to the unique personality exhibited by each person or entity, be it plant, animal, or other material forms. The third soul is called "Sicun" and is that special property, power, or way of being that sets it apart as a group or family. For example, Grizzly Bear, White-tailed Deer, Blue Spruce Tree, Sweet Grass or Obsidian Flint would characterize distinct groups or entities with special traits and properties. The fourth soul, the "Nagila" is the universal base energy that courses through all things; it is the ground energy of the Universe, the breath of the Great Mystery, the "Takuskan Skan" in all things.[2]

During the Lakota Sundance, the "Hanbleceya" (crying for a dream) is the time, after extensive fasting and physical sacrifice, that the four souls of the sundancers may be activated to interact with the souls of other spirits and entities of the world through a vision. If the sundancer is of good heart and has prepared properly, he may enter a visionary state of dream. The interactions that occur between souls therein impart important knowledge and understandings that the sundancer becomes obliged to share with others for the good and the life of the People. As Arthur Amiotte, Lakota artist and educator states:

> One is more than mere physical being, the possibility for interac-
> tion, transaction, and intercourse within other dimensions of time,
> place and being is what the dream experience is to the Lakota: an
> alternative avenue of knowing.[3]

As an alternative avenue of knowing and learning, dreaming has served Indian people in substantial ways. As with the Lakota, dreaming was recognized by all American Indian societies as a way of creating and understanding the essential nature of relationship within and outside one's self. The use and context of dreaming varied widely from tribe to tribe and region to region. But in every case, dreams and the more ritualized and structured form of visioning were an integral part of American Indian ritual, ceremony, and natural philosophy.

Among some tribes, dreams and their Tribal structuring through visioning were important enough to warrant a special status in the social organization of a tribe, with special roles and designation given to the dream interpreter or the dream societies that choreographed visioning ceremonies.

Dreams were deemed important avenues for glimpsing the future, finding that which had been lost, understanding the cause of psychological disharmony, and the origin of needs and wishes that must be honored. Throughout Indian America, dreams and dreaming were considered essential to success and happiness in life. This valuing of dreams set the psychological and social context necessary for receiving, remembering, and incorporating dreams into the reality of everyday living.

Indeed, Indian dreamers within a social context that valued dreams, developed extensive abilities to plan and manipulate the content of their dreams toward desired outcomes. In every tribe there were cultural and social rewards for dreams that helped the people. And through rewarding culturally significant dreams, Indians reinforced the role of dreaming in the fabric of their social/

cultural being. With such incentives, Indian dreamers actively sought to catch hold of any dream song or dream object that might symbolize an aspect of the deepest sense of themselves or of the people, their tribe or clan. It was through such dreams and visions that Indians created meaningful personal and group rituals, ceremonies or customs, many of which continue to be enacted today. Indians also gave their dreams creative waking form through art, song, dance, story, poetry, ritual, or ceremony. It is through art that Indian people continue to communicate their dreams today.[4]

Taken as a whole, Indians used dreams effectively in a variety of problem-solving and learning situations that required them to come to know their inner selves. To achieve this required the development of a direct and practiced understanding of an ecology of the mind and spirit seldom equaled in contemporary times. From the earliest ages, children were conditioned, not only to honor their dreams, but also to learn how to manipulate them toward desired outcomes. In short, many Indians learned how to dream for effect. By coming to terms with their fears, their hopes, their ambitions, and their shortcomings through honoring their dreams and learning from them, many Indians developed a steadfast and self-reliant nature that enabled them to cope with stressful situations and face the trials and tribulations of their lives with a high level of integrity.

That legacy of dreaming, which at the time of the first contact with Europeans was so apparent, can be revitalized in a contemporary reassertion of the Indigenous education process. The enabling power of understanding and honoring the dream process within the context of a new form of Indian education is largely an untapped domain. Today, Indigenous people everywhere suffer, in varying degrees, from "cultural schizophrenia." Being constantly faced with adapting themselves to two very different worlds of being has caused untold confusion and misery, as well as social and personal dysfunction among Indian people.

The educational process must again reconnect Indian youth with their dreaming and creative selves. Through the process of art making and the realization of the visioning process as a part of the educative process, great strides are possible in addressing the personal, social, and cultural disintegration that has become too much a part of the lives of many Indian people today. Denying the spiritual and psychological importance of dreaming, and not honoring its place in the educative process, leads to stunting an elemental process of human learning. It ensures that a cultural/social schizophrenia will continue to manifest in American Indians and take its toll on their lifeblood, be they young or old, reservation or urban, blue or white collar, full blood or mixed blood.

The key to this existential dilemma lies, in part, in learning and understanding how to apply the creative process of visioning in a meaningful and direct way within a contemporary Indian educational setting. Visions are essential: they are integral to individual and communal success, and they are a foundation of conscious evolution and human development.

The Role of Vision In Indigenous Education

Visioning embodies and focuses our creative power to visualize and realize new entities in communion with others and with our spirit. Visions always mirror what we deem sacred and intimately important to us. Also, visions relate, and act to integrate, all aspects of our lives. Visions are always about our individual movement toward wholeness. Whether the visions are for and about ourselves, our work, our community, or the whole world, they affect us at our deepest level of being. Honoring and living through vision is a quintessential learning process. Living through vision engenders living for a purpose and, as such, significantly enhances the meaning and quality we find in living. Vision forms a contextual frame of reference through which we can measure, relate, and act during our daily lives. As a whole, visions are the source of the important motivation of our lives and the straightest path to fulfilling our innate human potential.[5]

It is no wonder that visions held and continue to hold such an important place in many Indian societies. The process of visioning is a basic creative response to making meaning of life. Visions are, indeed, for life's sake.

The elaborations of visioning through ritual and ceremony by Indian people are pregnant with spiritual and psychological meanings. These elaborations themselves model the integration of myth, dream, art, ecological philosophy, communality, and spirit. In the Lakota Sundance, myth, art, ritual, depth psychology, and human community combine with dream to produce a fully integrated sphere of education toward the goal of developing a complete and fully potentiated human life. The Vision quest, among the Lakota, is to find life in one's being, in one's world, and in one's community of relationships.

'To find our life' is the translation of the Huichol Indians' pilgrimage to the mythical land of Wirikuta where Peyote, the Huichol sacrament of life, grows in abundance. During the pilgrimage, the Huichol make a variety of stops at sacred sites, which include springs, small hills, and canyons.[6]

At each of these stops the Huichol pilgrims retell the deeds of their ancestors at these sites during that first pilgrimage to the land of Wirikuta. At each site the Huichol, in a sense, bring themselves into resonance with a dimension of their souls and their guiding cultural myth in preparation for the vision that they will seek after picking the Peyote. In short, Huichol pilgrims form a communal bond with each other, their guiding myths and their sacrament, which is the Peyote. They delve deeply into the essence of their relationships. The pilgrimage embodies the preparation, sacrifice, and transformation that opens each pilgrim to the creative potential inherent in the process of visioning.

When the Huichol arrive in Wirikuta, they ritually hunt the Peyote as they would hunt a deer, that life-giving animal that for them symbolizes the spiritual yet illusive essence of peyote and the life-finding gift of vision that it presents.[7]

After collecting Peyote, the pilgrims present their offerings of yarn paintings and accompanying prayers and prayer feathers. These embody their wishes and their hope for a guiding personal vision that will help them to find their life. Their presentation is made to "Tate wa ri", the sacred fire, and "Kauyumari", the five-pointed deer, whose essence is the Peyote. As they sit around their sacred fire, they share with each other, as ritual food, selected peyote buds representing the "five sacred colors of corn".[8]

As they sit in vigil through the night, eating peyote, awaiting their individual visions, the pilgrims retrace their lives and the reasons and events that have brought them to find their life. One by one, each pilgrim receives a vision and direct insight about their spiritual selves. Each pilgrim receives the gifts of their creative vision that later may form the basis for a series of yarn paintings, a song, a personal ceremony, or even another pilgrimage to learn more and gather new insights and creative gifts.[9]

Such visioning is always a profound transformative experience that will deeply affect their lives and their relationships from that time on. As such, the Huichol pilgrimage outlines the archetype of questing for a vision. Both as a group and as individuals, the people who have journeyed to Wirikuta, the place where their Mother Peyote dwells, "have found themselves" as the Huichol say. They have received their life; they have received their vision.

> I have eaten the pure foam of the sea! Who
> now knows better how to sing, how to dance?
> Who now knows better how to paint with yarn?
> Who now knows how to plant? It is I, I now
> know how to do this best. I have eaten the pure
> foam of the sea! I have eaten the pure foam of the sea![10]

The Huichol pilgrimage illustrates vividly how dream and vision work in the Indigenous educative process. There are dozens of examples from other American Indian tribes and other Indigenous people around the world. What is important is that we understand that there are basic principles inherent in the process of visioning that have direct implications for a more complete approach to education, one that recognizes and claims an integrated process of learning. These basic principles as reflected in visioning, include:

1. Visions are always holistic. They are interdependent with and acted upon by every other aspect of a whole system, be that the individual, the family, tribe, or a social/physical environment.

2. Visions unfold through symbiotic cooperative activity with others in a complementary give-and-take relationship. Visions in groups are always about working together to gain common goals.

3. Visions have an innate pattern that is characteristic of both the individual and the inherent nature of the vision itself. Visions have a rhythmic life of their own whose cycles of evolution and development have to be understood and honored.

4. Visions and their implementation teach us about the nature of learning as a journey toward a greater level of completeness. In questing for a vision, we learn not only about trials, tribulations, sacrifice, and real work, but also about our strengths, weaknesses, and our innate creative potentials.[11]

The potential of teaching for vision and engaging students in the creative process of visioning is literally revolutionary in its implications for contemporary education. Through facilitating the understanding of their dreams and conditioning them for the creative process of visioning, we allow students an avenue for learning that capitalizes on one of the most basic and ancient contexts for developing self-knowledge.

This would require a complete restructuring of what we now know as the school. Whether or not this can become a reality in the institutions of mainstream American education is debatable. But for Indian people and Tribally controlled schools, a contemporary expression of this concept would seem essential.

The reintroduction of such a process into Indian education would allow Indian people to cultivate in themselves the efficacy of Tribal modes of knowing and understanding. It would be a culturally based methodology whose principles are recognized and applied in traditional Tribal settings where visioning rituals still exist. The difference would be only in the nature of the approaches used: that is, the Tribal setting focuses on Tribally specific ritual and values, while a school version would focus only on universals and views using combinations of tools and appropriate media.

Indian young people need to be given opportunities to learn again how to live through vision and reconnect their contemporary lives with that of their Tribal heritage. By living through vision, young people learn how to reconnect with and honor their own nature; they learn how to live a life in touch with their individual creative sources. They learn to live life purposefully and understand life and education as a process toward becoming complete.

As Linda Marks so beautifully states in her book, *Living with Vision*, to develop a visionary process means to develop the ability:

> "...to *see* the way things are; to see how things can be; to know what needs to be done from where we are to where we are going; to know what part we are to play in partnership with others; to feel the inspiration and call to act; and to be able to know and take appropriate action to live a life with purpose."[12]

The essential dilemma of many Indian young people is how to live purposefully. Indian youth need to see the relationships among Indian cultural values, finding a purpose for their lives, understanding the kind of work they need to act on purpose, and developing of a vision that guides them toward fulfillment of themselves as complete human beings.

This is exactly what the context and process of dreaming and visioning were able to accomplish for Indian people in the past. Visioning continues to do this today for those tribes and those individuals who have the remnants of this once-great and highly effective educative process. Will Indian people, Tribal leaders, Indian professionals, and Indian educators heed such a call? This question is yet to be answered, and it is a question that only Indian people themselves can answer.

Art and Alchemy

Art was a monumental evolution in the development of human learning. Art, which is the transformation of raw materials into a form that reflects meaning to both artist and user, is equally a reflection of an elemental transformation. Indeed Art, in its highest forms of expression, is a kind of magic. And in this magic of creation, the artist becomes immersed within his media and the mind of creation.

To honor this intimate and spiritual relationship, the artist must understand and master his own creative center through patient and exercised discipline. The artist must work with: clarity of purpose; an understanding and true appreciation of his materials and his tools; an inner harmony and vitality of spirit, mind, and body; and a focused meditative attention that exercises his full intelligence in a prayerful act of bringing an entity, a form that lives, into being.

The creation of art is an alchemy of process in which the artist becomes more himself through each act of true creation. He transfers his life in a dance of relationship with the life inherent in the material that he transforms into an artistic creation.

In each process of creation, there must be an initiation, purification, death, and rebirth of the artist through focused creative work. In working, reworking, and suffering into being a work of art, the artist is creating and recreating himself. It is, in a metaphoric sense, a matter of life, death, and rebirth.

This is the vital essence of artistic creation that the master Indigenous artist knows so well. This is the age-old ceremony of art whose aim is the making of one's self, the celebrating and symbolizing of an aspect of life deemed important to the artist, and the reality that he sees and shares with his tribe, his people, and himself.

The master Indigenous artist was set apart from others of his tribe only by his relative level of practice and skill in a particular art form. All Tribal people engaged in the creation of artistically crafted forms. Young and old, men and women, each in their own measure participated in the making of things. Whether songs, ceremonies, dances, pottery, baskets, dwellings, boats, or bows, Indigenous people were one and all engaged in creating the utilities of their lives. Art was an integral expression of life, not something separate; it rarely had a specialized name. The modern perception of art for art's sake, as it is defined and expressed in modern and usually egocentric terms, had little meaning in Indigenous society. Everyone was an artist, a maker of things, and the things made always had their proper form and use as well as inherent symbolic meaning. In each case, the traditional art form reflected the mythos of the tribe, that is, the way a people viewed and understood themselves. The Indigenous artist instilled meaning in every work he created. He made the divine, as he and his people defined it, visible through his art. Art was a way of expressing his whole being in relationship with his tribe and the spiritual essences that moved his world. Therefore, Indigenous art was functional and meaningful at the same time. There was no separation between craft and fine art as exists today in modern Western society.

> Primitive man, despite the pressure of his struggle for existence, knew nothing of such merely functional arts. . . . He could not have thought of meaning as something that might or might not be added to useful objects at will. Primitive man made no real distinction of sacred from secular: his weapons, clothing, vehicles, and house were

all of them imitations of divine prototypes, and were to him even more what they meant than what they were in themselves; he made them this 'more' by incantation and by rites… to have seen in his artifacts nothing but the things themselves, and in the mythos a mere anecdote, would have been a mortal sin, for this would have been the same as to see in oneself nothing but the 'reasoning and mortal animal', to recognize only 'this man', and never the 'form of humanity.'[13]

Indigenous Arts Are Mandalas of Creative Transformation

Traditional American Indian art forms are created for a specific purpose or activity and have been handed down from teacher to pupil through a symbolic initiatory process that significantly transforms the pupil. It also reflects the mythos of the tribe and has meaning and value for the tribe generations after its creation.

The educative foundation of traditional art forms is inherent in the ceremony of its creation. For the Indigenous artist, traditional art influenced the form and expression of life as well as providing a pathway to commune with the Great Mystery. The creation of art was a mandala of process for the re-creation of the Tribal artist. It was also a way to evoke and focus the re-creative and healing power of the foundational guiding myths and traditional knowledge of a tribe.

The outcome of this approach to art-making was a reforming of both artist and participants to a higher level of completion. Art, viewed in this way, becomes a series of acts for developing and perpetuating a process of life-enhancing relationships. In this context, the ceremony of making becomes far more than the product; the product becoming only a symbolic documentation of the creative and spiritual process that gave it form. However, because such forms were created with a specific intention, many were used to evoke creative magic through ritual and ceremony. Artifacts created in this way were used and reused as needed, while others, such as the Navajo ceremonial sandpainting, are destroyed after they have served their curative reharmonizing purposes.

The concept of the mandala is useful in understanding the inherent wholeness of this way of "arting" and how the transformation and rejuvenation occur. The word *mandala* comes from the Sanskrit and means 'center' or 'to circle' or 'in the middle place'. In every respect, the mandala represents a structural metaphor for wholeness or completion. The mandala is an archetypal structure whose variations can be found in sacred art traditions, ranging from architecture to iconography to weaving to sandpainting.

Wherever the mandala structure is found, it conforms to four basic characteristics. It has a center, reflects a basic symmetrical pattern, has a boundary defined by cardinal points, and has a specialized construction that provides a tool for concentration and meditation toward a pre-defined purpose. The creation of a mandala embodies a therapeutic ritual that honors our impulse toward wholeness through striving toward centering, healing, health, and transformative growth and development.

A primary function of creating a mandala is to engender a process that recognizes the relatedness of elements in a specific context to a person, place, or group. Mandalas show the relationships of elements to problems that are being addressed. In the reflection of relationships, mandalas also mirror the nature of self-relatedness to the creator or participants.

It may be said that each person is a living mandala at the physical/mental/social and spiritual levels. The mandala is an elemental learning tool. Through its construction each person must learn: to concentrate their various levels of being, to understand their basic orientations, and to know their center, in order to release the creative energy stored therein.

The creation of art by Indigenous artists mirrors the creation of mandalas. Some Tribal arts, such as the Navajo Sandpainting, *are* mandalas. In the creation of a mandala, distinct stages of development are readily apparent. For instance, the creation of a mandala begins with cleansing one's being through prayer, fasting or meditation to increase the receptivity of the artist to his/her creative task.

This is followed by an activity that helps to *center* the artist's mind, body, and soul through concentrating one's energy inward, thereby energizing the creative spirit. Then there is an *orienting* of one's self to the creative task by: ordering preliminary activities, preparing tools, testing patterns, immersion in preparatory actions, research, and gathering of necessary materials.

The next step, which is *construction* of the actual artifact, comprises the creation or putting together of the parts. This making of the artifact, dancing of the dance, or singing of the songs, is the direct expression of the activity completed in prior stages. In a mandala process the creation or performance is not the end, but rather the middle point.

To complete the whole of a mandala process, there must be a complementary side to that of production. This complement might best be termed the making of meaning or reflection. In the making of a mandala, there must be a stage of internalizing the inherent message of the mandala by the maker, the audience, the user. This is the point where all who have participated in the mandala process identify with its essence, its spirit. Once this identification has occurred, there is the need for a gradual detachment from emotional states that usually characterize the identification stage. This is a stage of letting go. It flows into the next two stages: *reintegration* into a more basic level of being, and *actualization* into everyday life what has been learned about oneself and the purpose of the mandala. This is exactly what happens in the whole-making process of the Navajo Sandpainting.[14]

A mandalic process characterizes the making of sacred or ceremonial forms among many Indigenous people. Traditional art forms among Indigenous people, regardless of their mode of expression, integrate and reflect the essence of the people. The mandalic process structurally articulates the sacred play between creativity and entropy for all those who participate in its unfolding.

The Ceremony of Art:
A Way of Seeing and Expressing In Indigenous Education

The human need to express through art has its roots in the deep reaches of man's hunter/gatherer origins. Art, as a human thinking and expressing process, is intimately connected to the creative explosion of human consciousness. As a facet of creative consciousness, Native American art presents a reality that is at once specifically unique, yet humanly universal. In addition, the process and product of Indigenous educational philosophy is intimately expressed through the various Native American art forms. Expression of Native American art presents what is inherently real about the Native American experience and understanding of the world — past, present, and future. Native American arts show the possibilities, the many different windows, from which to view the world. Each window, and the doorway that accompanies it, opens upon other possibilities of human experience that also have validity.

Traditional arts of Native America chronicle cultural realities whose richness and potential for human understanding are only now being revealed through contemporary research and American Indians telling their own story. An often hidden, yet all-important aspect of art is the nature of the work, or the process of creation of the art. This art provides reflections of the Indigenous educational process, that is, the conditioned way of thinking with its aesthetic, social, psychological, spiritual, and ecological perspectives. This approach to art was and is an integrated expression of an art of living. This sensibility for the art of living evolved over millennia and continues to be reflected in contemporary Indian arts, even with the incorporation of new materials, mediums, and Western European influences. As a whole, it is a process that engenders becoming fully human.

This reflection or sensibility is exactly what one must begin to see — to learn how to unpack the conditioning presents both the challenge and the fresh look at the educative process and the evaluating nature of Indian art forms. It was this brilliantly unique and inventive nature of Native American art forms that affected the sensibilities of modernist art as reflected in the work of artists Henry Moore, Martha Graham, Jackson Pollack, Georgia O'Keeffe, and many others.

The Tribal way of art allowed everyone to share in a particular expression and process of culture and living. Art was viewed as an expression of life and was practiced, to one extent or another, by all the people of a tribe. Traditionally, art was an anonymous activity expressing a unique cultural perspective of living.

Despite the anonymity of most American Indian art works, the creativity, craftsmanship, and ingenuity of the individuals with vision shone through with exceptional clarity. Such talent reflected the consummation and integration of the Indigenous educational aims of developing people with a heart, a face, and a visionary foundation. The Tribal artist individuated a tradition of creating through time and space.

Whereas myth is reflective of inner psychology and cultural concepts through imagery and symbol, art gives a concrete and tangible expressive form to these dimensions. Art, then, is a primary foundation of the Indigenous education process. As product, art makes tangible this process. As process, art is an integral part of the product itself.

Art As A Way of Ceremony and Transformation

Just as each individual sees reality in a unique way—so does each society, and each generation in a society, understand reality uniquely. Art is a way of seeing, of being, and of becoming. To see the expressive realities art presents, one must first learn how to look. To understand this development of art as a way of seeing requires that one recognize the inherent ritual and ceremony of art as an ongoing dimension of Indigenous education process.[15]

"The complex process by which an artist transforms the act of seeing into a vision of the world is one of the consummate mysteries of the arts—one of the reasons that art for tribal people is inseparable from religion and philosophy. The act of envisioning and then engendering a work of art is an important and powerful process of ritualization . . . The act of ritualization is a metaphoric process—whether we are speaking in terms of visual art and architecture, of epic poetry or the performing arts."[16]

Indigenous artisans selected those features of what was being depicted that conveyed its vitality and essence, and expressed them directly in the most appropriate medium available. This approach—as opposed to the attempt to conform to intellectualized theory or schools of thought or depict the exact form—reflects the basic foundation of ritual creation of traditional Tribal art. The emphasis in the creation of traditional art is on getting to the heart, the spirit, of an event or entity.

Art in primal societies reflected the ritualization of the life process. For much of Indigenous art, the aliveness of an artifact was the primary aesthetic criteria, rather than its beauty. This did not mean that Indigenous artifacts were not beautiful, rather their inherent beauty was a natural by-product of their life.

The life inherent in much of Indigenous art reflects a process/product of the Indigenous educative process. Gaining insight into the nature of Indigenous education, through an exploration of its foundations, represents important insight for the new paradigm of education. To get at the meat of the matter as it concerns the role of art in the Indigenous education process, an exploration of the ceremony of art is essential.

The ceremony of art touches the deepest realms of the psyche and the sacred dimension of the artistic creative process. This is the level that not only transforms something into art, but also transforms the artist at the very core of being. This way of doing and relating to art makes the process and context of art-making infinitely more important than the product. This transforming quality of creation is inherent in Indigenous American Art in varying degrees from the purely utilitarian artifact to the shamanistic talisman. The plants, animals, and the technique and media with which the artifacts are created reflect an integration and clarity of purpose with mind and heart that accomplished modern artists have difficulty emulating. The innate Nature centeredness of Indigenous art represents an educated soulfulness that unfolds through the creative process of the artist onto the medium.

Indigenous artifacts were created with an acutely developed acknowledgment of the natural elements from which they were made. The most elaborate examples of such understanding are Indigenous ceremonial artifacts. Each component of an artifact was carefully chosen for its integrity of spirit and its symbolic meaning within the traditions of a particular tribe. The use of particular natural pigment, clay, wood, stone, plant or animal parts, gathered from special places in ritually prescribed ways was common in the creation of ceremonial artifacts. From intention and conception to completion and use, every step in the creation of a ceremonial artifact had inherent meaning within a greater perspective of relationship to spiritual energy.

Spirit, soul, purpose of each component, and their transformation through artistic creation, were practiced and taught through the deliberate creation of a context in which process, product, and self might become one. The context that allowed this process of teaching to unfold might have been ritual, ceremony, dance, song, pilgrimage, or any combination thereof.

Creativity and transformation are interrelated in every context or act of artistic creation. Apprenticeships, formal and informal, were the primary vehicle for learning a particular art form. In such apprenticeship relationships, the mentor many times set up conditions in which the apprentice would learn how to identify with the creation of an artifact. In the making of ceremonial art these conditions were extended to include the transformation of the apprentice to a requisite level of consciousness. In this way art became a process of spiritual training that involved the spiritual development of the artist at every turn. It is no accident that the first shamans can also be considered the first artists.[17]

The contexts discernible in the creation of ceremonial art in Indigenous societies follow this general pattern:[18]

A. *Preparing*: This is a conscious effort to simplify, to become aware, to sharpen the senses, to concentrate, to revitalize the whole being. The idea was to develop the ability to imbue an artifact with pure and simple vitality, to have clarity of mind and the stamina to undertake a very difficult and sometimes dangerous task, for example, the initiatory paintings of the caves of Lasceaux, Tres Fries.

B. *Guiding Spirit*: Consistent adherence to original intent, the idea of applying one's will to concentrate one's whole being into a task, a creation, a song, a dance, a painting, an event, a ceremony, a ritual, etc.

C. *The Sources*: Attention to the nature of the sources of raw materials to be used in the creation of an artifact, especially one for ceremonial purposes, was essential. Not only the quality of materials was important, but how and where they were obtained.

D. *Adhering to patterns yet transcending them (form/design)*: "Generally, ceremonial artistry acknowledged the inherent mystery, the intrinsic integrity of both medium and material, but within the parameters and adherence to a sometimes strict cultural convention."

E. *Time*: A culturally defined dimension, and when combined with the intuitive and spiritually conditioned sense of timing applied by the master artist in the production of ceremonial art, time itself becomes an artistic and creative ingredient.

In the creation of ceremonial art, time becomes an important variable. Artists, in the creation of ceremonial art, concerned themselves with the timeliness of creation from beginning to end.

"If a tribal carver, blacksmith, weaver, singer, storyteller or whatever was not a diviner of time, such a person would be consulted, and a favorable time would be divined for the initiation of a ceremonial artifact. Through prayer and transcendence of mind, the artisans would attempt to 'dance' themselves into synchronicity with the appropriate sequence of moments for the creation of the ceremonial artifact. Through the entire creation process there were a series of 'right' moments or phases which might be suggested by a certain smell, a quality of the raw material, a feeling, emotion or dream, which might indicate whether or not to proceed to the next phase of creation," in short, an alignment of knowing.

F. *Right Place*: Time and place are integrally related. Therefore, the place of creation often becomes a consideration in the creation of ceremonial artifacts. Certain places were considered by Indigenous groups as being conducive to certain endeavors. Such places might be character-ized by invisible qualities, the availability of appropriate materials, environmental areas conducive to heightened awareness and creativ-ity, dreaming places, healing places, dancing places, living/setting places, singing places, and creative places.

Part of the reason for preparation before creation of ceremonial artifacts was to be able to locate at the appropriate place for creation, through sensitivity to feedback at several levels of awareness.

Location also included a sensitivity to the metaphor of space and orientation, and alignment of self with environment and the material used. Space and location orientation are important considerations in all Indig-enous people's activities.

G. *Letting Go and Becoming*: Self-effacement and surrender to the contin-gencies of the task of creation often characterize the production of ceremonial art. Such a state of being might result from the phase of preparation or at some critical turning point in the creative process. Regardless of how the state was reached, it was necessary for it to occur if artist and artifact were to become one, and if the authentic transfor-mation of both was to occur.

H. *Intrinsic well-practiced belief*: "The struggle to create the artifact which is imbued with power and authentically symbolizes an essence… is a struggle of finding and sustaining appropriate will. It is only appropriate will, sustained by an integrated and properly focused vigil, that will align with an eloquent expression of a 'truth' of a given indigenous group."

The struggle to express such a truth through the creation of a ceremonial artifact comes only from a long-practiced faith in the effect of one's work and purpose. The successful outcome of such a struggle depends on what can be termed appropriate will. Appropriate will results from a full understanding of the repercussions of undertaking a task and the purpose to be fulfilled by the work that is created. Appropriate will integrates the intention for creating work and puts in context the planning, vigilance, and devotion required to bring a work to completion.

I. *The Packing of a Symbol*: Symbol and symbolization are the essence of art in every form. Indigenous people believe that symbols have a power beyond their literal connotations. A symbol might protect one from a danger or invite it; a symbol might heal or kill, induce fertility or prevent it, communicate a universal or a specific, trigger empowerment or take it away. Through the ceremony of art, Indigenous artists "packed" a symbol with specific meaning and intent. Petroglyphs represent a clear exemplification of such a packing process. Each symbol represents a metaphor whose meaning is in the context of the myth, experience, or understanding of a Tribal group or clan. The Kokopeli among Puebloan people or the medicine wheel among the Sioux are but two of the hundreds of examples of such packed metaphoric symbols among Tribal people of the Americas.

J. *The Vigil*: Deals with the cultivation of patience and focusing intent and attention throughout the creation of an artifact. Sustaining appropriate attention to every aspect of creating an object is not only a reflection of vigilance but also an honoring of the process of making through which each detail of work is given its due. It is a way of prayerful work.

"A primal artisan would never for a moment leave the proximity of the setting of the task, not for a moment, not even if it were meat or clay cooking slowly in the perfect pit or oven."

K. *The Completion*: Is the completed gathering of everything that needs to be part of creating and packing into a tangible form. In this stage the intent of a created work is crystallized and given physical birth into the human world of use and understanding. This is where an artifact is brought into its full physical being, ready to be used and serve its purpose. As a form, it is packed with potential, but this is not the end of the Indigenous artistic process, only a transformation of orientation and focus.

L.   *The Give Away*: Is where the completed form, and the life and meaning inherent in its physical being, is given up to the purpose and process for which it has been created. The Give Away marks the entrance of the artifact into a community for symbolic recognition and use. The artifact may be used once or may be used and reused many times, but its meaning is always understood as long as a Tribal group remembers to remember the context, circumstances, and purpose of its creation.

M.   *Aesthetics and Appreciation of Intrinsic Meaning*: Reflected in the honored use of the artifact for its designated purpose from one generation to the next, or over the life span of the individual(s) responsible for its creation. The aesthetics and value of the artifact are directly related to what it means and the purpose it serves in a Tribal context. For instance, the potlatch "coppers" so integral to the Potlatch Giveaways among Northwest Indian tribes increased in value the more they were given away by the families who honored their aesthetic and intrinsic meaning. This is one of dozens of examples.[19]

The Ceremony of Art inherent in the philosophy and use of art among Indigenous societies presents an essential attitude for the learning, teaching, and using of art in a contemporary educational context for American Indians. Art and the making of art are natural cultural modes of expression for American Indians whose development and process is intimately intertwined with their spiritual orientation. However, the process and intent of art-making, and art as a way to educate, must build upon a revitalized foundation of Indigenous art in a contemporary setting. Art for art sake, art as individual writ large, art as intellectualization, art as commodity, art as social commentary are all dimensions of the modern contemporary art world whose consequences today's Indian artists must come to understand in the evolution of contemporary Indian art. This must be accomplished without contemporary Indian artists losing the under-standing of the intrinsic power and value of the Ceremony of Art that lies at the core of what art means and the role it plays in defining the soul of Tribal identity.

To accomplish such a task is a great challenge. Yet, it is of paramount importance to ensure that the process and meaning of traditional Tribal arts are not forgotten, because they are a unique and irreplaceable way for "seeing the voices of our hearts" and accessing wholeness through the creative process.

Art As A Way of Wholeness, Creativity, and Orientation

The making of art in Indigenous societies provided a pathway to wholeness for both the artist and those who utilized the artist's creations. Indigenous art provided a vehicle for approaching wholeness in that it required the artist to honor four orienting roles in the creation of a traditional art form, especially those created for ceremonial or spiritually empowering purposes. Applying the Indigenous metaphor of sacred directions, and the expression of dual yet complementary natures, these basic roles can be characterized metaphorically as follows. (See Diagram.)

In the East, which represents for many Tribal people of North America the place of new beginnings (heralded by the first light of dawn), there is the orientation of the Shaman/Priest. The pairing of shaman and priest in the East is metaphorically appropriate in that both archetypes preside over the visionary and spiritually transforming foundation (which provides the basic impetus for the making of Indigenous art) and the centering process (which prepares and guides the artist in the creative process). This is the seeing of what needs to be done.

In the North is the orientation of the Hunter/Warrior that represent the tracking, finding, and holding of the manifestations and symbols of both spirit and vision. This orientation concerns the application of one's innate intuition in finding those things needed to create art that properly addresses the essential elements of the vision to be created. Through this orientation the creator develops the courage and self-confidence to follow what has been seen. In this orientation there is also the process of centering, developing the heart and strategy to carry through the creative act.

In the twilight orientation of the West are the Artist/Poet. These archetypes creatively represent the unfolding of events, beginning in the visionary/spiritual orientation of the East, through the metaphoric use of images, words, forms, music, songs, and dance. In the roles as creative presenters of the Sun's illuminating light, Artist and Poet represent the images, forms, thoughts, sounds or actions that document and illuminate the path toward wholeness.

In the South is the orientation of the Philosopher/Teacher. These archetypes represent the quest for understanding and organizing the metaphorically coded messages inherent in the art that has been made. The creative play between understanding, which is the domain of the philosopher, and communicating, the domain of the teacher, form the infrastructure for the formal and informal transmission of knowledge and meaning of what has been created. This is the knowing of what has been made.

In some Indigenous orientations, the South is the source of the fertile, creative winds and the monsoon rains, which warm and nourish the arid lands of the Southwest. The philosophical and educational orientations associated with the South provide a poetic and natural frame of reference to reflect on the creative process of learning through art.

The Cardinal Orientations of Indigenous Creativity

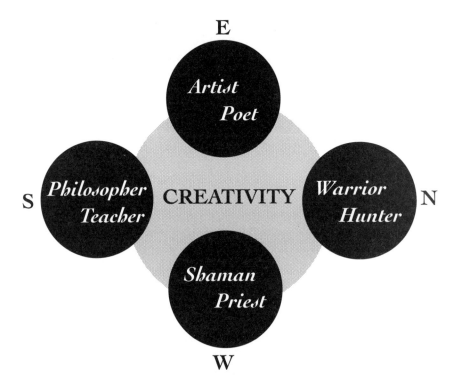

These orientations run parallel to contemporary understandings of the creative process. In essence, each of the orientations mentioned mirrors the generally accepted stages of the creative process. Viewed in reverse order, First Insight, the first stage of creation, might be associated with the Artist/Poet. In this stage creative thought begins with dreams, intuitions, exploration of archetypes, forms and images within the individual or group unconscious. The process then evolves to a perceptive play with Visual/Verbal/Spatial/Tactile or Auditory symbols and forms. Next comes a period of searching, introspection, and intellectualization, which develops the artist/poet's level of sensitivity and empathy for the creative work. Finally, the creator enters into the realm of macro vision, which is characterized by metaphoric thinking and transformative vision upon the metaphysics and spirituality of that which is to be created.

The second stage of *Preparation/Immersion* is closely akin to the orientation of the Philosopher/Teacher. This stage begins with a process of making meaning, addressing contingencies, and exploring key relationships relative to an approach to an artistic work. There is a learning of tools, research, and application of strategy and logic to find the best way to make what needs to be made. The process then moves to more reasoning, symbolization, responding, and searching, combined with establishing the proper emotional and intellectual context for the making of the artistic work. At the macro level, this stage is marked by inquiry, scholarship, accumulation of knowledge, and further reflection on the metaphysics of the work to be done. Through this stage, and the preceding one of First Insight, the form of the creative work gradually begins to take a tangible prototypical form.

The third stage of *Incubation* closely resembles the orientation of the Shaman/Priest and is similar to the beginning stage of First Insight. The difference between the two lies in the relative depth each stage submerges into the unconscious. While First Insight is more perceptual, Incubation is more primal and alchemically transformative. The learning that is characteristic of First Insight and Preparation moves to the deeper unconscious realms of dreams, drives, archetypes, intuitions, and preconcepts based on life/death symbols. Incubation, at its deepest levels of expression, gives rise to metamorphic processes and mythological thinking revolving around transformation and rebirth. These processes and thoughts are in turn expressed through forms of initiation, ritual, and ceremony. At the macro level, Incubation engenders hologizing, healing, and expressions of spirituality including those characteristic of various religious rites and practices. This stage cooks or fires the forms being created in the deep kilns of the unconscious.

The fourth and final stage of *Evaluation* is similar to the orientation of the Hunter/Warrior in that evaluation is like finding your prey, producing the work, and taking a stand in defense of what you have made. Evaluation primarily involves developing a strategy for presenting a work and addressing one's critics and one's shortcomings with courage. As a whole, this stage engenders self-confidence through boldly taking risks and defending the principles and integrity of the creative process that has led to the art. At the macro level, the realization of this stage results in a state of completion. A relative state of spiritual centeredness and holistic perspective, which is expressive of the good heart engendered by the completion of a creative work, characterizes this last stage of creativity.

Indigenous arts provided and continue to provide a foundational way to express and nourish the soul of the instinctual human need to learn and create. Art is an essential part of human learning and plays a pivotal role in the development of the inherent potentials of every person, regardless of social, cultural, or political status.

The place of the arts in Indigenous educational philosophy is without question. What is questionable is the reliance upon Western European concepts of art and the ego-centered, capitalistic, schooling for art that underpins the tacit infrastructure of the education of Indians in the arts. There is a Way of Indian art that is distinctly non-Western, non-European in its orientation, philosophy, aesthetic criteria, and aims. To understand this difference, it is important to understand the ceremony of art as it is practiced by Tribal people in the creation of ceremonial artifacts. For historically, Indian artists created for Life's Sake.

The Analogy of The Tree of Life

The tree of life, as an analogy for the educative process and quest for knowledge, presents a structural symbol for Indigenous education that embodies its life and Nature centered orientations. Traditional Tribal art is, in every sense, an expression of the relationship of Tribal people to life and Nature. The tree presents an archetype of life, learning, and development that begins with the sprouting of a seedling embedded in fertile ground, then moves to the various stages of growth and development, through all seasons of life and its trials and tribulations until it begins to form seeds of its own. What an amazing natural analogy for a life of learning. Each specie of tree is a particular tribe originating and rooted in the soil of a particular place, living and growing into its own particular form and completing itself in the distinct way of its species, yet having its own unique expression of life. The leaves, fruits, and seeds of each tree are the outward expression of its life and its treeness. Each of these is the expression of the art and soul of the tree and of Tribal people. What better analogy for the process of Indigenous art could one find?

The sacred tree is a symbolic ecological metaphor represented in myth and ceremony everywhere in the Americas. Many Indian myths refer to the Tree of Life, which nourishes and connects all life. It is a symbol of the core orientations of Indian philosophy, holding life and rooted to the Earth. It is the central axis around which all life and activity revolve. It is the living symbol and source of that divine creative energy of life expressed in language, song, dance and craft. The roots, trunk, branches and leaves of this sacred tree may be seen as symbolic expressions of various dimensions of Indigenous education and art orientations.

The thousands of expressions of Indian art are the leaves of this great Tree of Life. May the Great Tree flourish once again and flourish in the hearts of all mankind.

A Tree of Life and Indigenous Artistic Expression

ARTISTIC
EXPRESSIONS

THE
INDIVIDUAL

CONTEXT   SOCIAL GROUP   ENVIRONMENT

ART
SPIRITUALITY
RITUAL
MYTH

CULTURAL/ENVIRONMENTAL ORIENTATIONS

THE CEREMONY OF ART

SPIRITUAL ECOLOGY AND THEOLOGY OF PLACE

VII

WE ARE ALL RELATED

The Communal Foundation of Indigenous Education

Introduction

Mitakuye Oyasin, "We Are All Related," personifies the integrative expression of what Indian people perceive as *Community*. Understanding the inclusive nature of this perception is key to the context in which traditional Indian education occurs. Context is essential in education and determines both the meaning and application of teaching and learning.

Relationship is the cornerstone of Tribal community; the nature and expression of community are the foundation of Tribal identity. It is through community that Indian people come to understand the nature of their personhood and their connection to the communal soul of their people. The community is the place where the forming of the heart and face of the individual as one of the people is most fully expressed. Community is the context in which the Indian person comes to know the nature of relationship, responsibility, and participation in the life of one's people.

> The Indian individual is spiritually interdependent upon the language, folk history, ritualism, and geographical sacredness of his or her *whole* people. Relationships between members of families, bands, clans, and other tribal groups are defined and intensified through relational and generational language rather than through personal names, which are considered to be sacred and private to the individual. The relatedness of the individual extends beyond the family, band or clan to include all things of the world. Thus nothing exists in isolation. Individualism does not presuppose autonomy, alienation, or isolation. And freedom is not the right to express yourself but the far more fundamental right to *be* yourself."[1]

Indian community is the primary context for traditional education. Community is the context in which the affective dimension of education unfolds. It is the place where one comes to know what it is to be related. It is the place of sharing life through everyday acts, through song, dance, story, and celebration. It is the

place of teaching, learning, making art, and sharing thoughts, feelings, joy, and grief. It is the place for feeling and being connected. The community is the place where each person can, metaphorically speaking, become complete and express the fullness of their life. Community is "that place that Indian people talk about", it is the place through which Indian people express their highest thought.

How, then, does Indigenous community work? How does it context learning? What happens in Indian community that makes traditional education what it is? What are the educational structures of Indian communities, and how are their roles played out in the process of education? How does the community link its members to the natural community of their environment, their place? How is the communal soul linked to the expression of the individual's role in a tribe's spirituality? What are the implications of community for contemporary Indian education? These are some of the questions that we will touch upon in this chapter. *Mitakuye Oyasin*, we are all related, we are all *Of Community*. In engendering an understanding of this fact in the educational structures and processes that we create, we honor what is truly most human in each of us.

Cultures As Environments

Human cultures are constructs that create environments through which humans are able to live. As human social environments, they conform to the same general ecological principles as physical environments. For example, cultures evolve, adapt, and react in response to ever-changing internal and external environmental factors. Like micro-organisms, human communities act on their external environments to create conditions favorable to their continuation. Human communities are born, evolve through several stages of succession, reach climax, and then gradually decline, giving way to new communities that spring from the compost of the old.

Indigenous communities reflect this human ecology. It is therefore no accident that traditional forms of education expressed in Indigenous communities transferred the recipe for making a living in a given environment. Traditional education is a vehicle for transmitting the social and ecological messages of the life of a people. Traditional education is a vehicle for the ecological sense and the spiritual ecology of the people. Humans create culture as a construct to organize the social/communal instinct of our species toward survival and sustainable communities. Culture is the expression of our social genes. Understanding and transferring knowledge of its complex, ecological messages remain the most essential educational challenges of our time.

How Does Indigenous Community Work?

Community, in a universal sense, may be said to be founded on a set of timeless rules guiding individual and group identity within the web of all-interpenetrating symbolic culture.[2]

Community is the natural context of human life and activity. We are, one and all, social beings living *in relation* to one another. Our physical and biological survival is intimately interwoven with the communities that we create and that create us. The community is a complex of physical, social, and psychical relationships that are ever changing and evolving through time and the generations of people who identify with it. The community began in its first forms with the extended family, with shared lineages and ways of life. Until relatively recently in human history, all human communities were made up of people who were biologically related through family, clan, and Tribal ties. Each person in these early communities survived through their relations!

Human language, religion, art, technology, laws, ethics, values, forms of education, and other institutions all serve as particular expressions of community. In the context of community, the medium is the message. In other words, at a conscious and unconscious level, the community is each of us, no matter who, when, or where we are. It is through the medium of community that our first human ancestors created the phenomena of culture. And it is through community that each successive generation of people has expressed the million faces of culture. Civilizations are not the enduring human systems—communities are!

Indigenous communities mirror the earliest expressions of human culture. In some cases they are unbroken lines of ancestry originating thousands of years in the human past. It is not unrealistic to say that Tribal people share a deep and abiding relationship to Place with other members of their community. Early Tribal communities reflected natural community in terms of structural and mythic orientation. This is to say that early Tribal communities intimately oriented themselves to the stars, to mountains, deserts, rivers, lakes, oceans, plants, animals, and spirits of a Place. Those natural geographies that were important to the identification of a Tribal people, as a People of Place, were deemed sacred. Simon Ortiz, Acoma Pueblo poet, relates the Acoma story of place in the following way:

> Acoma Pueblo people began to live atop
> its monumental sandstone pinnacle
> many, many centuries ago:

Ancient stories
of their existence speak of a journey on a Life Road
from a time when All Things were in A Place Below
from where they Emerged.

Eventually for an era
of time, they lived in a wondrous place
where all living things, all people were together,
but from where they had to leave.
Guided by the Creator of All Things,
they had to make their way on the Life Road,
make decisions on how to live, what they should do,
and where they should go.

And they came
to a Place That Was Prepared,
the tall, massive stone they know as Aacqu.

Like all the other Pueblo people, the Acoma
have always known where the Center is.
From the Center place of knowledge
within themselves they have learned
from the generations before them,
they have always known the Blue mountains
and high places to the North, West, South, and East,
and they have known the Yellow and Red and White
hills and sandstone cliffs.

And upon the land
they have seen tall, slender evergreens, the sagebrush
and yucca, sinewy grasses and brilliant flowers,
and they have seen and heard flying hawks,
crows, and wrens, and they have seen and hunted
deer and rabbits, and they have watched the tadpoles
come alive after the rain.

All this and more,
they know about their place. All this and more
they know about the time that is now. From

the beginning, the story tells of who they are
and where they live and all the things that
relate to them and live with them in this world.
From the beginning to the present and into the
future, they know they must keep this Story alive![3]

The harmonizing of natural community with human community was an ongoing process in Indigenous education. It was both a formal and an informal process that evolved around the day-to-day learning of how to survive in a given environment. This learning entailed involvement with ritual and ceremony, periods of being alone in an environment, service to one's community through participation in the life making processes with others, and engendering a sense of enchantment for where the people lived. All of these processes combined toward realizing the goal of finding and honoring the spirit of place.

This was essentially a deeply felt ecological relationship borne of intimate familiarity with a homeland, and the homeland became an extension of the "great holy" in the perceptions, heart, mind, and soul of the Tribal people who lived in it. From this perspective, it is easy to understand why Indigenous people around the world lamented the loss of their land. For in truth, from their perspective and reality, it was a loss of part of themselves.

What then are Indigenous communities, and what do they do? First, Indigenous communities are models of interconnectedness, and are the intimate human social structures through which we learn about basic human relationships. For instance, Indigenous communities embody and harmonize the duality of maleness and femaleness. Understanding the biological and psychological nature of these complementary relationships ensured the group's survival in the face of its most basic challenges. The mythic and spiritual qualities of maleness, femaleness, childhood, middle, and old age are celebrated as a dynamic of natural life and blended in ways that enhance and express the fullness of the spirit of community. This helps members to perceive relationship as a way of life.

Indigenous community is about living a symbiotic life in the context of a symbolic culture that includes the natural world as a necessary and vital participant and co-creator of community. The life of the Indigenous community is mutually reciprocal with the living communities in the surrounding natural environment. Through a rich and dynamic oral tradition, Indigenous communities reflected the stages of creative evolution and the characteristics of the animals, plants, natural phenomena, ecology, and geography found in their place. The oral tradition became an essential aspect of traditional teaching. Thus, story becomes a source of content and methodology for Indigenous community education. Story allows individual life, community life, and the life and process found in the natural world to be used as primary vehicles for the transmission of Indigenous culture. The vitality of Indigenous cultures is dependent on the life of individuals in community with the natural world. Indigenous cultures are extensions of the story of the natural community of a place, and they evolve according to ecological dynamics and natural relationships.

> One way traditional people have always expressed their own symbolic culture is through the ongoing retelling of the animal myth-dreams that concern their own deepest connections within the larger field of nature... the message of totemism identifies a human society interacting with groups as teachers and students within a neighborly world. We learn how to structure both our lives and culture not merely by observing nature, but by participating with nature.[4]

In this sense, Indigenous community becomes a *Story* that is a collection of individual stories, ever unfolding through the lives of the people who share the life of that community. This large community is always a living and animate entity, vitalized when it is nourished through the attention of its tellers and its listeners. When a story finds that special circumstance in which its message is fully received, it induces a direct and powerful understanding: this becomes a real teaching.

In Indigenous communities the elders, the grandmothers and grandfathers, hold the stories of their families and their people. It is they who give the stories, the words of good thought and action to the children. They tell the children how the world and their people came to be. They tell the children of their experiences, their life. They tell them what it means to be one of the People. They tell them about their relationship to each other and to all things that are part of their world. They tell them about respect—just as their grandparents told them when they were children. So it goes, giving and receiving, giving and receiving stories—helping children remember to remember that the story of their community is really the story of themselves!

A Personal Story

To remember is a way to re-know and reclaim a part of your life. The following are personal recollections of my childhood, growing up in the context of my community of Santa Clara Pueblo, New Mexico. Remembering these kinds of stories is a way of revitalizing the experience of Indigenous education in community.

I remember listening to sounds that, as I grew older, I learned were called singing. I remember hearing and seeing the faces of many people. I remember swinging through the air wrapped up in something that I later came to know was a traditional cradle, suspended from the *vigas* (ceiling rafters) in Pueblo homes. What I remember most of that time was always being with people. These were the first encounters I remember with community; just sounds, sights, and the feeling of being warm and safe. I remember it was a good feeling!

When I was about five, I remember going with my grandmother to visit with her friends and relatives in the Pueblo. I remember those days vividly because each visit was an adventure, a break from the usual routine. I seem to remember every thing and every place we visited during that year. It was the year before I started first grade at the local elementary school. I learned so much with my grandmother during that time before school.

My grandmother was in every sense a matriarch, well known and respected in the Pueblo as well as the Hispanic villages nearby. She was of a generation born before the turn of the century. Her world and frame of reference were therefore of the old times, of old New Mexico, a time when Pueblos reflected more complete expressions of symbiotic relationships with their respective environments.

I remember helping the old people prepare, plant, and hoe their gardens. I remember sitting with those old ones during the hot lazy afternoons eating Indian cookies and listening to all their stories. I remember spending days in the foothills and mountains near the Pueblo gathering plants that my grandmother and other old ones directed me to. I remember playing with the other children who came with their grandmas and grandpas. I remember eating native trout baked in a fire pit with wild peppermint and watermelon and wild cherries with the older people and their children. Afterwards, all the children would jump into the stream to play and try to catch tadpoles, and the old people laughed and laughed. I remember always walking. I remember my grandmother telling me that all older people were my aunts and uncles and their children were my cousins and that I should call them such and treat them kindly. I remember that every one, young and old, shared with one another. When we went to visit older people we would take gifts, usually food, cloth, or meat. We would return with fruit, vegetables, and other gifts. It was a form of reciprocal giving; that was how things got spread around. But that wasn't all—community news, prayers, shiny marbles, comics, toy soldiers, baseball cards, and a hundred other things got traded too.

When my grandmother and I attended a feast day at a neighboring Pueblo, I remember the kindness with which we were received, especially by the other grandmas. In these visitations, I came to know the differences between Pueblos and other people, as well as the sense of oneness of the greater Pueblo world. I felt that, indeed, we were all related. I remember those times when I sat with my grandmother and other older ladies and men in what is called the "Saints' house", a small cottonwood leaf lined shelter set up especially for Pueblo feast days so that the saints might also enjoy the dances. In the Saints' house the old ones sat with the saints praying the rosary, visiting and talking about the community news and of course the old times. In this way, they reaffirmed their faith in a Christian god and simultaneously, the traditional sense of Pueblo community, values, and way of life. Pueblo life has always revolved around tradition and age-old practices. Catholicism has been adapted to these ancient communal themes and thereby has been given a place in Pueblo community.

I remember watching my grandma and other women and men of the Pueblo replastering their houses with adobe mud, laughing, and working as if they were one body. I remember my grandmother and other aunts baking bread in the special outdoor Pueblo ovens called *ornos*. My cousin and I would then sneak about and try to be the first to taste the fresh bread, pies, and cookies they left cooling near the oven. I remember those special feasts when all my relatives would come to my grandmother's home or those times when she would go to help others prepare feasts for weddings, baptisms, and even funerals.

There are many other memories, many other events of communal life, which formed me. But those early memories still have the greatest vividness and remain with me even to this day as the good sense of community. Our sense of being and our perception through community evolves over time. They mature through time in sync with the changes in our lives. In this way they form a foundation for personal history. These memories provide me with my sense of rootedness to place and people that I carry wherever I go. There were, of course, sad memories as well; memories of hardship and pain, memories of doubt and anger with regard to community. But, in all, I cannot remember a time when I didn't learn something through my participation in community, when I didn't see something differently or when I was not shared with in a direct and significant way. I don't remember a time when my community wasn't involved in teaching something, or when I wasn't impressed with the strength and continuity of Pueblo community.

The elders tell us, "Celebrate your life, be happy with what you have, care for one another, be of good thoughts and words, help each other, share with one another the life you have been given. This is the way our People continue to live — through you and in you, be glad — you are one of the People!"

For The Good of The People:
Foundations For Leadership, Service, and Community Values

People were formed in the context of Indigenous community. They are given a context through which they can realize themselves by being of service to their community, their people. The completion of themselves as Tribal men and women was the communal and religious ideal they sought — an ideal whose depth of expression is almost never achieved in contemporary communities today.

> Tribal man is hardly a personal 'self' in our modern sense of the word. He does not so much live in a tribe; the tribe lives in him. He is the tribe's subjective expression.[5]

A depth of Tribal understanding was achieved through the following key elements that structured and formed the experience of each Indigenous community member from birth to death.[6]

Guidance. In Indigenous community, parenting was actively undertaken by all the adult members of a child's extended family, clan, and tribe. All adults were considered teachers and any adult member of a group could guide, discipline, or otherwise play a direct role in educating a child. Every adult was conditioned to care for the well-being of the group and each of its members. Every adult was admonished to concern themselves with the development of each child into becoming a complete person, for the good of the people.

Kinship. The network and full expression of the extended family and clan within Indigenous community provided a web of relationships that profoundly affected the perception of children. Therefore, children learned early the significance of family, responsibility, respect, and the foundations of relationship and kinship. Father, mother, aunts, uncles, cousins, and grandparents, each in their special way, influenced and formed the family's children. Older children in the family learned early to care for younger ones. Through such experience they learned how to share, nurture, and support others.

Diversity. In the context of the close-knit, interdependent, Indigenous community, children were exposed to a diversity of people. This included: a diversity of ages, married and unmarried men and women, a diversity of personalities and statuses, the handicapped and the "contraries". In the course of living in community, children interacted with all the people on a daily basis and in a variety of ways.

Special status. In Indigenous community, all children were considered special, sacred gifts from the creator. They were seen to have a quality all their own that was respected and prized by the community. They were considered to have a direct connection to spirits in Nature. They appeared as special players in the guiding myths of some tribes. They were bringers of light and good fortune to the community. Indeed they were the physical example of the vitality of a tribe. They were the carriers of the future.

Ethical models. Morals and ethics were modeled by the family and community. Respect for the elderly, honesty, care for the ill, appreciation of differences, respect for privacy, proper behavior during ceremonies, and proper treatment and respect for plants and animals were practiced daily in direct and tangible ways.

Clear roles. In Indigenous community everyone knew their relationship to other people, Nature, and the things of their society. Relationship was the basis of the community and therefore intimately understood in its various contexts for teaching, learning, and action. The roles of each individual were clearly defined and recognized so that expectations could be clearly defined. Traditional protocol reinforced the relationships and responsibilities associated with major roles in the clan, society, or tribe.

Customs and practices. Customs associated with each community role or change of roles served to define specific relationships. Customs and other practices reinforce community values and activities on a regular basis. Births, marriages, deaths, initiations, cyclical events based on a ceremonial calendar, dances, and other special celebrations combined to support and embellish community values and relationships.

Recognition. Recognition in the form of naming, rites of passage, gifting, feasting, and other social events honored achievement that benefited and enhanced the people. These forms of special recognition were valued by each member of the community and provided motivation for many to seek ways to perform extraordinary acts of service for the community.

Unique learners. The uniqueness of each child who learned in their own way and at their own pace was naturally accepted and honored. Indigenous teachers understood that people learn in many ways and that each person learns to perceive, then think, and then act in their individual ways. Given this understanding, most of Indigenous education was experiential and occurred in the course of doing work. When the time came to learn specific things, general rules were given and a general context was established. Ultimately, however, each person chose the way they would learn, and the extent that they wished to learn, based on their own way of learning and doing.

Community work. Community interdependence characterized activity related to all major events and tasks in Indigenous community. Community work, organized through clan or society, involved every member of the community in projects that were for the good of the people. These activities ranged from agriculture to hunting, from building to art making, and from food gathering to ceremony. As a matter of common survival and tradition, people of a community came together as an integral unit for the benefit of all. In work, in play, and in ceremony, community was constantly being reinforced and experienced by every member of a group. It is this day-to-day practice at community that forged the communal spirit and provided such a powerful foundation for learning and understanding the nature of relationship.

Environment. Living in the natural world was a common context for the development of both the individual and community in Tribal societies. Nature was the essential frame of reality that formed the learning experiences of all Indigenous people. Indeed, Indigenous societies attempted to resonate all aspects of their social organization with their understanding of the natural world. Indigenous cosmology was informed throughout by natural reality. The geographical and structural orientations of Indigenous communities to their natural place and the cosmos reflected a communal consciousness that extended to and included the natural world in an intimate and mutually reciprocal relationship. Through clan and societal symbolism, ritual, art, and visionary tradition, Indigenous communities connected themselves to the plants, animals, waters, mountains, sun, moon, stars, and planets of their world.

Spirit. Spirituality and a sense of the sacred permeated all aspects of Indigenous community. Life was sacred, relationship was sacred, Nature was sacred, and the tribe was sacred. Each of these processes and structures was a creation of the highest thought and tied to the guiding myths and foundations of the religious expression of a tribe. Among Indian people, as Vine Deloria so aptly states,

> Religion is not conceived as a personal relationship between the deity and each individual. It is rather a covenant between a particular god and a community. The people of this community are the primary residue of the religion's legends, practices, and beliefs. Ceremonies of a community scope are the chief characteristic feature of religious activity . . . Stories, songs, games and art were used to instill respect [for the sacred]. Life, as a whole, was tied to spirit.[9]

Therefore, the ultimate quest of both individual and community was to find life, to find "that place that Indian people talk about". Through these contexts of learning, the individual became intimately conditioned to the nature of right, or successful relationship and the importance of each role and individual in the complete expression of community. This understanding, in the context of Tribal communities, formed the foundation for the development of extraordinary leaders. In Indigenous community, individuals rose to positions of leadership based on their service to the people. To be of service to one's people was a major goal of every adult member of a tribe.

Leadership in and of itself was never a goal of Indigenous education but rather a result of living in community and striving toward becoming complete. Traditional learning was always geared toward understanding and applying what was useful and beneficial. Indigenous community was predicated on the perception that all things can be useful, and the qualities of being useful and beneficial intertwine. These perceptions imply reciprocity, support, benefit, purpose, and vision. These perspectives—combined with an ingrained love for one's people and orientation to act for the good of the people—formed the foundation for the expression and development of Indigenous leaders. Leadership was a role that had to be earned in Indigenous community. It was earned by achieving a level of integrity that was irreproachable.

Indigenous leadership was about commitment to nurturing a healthy community and enriching the cultural tradition of one's people. Indigenous leadership was about service and support of community values and life. Indigenous leaders were predisposed to care deeply and imagine richly with regard to their people. They listened to their own visions and the visions of their people; they used their imagination and creativity; and they gathered the people and moved them together to find their life.

The Natural Sense of Community

Community in its natural, social, and metaphysical sense is indeed, as Acoma Pueblo poet, Simon Ortiz, so aptly poses, "that place the Indians talk about."

Pueblo communities are about creation. They are expressions of a natural creative process that is described in a mythical sense through Pueblo Storytelling. All things that Pueblo people do celebrate the life that *is* the community. This engenders a deep and abiding belief in the creative power of life in all its forms. Pueblos believe that without regularly practiced belief in community, the stories, the songs, dances, prayers, and way of life lose not only their meaning, but also their natural power to move and enliven us as living People. It is in this belief that thoughts are regularly extended to all creation with love, respect, and reciprocity.

Knowing we are People, significant but equal and not one
being more important than the other; this is the way we must see

ourselves. This is the way we share the fruitfulness and difficulties of life. In this way we will always strive for harmony with all growing things, and we will always keep a reciprocal and grateful relationship with the land and waters on which we depend. In this way, we will always have something to do with the stars, which are far away yet as close as our eyes.[8]

Pueblos, like other Indigenous people, extend their sense of community and responsibility to include maintenance of all the natural world. This is part of the reason for the continual Pueblo insistence, in the face of great odds, on preserving their aboriginal lands. It is a foundational Pueblo belief that the ongoing life of the world can only be maintained through a proper and respectful relationship with the land, waters, other life, people, and the rest of creation. For the Pueblos, this is a responsibility that must be decisively chosen since, without such a choice, creation, and true and complete community, is not possible.

This commitment to care for the world also entails ensuring that Pueblo tradition and community remain whole. This is to have a structure through which the care and relationship to the natural world can be maintained. Even though Pueblos are independent and separate, there is a sense of oneness, a recognition and respect for one another that transcends their differences in language and custom. It is to this greater sense of community, unity, and solidarity that Pueblos have chosen to commit themselves. Pueblos reflect thoughts and approaches to communal education similar to that of other Indigenous people. It is the way they have actively strived to maintain "that place the Indians talk about."

Elements of The "Soul" In Indigenous Community

In Indigenous community everyone was a teacher, and everyone, at one time or another, was a learner. By watching, listening, experiencing, and participating everyone learned what it was to be one of the People, and how to survive in community with others. Learning how to care for one's self and others, learning relationship between people and other things, learning the customs, traditions, and values of a community: all of these understandings and more were the daily course of Indigenous education.

In Indigenous community a universal expression of ritual tradition was reflected that permeated all community activity with a sense of harmonious relationship. Integration and connectedness were consciously sought at all important levels of community structure and activity. Such integration was achieved through a series of rites that symbolized the importance of relationship and responsibility within community. These rites evolved through concentric rings of interrelationship, beginning with family, then clan, band, and tribe. They extended to the place of the people, and finally to the universe as a whole. Through these integrated rings of relationship and action, Indigenous communities directly expressed their mutual relationship with each other, other groups and the natural world. In addition, Indigenous communities expressed the cycles within cycles and honored, through ceremony, all important human and natural cycles within the boundaries of their world.

For Indigenous communities breath, water, and spirit were the components that tied all life together. The people understood that the community's continuity was carried within each individual, making each individual needed in the perpetuation of the life of the community. There was a place for everyone, the child, the adult, the old ones, the mentally impaired, the "he-she". Each person had something to offer, a special gift, and was allowed to participate to some extent in the life of their community.

Traditional sports and competitions held a special place in the hearts and minds of Indigenous people and acted to identify and bind communities together. Traditional games provided ways to settle disputes between communities and tribes. They were a way for Indigenous people to play with each other, to share themselves, other than in work or ceremony, yet integrally connected to both. Traditional games provided a way to gain recognition and practice skills valued in Indigenous community, skills such as caring, leadership, honesty, fairness, and loyalty. In addition, traditional sports developed the whole person, physically, psychologically, mentally, and spiritually. Therefore, traditional sports formed a natural framework for Indigenous teaching and learning. Traditional sports were about developing face (character) and heart (emotional development). These carried over into communal values that directly affected the life and quality of the people who made up the community. A more complete exploration of the nature of Indigenous sport will be presented in the segment dealing with Indigenous health and wholeness. Indigenous sports were a major form of re-creation for Indigenous community.

Ritual and ceremony combined to form a community complex for finding, maintaining, and perpetuating The Center, or soul of their people and community. Indigenous communities were collective expressions of the soulfulness of a people. It is through collective community as well as the individual, that the vitality of the human soul and the spiritual resolve of a community is engendered. Each Indigenous community tried to model themselves after their perception of the Cosmos. This cosmic orientation, combined with myths, dreams, visions, and special teachings gained through ceremony, played a direct role in reinforcing, enhancing, and extending the community's relationship to all things. It is this that the community taught (through story, art, dance, ceremony, and prayer), as the culturally patterned knowledge and experience.

The Navajo Sing embodies a communal complex. This complex exemplifies the identification of the Indigenous individual with their community educational process and their family, clan, tribe and natural universe. The Sing incorporates art, ritual, and communion with internal and external forces to restore the harmony between an individual and the rest of the world. In the Sing, the ritual creation of a sandpainting provides an expression, and a context, for learning about Indigenous health and wholeness.

Navajo sandpaintings "are made in a rich ceremonial context for the curing of individuals who have gotten out of balance with their world . . . . At a certain moment during the ceremony the ill person is placed at the center of one of the dry paintings; the understanding is that the person thus becomes identified with the power that is in the image painted and pressed into the body of the ill person; again to emphasize the element of identity: the painting is not a symbol of some meaning or power, the power is there present in it, and as the person identifies with it, the appropriate cure is accomplished."[9]

Through the Sing, the individual re-establishes a harmonious relationship to his or her community, as traditionally identified by the Navajo and as related by the mythic story behind the ceremony.

The Sing exemplifies the fact that communities are organic and very human. In their complete expressions, they reflect an integral wholeness and are, themselves, vehicles for human wholeness. The Sing is thus an example of how Indigenous communities reflect contexts for achieving health and wholeness.

Health, Wholeness, and Indigenous Community

There is a direct relationship between Indigenous community, the learning process therein, and the quest for health and wholeness. Much of the formal and informal learning that takes place in Indigenous community might just as easily be called endogenous education. A significant part of experiential education that occurs in community involves learning about one's inner self. This is done by participating in a process of illumination that comes forth from an individual's ego center. This aspect of Indigenous education, which has an individual as well as communal dimension, is embodied in the variably translated metaphor, seeking life or for life's sake. Health, wholeness, and harmony of the individual, family, clan, and Tribal community were the ideal state of life, and therefore the ideal goal of life in community. To reach this ideal state, the tools of ritual, medicine, art, sport, and other formal and informal teaching were used in the context of Indigenous community.

The whole human being and the whole community are integrally related. The whole person, as the whole community, is an amazing complex of diverse aspects. The human being holds together because of an integrated and organic relationship among constituent systems based on the Life Principle. The Life Principle is that dynamic combination of the physical, social, psychological, and spiritual being into the animated organic form that we recognize as Life!

The understanding of this principle is not new. All human cultures have recognized that life is wondrous, sacred, and systematic in its development. The educational dimensions of health, wholeness, self-knowledge, and wisdom have been espoused by most, if not all, traditional educational philosophies around the world. It was a natural outcome that Indigenous education engendered the development of a person with well-integrated relationships among all aspects of self and the world.

The "right" education was, of course, a culturally defined construct that had as its main criteria the harmonization of the individual with his or her culture. The process of teaching is considered right to the extent that it effectively accomplishes this feat from the perspective of the culture it is designed to serve. Indigenous community measured its teaching against its ability to produce harmonious social integration of each individual within the fabric of the community. The wholeness of the community was directly dependent on the wholeness of its members. So success in properly educating each community member was a matter of survival and continuity for the whole culture.

Achieving harmony, peace of mind, and health were ideal goals that were anything but easy to attain. They had to be actively sought, sacrificed, and prayed for. The elders of Indigenous community knew by experience that true learning causes change and at times may elicit a transformation of self at a person's very core. Transformation is a breaking apart to reform at a higher level of being and understanding. In its real expression in people, transformation is anything but peaceful and harmonious. Indigenous community recognized this aspect of true learning and provided for it though ritual preparation, rites of passage, and initiations. Society, rituals, healing ceremonies, sports, pilgrimages, vision quests, and other rites provided the communal context in which individuals might attain one of Indigenous education's highest goals, that of completing one's self.

The path to completeness within the context of Indigenous community required development of the whole person, expression of the highest thought, and walking the "Good Road." Inherent in Indigenous approaches to education is the recognition that there is a knowing center in all human beings. Community, healing, and whole-making rituals provided a kind of warp to help individuals access the potential inherent in each person's knowing center. Elders knew that encountering one's personal center (which was a manifestation of the greater universal center) was not always comfortable or without real peril. Therefore, coming into such contact was choreographed through specific and appropriate preparation to help each pilgrim negotiate their journey to their own source of knowledge, their knowing center, their soul. This was done because it was in the best interest of community to develop complete men and women.

The potential of human learning unfolds through our life cycle just as our journey toward wholeness evolves in meaning. Learning and becoming whole are, at every level of expression, intimately intertwined. Indigenous communities provided a fertile and supportive context for the unfolding of what Jungian psychology terms "individuation" or becoming individually whole and complete.

The difference between Indigenous individuation and individuation in the Jungian sense was that of orientation. Indigenous orientation was focused on the community and the spiritual as culturally defined by a specific tribe. Jungian individuation is oriented to the individual ego in the context of a modern Western cultural orientation. However, both orientations share a focus—the goal of completeness and inner growth—that forms a possible bridge for integrating them in a contemporary context of Indian education.

> Individuation is a work, a life opus, a task that calls upon us not to avoid life's difficulties and dangers, but to perceive the meaning in the patterns and events that form our lives. Life's supreme achievement may be to see the thread which connects together the events, dreams, and relationships that have made up the fabric of existence. Individuation is a search for and the discovery of meaning, not the meaning that we consciously devise, but the meaning embedded in life itself... (There is no sure road to individuation, it is a path riddled with doubt and uncertainty. It takes courage, perseverance and unmitigated faith in one's Center to seek to become truly whole.). . . .
>
> Becoming whole does not mean being perfect, but being completed. It does not necessarily mean happiness, but growth. . . . It is not getting out of life what we think we want, but the development and purification of the soul... to be healthy, then, has nothing to do with serenity, and less to do with adjustment, to be healthy is to become whole. We can, perhaps, say that the truly healthy person is the person who is involved with a life long process of individuation.[10]

Learning about self and individuating was rarely considered the sole concern of traditional American Indian teachers. However, the process of individuation explained by Jung was well understood and accommodated in Indigenous approaches to education. In these approaches, inner peace was not directly sought, since it was traditionally felt that to seek inner peace overtly was paradoxically to ensure that one would never find it. Rather, inner peace and wholeness were sought by way of ceremony, ritual, and living everyday life in community. Individuation in the context of Indigenous community came of its own, but it had to be worked for! Many paths of individuation, and the maintenance of health and wholeness, were developed by Indigenous people. One such path was that of running and Indigenous games.

Indigenous Games For Life

Indigenous games were intimately related to all aspects of Indigenous community and perceptions of health and wholeness. The realm of traditional games provides an ideal way to connect the ideas presented in the prior segment on health and wholeness.

Games were a community event whose purpose was not only to entertain but, as in all aspects of Indigenous community, a way to seek life and attain a level of physical and spiritual completeness. From the earliest ages, children in Indigenous communities were introduced to a variety of games that developed physical skill, thinking, and personal character. What was learned through their participation in games prepared them for a full life in community. They ran, they played, they swam, they jumped, they threw, and they faced and overcame hardship for the good of the people.

Indigenous games were tied to the guiding myths of the people and were themselves sacred activities because they required the participation of the whole person. As with all Indigenous communal activities, sports were imbued with ceremonial and ritual activity. Offerings, prayers, songs, and gifts were prepared and given to entreat the spirits of life to look with favor on the sacrifices of participants. For many Indian tribes, the games—just as hunting, warfare, or ceremony—were a way of making one's medicine.

Indigenous games reinforced, as well as expressed, community values related to respect, honor, interdependence, and service. Indigenous participants carried all that they were and all that they valued into the realm of the games.

Indigenous games included an array of events: ball games using sticks of various sorts, kicking of a ball while running, foot races of every length, dancing contests, contests of archery skill, spear throwing, swimming, games of chance, games matching strength, endurance or thinking. Games were played by men, women, and children and might include several hundred players and be several days in length. During the time when these community-wide games took place, they became the center of a community's life. In every respect these games reflected the spirit, health, and vitality of the community. They were directly connected to the way a community defined what it was to be healthy and whole.

> In most traditional Indian societies, games of skill or dexterity were rarely played by adults for mere amusement or fun. Rather, they were played for some purpose that was of importance to the community. To a considerable extent, sports were enjoyed in the same manner as are popular sports today; in addition however, they were interrelated with social issues . . . . Although it may not be apparent in most of today's Indian communities, sports were originally meshed with tradition, ritual, and ceremony.[11]

Dr. Joseph B. Oxendine, a Lumbee Indian and author of *American Indian Sports Heritage*, states that the major factors that characterized traditional Indian sports included:

1) a strong connection between sports and other social, spiritual, and economic aspects of daily life

2) the serious preparation of mind, body, and spirit of both the participants and the community as a whole prior to major competition

3) the assumption that rigid adherence to standardized rules and technical precision was unimportant in sport

4) strong allegiance to high standards of sportsmanship and fair play

5) the prominence of both males and females in sports activity, but with different expectancies

6) a special perspective on team membership and on interaction and leadership styles

7) the role of gambling as a widespread and vital component in all sports

8) the importance of art as an expression of identity and aesthetics[12]

Running For Life

The realm of Indian running presents an ideal model of the integration of games of sport with community ideals, values, spirituality, and orientation to health and wholeness. A large portion of Indian games involved running, since for all Indian tribes running was part of their everyday life.

From Alaska to the tip of South America, Indian people ran for competition, communication, transportation, and ceremony. Running was a way of learning, ritual practice, training, and being alive! Running was celebrated and often formed the context for mythic adventure in the folklore of many Indian tribes. Animal and human characters were often pitted against one another to compete for a prize, favor, or special blessing. It was in the context of the racing story and the process of the race that the lesson of the racing tale was discovered. The racing tale concerned the nature of inner and outer strength. Sometimes the lesson was about something important to know and understand related to the values of a community. The moral might be about fair play, honesty, or perseverance. The moral might deal with the wisdom of strategy and knowing yourself, your course and your opponent. The tale might explain in a mythic sense why certain things are done by a tribe or why certain present-day situations exist. In every case, running brings out a truth important to self-knowledge and individual or communal well-being.

> Many Southeastern tribes, such as the Alabama and Cherokee, tell of proud Hummingbird being challenged by Crane to race. Overly confident, Hummingbird zips ahead in daylight, but stops at night to sleep, while crane flaps patiently along. On the final evening, to avoid waking Hummingbird, Crane heads for higher altitudes, reaches the ocean, and wins the right to inhabit marshes and rivers forever. The lesson: racing is as much an exercise of consciousness as of speed.[13]

Indians, such as the Tarahumara (which means footrunner), identify themselves with running to such an extent that not one aspect of their social, spiritual, or economic life does not reflect its direct influence. Tarahumara feats of long distance running are renowned in modern times. Introduced to the running-way of being as soon as they are able to walk, the Tarahumara continue to run for purposes of communication, work, competition, recreation, and ritual. However, their running way of life reflects what was really the commonplace integrative expression of the natural human activity of running among practically all Indian people.

Running formed the basis of the oldest form of communication among Indians. Through an elaborate system of paths Indian people criss-crossed the Americas. Many of their pathways have today become the paved roads and interstates that connect all regions of the United States.

Running is also a metaphor for overcoming the difficulties of life. It embodies an important dimension of Indian spirituality attained through physical training. It was a way of training heart, mind, body, and soul. Plenty Coups, a famous chief of the Crow, provides the insight into such training in the following excerpt from his autobiography:

> The day was in summer, the world green and very beautiful. I was playing with some other boys when my grandfather stopped to watch. 'Take off your shirt and leggings,' he said to me. I tore them from my back and legs, and naked except for my moccasins, stood before him. 'Now catch me that yellow butterfly. Be quick!' Away I went after the yellow butterfly. How fast these creatures are, and how cunning! In and out among the trees and bushes, across streams, over grassy places, now near the ground, then just above my head, the dodging butterfly led me far before I caught and held it in my hand. Panting, but concealing my shortness of breath as best I could, I offered it to Grandfather, who whispered as if he told me a secret, 'Rub its wings over your heart, my son, and ask the butterflies to lend you their grace and swiftness.
>
> 'O Butterflies, lend me your grace and swiftness!' I repeated rubbing the broken wings over my pounding heart. If this would give me grace and speed, I should catch many butterflies, I knew. But instead of keeping the secret, I told my friends, as my grandfather knew I would,' Plenty Coups chuckled, 'and how many, many we boys caught after that to rub over our hearts.... We worked very hard at this, because running is necessary in both hunting and war ....'[14]

In the act of running, and through the creation of games associated with running, Indian people expressed themselves as human beings in the most direct and physical way. Running, like dancing, provided a way to connect the human spirit with the spirits of the natural world.

Through running, Indian people connected themselves with their inner and outer realities. They learned how to play and re-create themselves in deeply profound ways as they ran for life. They learned how to be of service to their people and their community. They connected themselves with their mythic stories and the spirits of those stories who also liked to run. They learned about themselves and about their physical and spiritual abilities. They "saw their life" as in the Papago vision runs that occurred during their pilgrimage to the sea to collect salt. They developed their bodies, hearts, and souls, and thereby came to know the nature of what it meant to become complete, whole, and healthy.

Running was only one of the Indigenous ways of communal sport and life. But a seed is contained in this expression of community. It is about the nature of the individual in community and the community's place in the education of the whole person. The implications of this individually and community-oriented process of education remain significant for a contemporary approach to Indian education.

✵ VIII ✵

LIVING THE VISION

INDIGENOUS EDUCATION FOR A TWENTY-FIRST CENTURY WORLD

Introduction

THIS WORK HAS BEEN A PILGRIMAGE, tracking the spirit of Indigenous education through concentric rings of relationship. Images and meta phors have been portrayed as reflected in the words of many people, Indian and non-Indian, artist and scholar. Through creating a symbolic web of structures and images based on metaphors about "that place that Indian people talk about", we have explored the character of specific concentric rings. In doing so, we have gained some perspectives on the Center of the human process of learning and teaching. Metaphorically, we have looked to the top of an *inner* mountain to gain a perspective of where Indian education has been and where it is now.

We are poised to see where Indian education may go and the best paths it might take to get there. The top of this mountain is a place to contemplate the choices that we must make about the future of education. Each choice implies an orientation, inherent consequences, and a set of possible paths. I believe this is the place that all education has reached in our global village. All education is rooted in or has evolved from, an Indigenous past. In reality, all education is founded upon Indigenous basics.

In its most holistic sense, this work has been about the foundational aspects of education in all human cultures. It can be viewed as inclusive of all people and time periods—even those of modern education. However, my particular orien-tation is that of an American Indian educator living in contemporary times and playing a new role in the history of American Indian people. I have attempted to present a perspective that reflects the thoughts and feelings of many contempo-rary Indian people. For American Indians and education, this is a time of choice. In many respects, the survival of the unique cultural identity of American Indian people depends on the choices we make now. In making these choices and attempting to understand the consequences of each, it becomes crucial that we ask questions about spirit, philosophy, structures, roles, contexts, and intent of American Indian Education in the twenty-first century.

In the "tracking the spirit of vision" model presented previously, there is a set of concentric rings called The Asking. This represents the first stage in the search for meaning and establishment of relationships around one's vision. The Asking is the first stage of focusing the dreams, intuitions, and desires that motivate the questing for vision generated from the Centering Place. The Asking is the place of questions, and this is the place that, I believe, American Indians are in tracking a collective vision of Indian education.

Questions are the basis of dialogue and stem from the basic human desire to know, to understand, to explain, and to story. Essential questions have guided the development of this work, questions that I felt were profound and urgent in their need for exploration and explanation. This place of Asking begs for dialogue at all levels of relationship, structure, and expression. Such dialogue has been going on in small ways, in informal and formal ways, here and there. We all share in those first intuitions, those dreams, because we share essential metaphors, and we are, indeed, all related. Thought Woman is whispering in our ear and again turning the wind that stands within each of us.

What are the essential questions that must be posed to enact a collective transformative vision for American Indian education? From my perspective they include the following:

How can we empower ourselves to vision and find our life in a twenty-first century world through the path of education? How do we prepare ourselves for a challenging visionary transformation? What are the dimensions of the kind of revitalized Indian educational leadership that must be addressed? What are the educational models we have already tried, and what have we learned from them? What are the structures we need to create? What are the implications of the Foundations of Indigenous Education for modern global education?

I do not pretend to have the answers to these questions. I do, however, see paths, models, and images that invite further exploration. I present one of the models, guided by an insight from my own vision, as a seed for thought and dialogue. It is a Model for Teaching Indigenous Science. I present this model because Western Science has been the single most powerful paradigm of modern Western culture. There is a parable that often flashes through my memory during times of quiet, deep relaxation, or just before I fall asleep:

> It is an essential, life-sharing act of each generation of a People to nurture that which has given them Life and to preserve for future generations the guiding stories of their collective journey to find life.

The Need For Indigenous Approaches To Education

Alienation from mainstream approaches to education have been one of the consistent criticisms leveled against modern education by Indian students. Beyond compensatory programs, remediation, and programs that attempt to bridge the social orientations of students with those of the school, they have been given few choices of school curricula that truly address their alienation. Most attempts at addressing these issues have revolved around refitting the problematic Indian student to the system that caused their alienation. Too often, the Indian student is viewed as the problem, rather than the unquestioned approaches, attitudes, and curricula of the educational system. The knowledge, values, skills, and interests that Indian students possess are largely ignored in favor of strategies aimed at enticing them to conform to mainstream education. Few comprehensive attempts have been made to create a body of content and teaching models that are founded on contemporary expressions of American Indian educational philosophy. The inherent worth and creative potential of Indian students and Indian perspectives of education have not been given serious consideration by mainstream education. As a result, many of the brightest and most creative Indian students continue to be alienated from modern education and drift about in a malaise of apathy and self abuse.

The alienation of Indian students from education and the resultant loss of their potentially positive service to their communities need not continue, if we revitalize our own deep heritage of education. Indigenous approaches to education can work if we are open to their creative message. We must apply our collective creative energy to revitalize and reintroduce their universal processes of teaching and learning. Indigenous educational principles are viable whether one is learning leadership skills through community service, learning about one's cultural roots through creating a photographic exhibit, or learning from Nature by exploring its concentric rings of relationship.

The creative potential of building upon and enhancing what students bring with them culturally has been explored at a number of Indian educational institutions. The development of Tribal community colleges and the evolution of contract schools governed by tribes offer plausible structures for developments of this nature. Such structures are, however, only a first step toward a much more comprehensive vision of what Indian education can be.

Empowering Ourselves

Every journey toward transformation begins with reflection on those things for which one cares deeply, and the relationships that exist in one's inner and outer worlds. Today, words like transformation and empowerment are the modern catch-terms for processes that Indian people traditionally termed "making or finding one's personal medicine". Creation, identification, and empowerment of American Indians—as Tribal people in the face of modern constraints—have been the central dilemma of American Indian life since the time of the first European contact. The struggle to maintain American Indian identities, in a modern context, has continued to intensify and become more complex since the turn of the century. The struggle to maintain who we are, and what we believe in, has resulted in expressions of hopelessness and accompanying forms of disempowerment. Collectively, American Indians continue to suffer from "ethnostress" that began during the time of first contact. Ethnostress is primarily a result of a psychological response pattern that stems from the disruption of a cultural life and belief system that one cares about deeply. Such a disruption may be abrupt or occur over time and generations. Its initial effects are readily visible, but its long-term effects are many and varied, usually affecting self-image and an understanding of one's place in the world.[1]

Among American Indians, the long-term effects of ethnostress have become all-too-apparent in community disintegration, declining health, inadequate education, and in the rates of alcoholism, suicide, and a host of other self-destructive behaviors, including child abuse. In response, a slew of Federal programs have been introduced, supplemented by State and private initiatives, to address the most pressing of these situations. Few of these efforts have addressed the phenomena of ethnostress or the fact that the central issue is authentic empowerment. As a result, when the money runs out, so does the empowerment, because money alone empowers very little except temporarily addressing an obvious physical need. The unfortunate state of Indian affairs today resembles a video-arcade game of musical chairs. The chair an Indian individual, tribe, school, or organization gets depends not only on how well you have learned to play the game, but how many compromises of spirit and authenticity you are willing to make to appease the political, bureaucratic, and industrial controllers of the game. Each time you turn around more chairs are missing, and you have to be faster, shrewder, and more competitive to stay in the game. The more you play, the more you become like the controllers and a part of the Real World. The real object of the game is to become another byte in the Great Computer's memory. The Great Computer and the Great Mystery are parallel constructs of human cosmology; the essential difference lies in your perception of authenticity. The Great Computer is contrived to support and legitimize its controllers. The Great Mystery, on the other hand, is the field of all natural relationships.

Ethnostress has many faces in Indian life, each presenting barriers to attaining authenticity in ourselves and our communities. When we don't acknowledge and deal with the reality of ethnostress, we act out its all too familiar effects. We do this by perpetuating dysfunctional relationships, divisive behavior, cynicism, mistrusting our own thinking, and other forms of self-invalidation, both of ourselves and of our culture. We enact the negative elements of the old communal tale of the "crabs in the bucket". In this tale, rather than support the empowerment of each other, we present obstacles, feeling that if we can't have it no one else should either. In defeating others in their attempts toward authenticity, we defeat ourselves, and we remain unempowered.[2]

To have authentic empowerment you must have a system of educating that not only trains for vocation but prepares individuals: for self-actualizing themselves, fulfilling their human potentials, enlivening their creative spirit, and finding their personal meaning, power, and what in earlier times Indian people called medicine. This is exactly what traditional Indigenous processes of education did. This education helped people find their way to the center of their individual and collective power. This is the essential meaning of the word empowerment. The implementation of Indigenous ways of educating is toward this most basic of human need. It authentically empowers and perpetuates the development of the spirit of families, communities, and tribes.

Indian self-empowerment takes commitment; it takes hard sustained work by individuals and communities. It also requires an honest self-examination of where we are individually and collectively.

There are some baseline concepts that we can use to assess "where we are at." For instance, some Indian people seem to suffer a "hostage syndrome" that mirrors the documented psychological effects of individuals who are kept in captivity for a long period of time. The syndrome is characterized by the states of alienation and confusion. These are emotional and thinking processes that individuals experience when they have adapted to the loss of their freedom and the demands of their captors. For individuals in confinement, these effects become readily apparent and observable. For groups, the effects are less apparent, but no less telling in the way that adaptive behaviors, attitudes, and states of mind may be generated, even over a long time. Reservations, and the status of being wards of the government, have had syndrome-like effects on the individual and social psychology of Indian people. These effects range from total rejection of the perceived controllers to an attempt to identify with them and become the same. Reading the case histories of prisoners of war, echo the range of adaptations American Indians made during their early years of reservation life. There are numerous examples of mind games engaged in by the controllers. The clichés used in such relationships speak to the true nature of the hostage syndrome. Here are just a few: "tradition is the enemy of progress," "command and control," "divide and conquer," "leave your past behind," "breaking the spirit," "incentives and initiatives," "total quality management," "zero-based budgeting," "re-education," "cultural development," "culturally disadvantaged," "assimilation," "relocation," "psychological realignment," "at risk." Sound familiar? There are new political, bureaucratic terms being coined every day. The message is more subtle; the intent has become more unconscious, but the effects are much the same.

The hostage syndrome has given rise to a view of Indian culture as being of the past: the so-called "culture under glass" that has dominated the view of most Americans since the late 1800s. Anthropologists, archeologists, and ethnologists of that era perpetuated a view of the "vanishing Red Man," the ghost of which still haunts us today. Their perspective formed the foundation of what contemporary America images as Indian. Many Indian people in their search for authenticity have based their perceptions of identity on these early ethnological perspectives. Although these perspectives were grounded in the reality that scholars presumed would happen, they underestimated the tenacity and adaptive ability of Indian cultures.

It is true that much has been lost in the wholesale assaults on Indian culture during the past 500 years. But, the cultural roots of Indian ways of life run deep. Even in communities where they seem to have totally disappeared, they merely lie dormant, waiting for the opportunity and the committed interest of Indian people to start sprouting again. Indigenous education is one of those dormant roots. The tree may seem lifeless, but the roots still live in the hearts of many Indian people.

Culture is an environment subject to the same ecological principles and truths as a physical environment. Culture is a dynamic human creation that is always in process at one or several levels simultaneously. Each generation of a People *is* their culture. Just as the life of a person can't be frozen in time, so it is true of living cultures. As individuals and groups of people in a culture reassess, revitalize, reaffirm, and recreate themselves, the culture as a whole transforms. It is an active and perpetually creative process. Living cultures cannot be put under glass, and Indian people, individually and collectively, must learn how to apply this active ecological principle of their cultures to empower themselves. Learning this and applying it with deepened understanding is a first step for Indian people in liberating themselves from themselves and the response patterns of victimization, apathy, abuse, fear, anger, alienation, powerlessness, and despair. By doing this, we cease to perpetuate the hostage syndrome in the perception of ourselves and our communities. This is a powerful communal act that cuts to the heart of self-determination and expression of Tribal sovereignty. It is more than a political act; it is an act of the soul!

Preparing Ourselves For Transforming Vision

The seeking of any vision requires a period of preparation. There is the initial preparation of setting one's intent, asking questions, and psychological empowerment. Then there is the process of seeking, a preparation accomplished by exploring the paths of the landscape through which one must pass, learning its story, and physical nature. That landscape may be internal as well as external. It is essentially coming to know those things, stories, people, or events important to your self-knowledge and your quest. It is about history, not the kind of history that is in books (although that is a place you may begin or end), but the kind of history that lives in the minds and hearts of a People. It is the oral history that presents how a people see themselves in their journey as a People. The key is learning to seek in a way that reclaims a people's oral history and cultural tradition for the purpose of constructing a transformative vision. We must establish dialogue about what our visions might be and try things out. We must appreciate what others have done in formal and informal ways, big and small, past and present. In this way we energize our visions as we live and grow. This is not as complex as it may sound since Indigenous educational processes have numerous vehicles for doing exactly this.

Seeing, talking, and doing are the basis of most learning. All cultures of the world have evolved formal and informal contexts in which this way of learning forms an integrated relationship with personal history, oral history, folklore, and the arts. Any number of historic and contemporary American Indian mythic and social structures might serve as a basis for developing symbiotic models based on dialogue, communication, and experience. Every traditional American Indian social event presents a context for story, sharing, and experience. The key is to organize these events—combined with other communal events and contexts—to form reflective centers for learning and empowerment. Then work the concentric rings of relationship toward preparing ourselves for new visions and realizing our collective potential for educating and thriving in the twenty-first century.

Intellectual, social, and spiritual learning unfolds in a definite context of relationships. We encounter this, and try to understand it to obtain meaning and orient ourselves. For Indian people, this primary context of relationship and meaning was found in the natural environment. In a sense, all traditional Indian education can be called environmental education because it touches on the spiritual ecology of a place. Indian people expressed a way of environmental education that oriented them to "that place Indians talk about."

The description that follows is an expression of how Indian perspectives of Nature and their relationships therein can form the basis of a contemporary environmental education curriculum. This is my own work based on exploration of environmental education as seen through the metaphors, concepts, and reality of Indian people. It is a work that spans the breadth of my career as a teacher and incorporates perspectives gained from my own Indigenous roots and my creative process as an artist. It has been my way of living the vision that has evolved from finding my face, finding my heart, and finding that work through which I am currently expressing my life.

Indigenous Science: Seven Orientations of Environmental Knowledge

The Rational:

There are many possible ways of defining Indigenous Science based on the theoretical orientations of anthropology, sociology, theology, or history of science. Each of these disciplines studies the epistemology of groups through their particular perspectives, to gain insight into how groups approach classifying, learning about, and transferring their knowledge of reality.[3]

"Ethnoscience" is a term invented by ethnologists to define and describe the methods, thought processes, philosophies, concepts, and experiences by which a primal group of people obtains and applies knowledge about the natural world. It was coined for use in non-Western cultures who lacked a word to describe the science-like epistemology, perceptions, interpretations, and applications related to knowledge of the natural world. The use and application of the term "ethnoscience" are very telling of how Western scholars and educators have viewed non-Western cultures. The term has often been used to set apart so called non-objective, non-literate, irrational, and primitive orientations to the natural world from the objective, rational Western reality of *Science*. Yet the term, ethnoscience, is useful for describing some of the key elements I mean by Indigenous science.

The implied separation, both in language and reality, reflects a dilemma that has been historically associated with the orienting, teaching, and learning of science, especially pertaining to the education of non-Western, traditional people. Ethnoscience denotes a culturally based science, while *Science* is perceived as the "truly objective study of natural reality, and the standard against which all others must be compared." The implication is that ethnoscience is cultural while *Science* is somehow a cultural. This is a perception commonly held by many educators, scientists, and the public and reflects a conditioned response emanating from the hidden curriculum of modern Western education. It is a perception that lies at the root of an attitude and approach that has caused significant alienation of many Indigenous people from mainstream Western approaches to science education. This perception—combined with my own cultural orientation to the natural world and the alienation experienced by many Native Americans to conventional ways of teaching science—motivated my exploration of ethnoscience.

Through the study of ethnoscience, one begins to develop an intuitive understanding of a people's way of living, perceiving, learning, and acting in relationship to their particular environment. Science, in its universal sense, along with Art and Religion, form a three-way path through which the nature and expression of the cultural mind and its core orientations may be explored. All three systems express, translate, and transfer the culture from which they are formed to its members, through their unique, complementary, and ever evolving processes.

Until recently, ethnoscience has remained an isolated thematic area of study in cultural anthropology. Here it has played a valuable role in the study of cultural thinking and learning. However, ethnoscience has taken on new significance as a result of work in cognitive psychology, linguistics, mythology, deep ecology, and even theoretical physics. The integration of a variety of orientations is characteristic of ethnoscientific inquiry since, by nature, it involves a multidisciplinary approach to research. Ethnoscience uncovers the processes through which a culture develops strategies and classifications for making Nature accessible to explanation and understanding. Through ethnoscience one is able to study, understand, and explain the similarities and differences in the way cultures apply the process of science. Science is essentially a cultural extension of man, a cognitive tool for trying to understand and explain the reality of Nature.

Therefore, the study of the ethnosciences of American Indians becomes a valuable tool for understanding, the cultural influences in science. It provides a way for Indians and non-Indians to gain insights about themselves and cultural conditioning in the natural world.

The ethnosciences of American Indian tribes are unique within themselves, yet many share characteristics because of adaptation to the same geographical area or because they are reflecting the same guiding values. In spite of diverse expressions there are tangible strands of relationship that allow American Indians to understand one another's approaches to knowing and relating to, the natural world. The approaches associated with healing, hunting, or the arts reflect this unity-in-diversity of cultural thought.

Variations of the mythic structures such as the "Trickster," "Sacred Twins," "Earth Mother," "Sun Father," "Corn Mothers," "Great Serpent," "Mother of Game," "Tree of Life," "Holy Winds," "Sacred Mountains," "Changing Woman," "Creation/Emergence," "Celestial Beings" and the "Great Mystery," occur in all Indian cultures and exemplify their inherent interrelatedness. These are the mythic structures that symbolize the processes of Nature and represent primal and mythical ways of perceiving the world. They represent distinctly Native American ways of perceiving the natural world. They are also extensions of science in that they reflect unique cultural interpretations of phenomena of the natural world. They explain the world, which is exactly what science is supposed to do. *Science is Story*!

The story of science was integrated with all other aspects of Indian life. When you apply holistic thinking to interpret the symbolic language, art, dance, music, ritual, and metaphors through which the story of Indian science has been transmitted, you begin to realize that they reflect tremendously perceptive and sophisticated ideas about the processes of Nature and the Universe. Recent research of ancient and contemporary Indigenous philosophies by scientist/ philosophers David Bohm, Fritjof Capra, and others, has made it apparent that many Indigenous people have incorporated understandings into their systems that are only now being explored or confirmed by the most advanced research in Quantum Physics. It appears that these preliminary realizations are only the tip of the iceberg. Exploration and re-examination of the philosophical and ecological foundations of primal cultures have begun in earnest.

Many aspects of American Indian cultures are now being examined through more enlightened perspectives that have evolved from theoretical physics, ecology, theology, ethics, mythology, and the psychology of consciousness. This examination has great potential for American Indians. It presents a contemporary foundation for interpreting important elements of the traditional paradigms of Native America in the context of a twenty-first century world. Native American youth must be prepared to take an active part in all areas of such a renaissance.

A renaissance of this nature requires an exceptionally creative approach to American education, and Indian education specifically. In most American schools, curricula in the arts, sciences, social sciences, and humanities remain cloistered in conventionally sterile boxes where they reside lifelessly in a state of perpetual dysfunction and impotence. They lack any semblance of an integrating Center. The educational outcome in these schools is mediocre at best. At worst, they become battlegrounds wrought with fear, hopelessness, and despair: school becomes a place of unfulfilled promise and alienation. Science, taught from a Western American cultural perspective, presents the antithesis of traditional culture for many Indian youth and initiates real psychological conflict and displaced anxiety. Native American students generally respond by being apathetic or rebellious, or they drop out.

For many Indian students, conventional science courses are seen as dry and mechanical, comprised of memorizing facts and formulas, taking tests and answering questions from the back of their text book. The process has very little to do with their lives. For the more traditionally raised students, school science is viewed as a tool for desecration and exploitation of their reservations. Alienation from science, as it is conventionally taught, is widespread among Indian students. This affects student performance in math and science as indicated by their generally low test scores in science related areas. This alienation from science has resulted in lack of scientific expertise among all tribes, leaving them vulnerable to exploitation and dependency on non-Indian consultants for decisions related to resource development, health, and other areas requiring scientific expertise. Tribal self-empowerment, self-determination, development of the leadership and capacity to live according to their own story become even more difficult to attain.

Science is a way of story; it is a process and structure of thought that is a natural part of human thinking. Every culture has used and developed this storymaking tool in its unique way. The core of the problem of science education today lies in the way Western educators have scripted the story. That script is called "curriculum modeling", and like the screenplay that brings a story to life for an audience, the conventional models of science education have grievously neglected their audience. They haven't updated the play, and they haven't presented a culturally empowering performance to American Indians. Therefore, the problem is one of content and presentation. Creativity in presentation, and cultural sensitivity in content are the essential ingredients of a winning production. This is the key to science education that is culturally relevant and empowering for Indian people. Science is a cultural system, and objectivity is really a subjective matter. Objectivity is a relative cultural system you happen to be applying. As such, the study of science from American Indian perspectives can provide invaluable bridges for cross-cultural learning and understanding.

This ethnoscience curriculum model incorporates an Indigenously derived structure called a "curriculum mandala". The mandala represents the integrated concentric rings of relationships among seven courses that comprise the curriculum. The seven courses are founded on the shared metaphor and meaning of sacred directions among Native American Tribal groups. From this shared cultural perspective, directions represent not only geographical orientations, but consciousness as well. Sacred directions provide a way for individuals and groups to place themselves physically, psychologically, mythically, and spiritually. This is an inherently environmental model in that Indian tribes traditionally associated a specific color, a kind of natural phenomena, an animal, a plant, a tree, certain spirits, and a kind of thinking—all of these have symbolic meaning in the cultural perceptions of a tribe—with a specific direction. These symbols are essentially ecological in that they related to a people's perception of themselves in relationship to their environment. Each entity associated with each direction symbolizes a quality of thought and being. For every tribe, the combination of these qualities formed the foundation for wholeness and the dynamic process of natural reality. The Indigenous science curriculum follows the logic and integrative process that is inherent in the orienting of Indigenous learning.

THE MODEL

The Center

The first course of the curriculum is entitled, "Creative Process: The Centering Place." It is the Center of the curriculum, the place of emergence. It explores the elements of creation and learning that are the first and most basic kind of orientation. Learning how you learn and create, by exploring the way others have approached learning and creating, allows you to establish a relationship to the human enterprise of creation. By exploring the ways Nature creates, you experience the wonder. You establish a meaning and context for the learning that you engage in. In this orientation, students explore their creative nature through making art, creative encounters with Nature, writing journals, researching creative expression in Indigenous cultures, and a variety of other creative learning activities. They learn to appreciate the quality and depth of understanding that Indigenous people possess related to the nature of creativity and its relationship to the human spirit. The centering place is a preparation for the holistic journey of learning based on the understanding of one's own creative spirit and capacity. Through this orientation, students begin the process of finding their own center, "that place that Indian people talk about", that place of self-knowing and empowerment that forms the foundation for a transformative process of learning and creation.

East

The East is the next orienting direction. East is the place of the Sun's first light, the place of first insight and illumination. The course associated with this direction is entitled, "Philosophy: A Native American Perspective". In the East, students are oriented to the natural philosophy that guides the attitudes, expressions, and applications of Indigenous knowledge. "Ecosophy" is the most recent term for the integration of environmental knowledge with physical, social, mythological, psychological, and spiritual life characteristic of Indigenous societies. The symbolism of wisdom, first light, rebirth, the Sun, and the dawn of thought associated with the East provides a context for the creative study of ecosophy. Students come to understand how philosophy is the foundation for the formation and expression of the knowledge systems of a culture.

The ecological paradigms inherent in Native American philosophies are compared to the various schools of Western and Eastern philosophy to gain insight into the differences and similarities of orientations, epistemology, and views of man and Nature. Students learn how philosophy expresses the way cultures view the world. These views form the images, myths, symbols, ethics, aesthetics, and visions by which a culture creates itself. Students explore the nature of the theology of place that binds Indigenous people to their place and forms their ecological understanding of their deep and abiding connection to their land.

In the East, students learn how to think about the world in relationship to the social structures, concepts, ideas, and values that reflect the special character of individual cultures. The East is where students may create their own foundation of thought in preparation for their personal journey of learning.

West

The West is the next circle of orientation. It is the place of sustenance, the group mind, social well-being, and community. The course associated with this direction is entitled, "The Tribe: Social Psychology from a Native American Perspective". In this orientation, students explore the social and psychological implications of the concentric rings of environmental relationship. Tribalism as a form of social organization is explored in relationship to other forms of community. Students apply principles and concepts from human ecology, environmental ethics, mythology, cultural anthropology, sociology, and social and Jungian psychology to examine the social ethos of American Indian Tribal communities.

Students are encouraged to explore questions of critical concern such as: Why is community important? What is Tribalism, and why has it been the social organization of choice and necessity for 495 of the last 500 generations of mankind? What are the thinking patterns of The Tribe pertaining to its valuing people, Nature, and social relationship over materialism, exploitation of natural resources, and individualism? What kind of ecology of mind is perpetuated in Tribal community? How has the disintegration of Tribal community affected the social psychology and well-being of contemporary American Indians? What is the contemporary nature of multiculturalism and its promise for American Indian community?

In the Western quadrant, students are immersed in exploration of social experience, and through dialogue, research, creative learning activities, guest speakers, special projects, film, and the arts students develop their understanding of the social environment in which they live and the concentric rings of relationship that extend from the community to the natural world. In short, they encounter the group mind in themselves and in others. Through such an encounter, they come to understand more completely the inherent ecology of human community and its reflection in themselves.

South

The next orientation is that of the South. The South is the domain of plants, fertility, the healing wind, good fortune, and spiritual wholeness. The course of this direction is entitled: "Herbs, Health and Wholeness: a Native American Perspective" and has two primary dimensions. In the first part of this orientation, students explore the nature of human relationship to plants and their role in our perception of, and dependence on, the natural world. Plants are explored within the context of their natural ecologies, traditional uses, and concepts of health and wholeness held by American Indian groups. Methods and content from plant ecology, botany, pharmacology, and traditional systems of medicine are applied to help students gain direct knowledge of how American Indians historically used plants for food and medicine. Through direct encounters with plants in their natural environments, students establish their own relationship with plants and the natural world. Students gather plants, make teas and other herbal preparations, draw and create natural art forms using the plants that they have gathered, keep journals and create stories related to what they are experiencing as they encounter plants and Nature. They connect themselves and learn by being with and in Nature.

In the second part of this orientation, concepts and principles from systems of ecology, mythology, storytelling, holistic health, Jungian psychology, traditional American Indian systems of medicine combined with other medical systems such as Chinese Herbology and Ayerveda are all used to examine the nature of health and wholeness.

Students are introduced to the metaphors, symbols, and lifeways traditionally incorporated by American Indians to gain insight into the communal and cultural domain of healing. Harmony, as a guiding concept, is explored in various expressions of American Indian ritual, dance, art, and medical practices such as the Blessing Way of the Navajo and the Yuwipi of the Sioux. The metaphor of seeking life is also examined as an expression of Indigenous orientations of the Life Principle, that dynamic interaction of physical and spiritual reality that we recognize as life. Students explore the matter of wholeness as a reality that each living thing participates in. Students begin to internalize that health is a dynamic state of being whole and in harmony to all aspects of their environment, internal as well as external. Healing is the restoration and maintenance of a dynamic state of health through revitalizing and centering a person or situation with creative application of natural processes. Students learn about the road to their healing center and how to work with the creative flow of the wholeness of Nature. They begin the journey for empowering of themselves by becoming their own healers.

North

North is the orientation that is associated with animals, and human relationship to this other community of life. The North is the domain of inner forms, the cold hardening winter wind, the unconscious, the origins of dreams, and the symbol of life begetting life through death. In this direction, myth becomes the vehicle, and animals the focus, for the exploration of the concentric rings of physical, social, ecological, and spiritual relationship between man and all other living things. The course associated with this direction is entitled, "Animals in Native American Myth and Reality".

In this realm, students explore the reflections of animals in our human selves. Animal is an arbitrary term since, biologically speaking, humans are part of the animal kingdom. Animals inhabit an important place in human thought and culture precisely because we are intuitively aware of our primal and essential physical relationship. Animals appear in the first stories, the first arts, the first expressions of ritual among all cultures. Animal life and behavior have been a model for human understanding of what it is to be human. Our reliance, love, respect, and even fear of animals are deeply embedded in our psyches. The ancient stories that we tell are stories of our relationship to our animal brethren.

The development of myth, Tribal community, art, and ritual can be tied to our need as humans to come to terms with the animals in the places where we have lived. Hunting and the quest of the Hunter of Good Heart are explored as the story of our mythic relationship to animals.

In this orientation, students are presented with concepts from wildlife biology, ecology, mythology, and theology that help them put in context the animal myths that they study. This is combined with students establishing a direct personal relationship with the animal world. This may take the form of drawing animals, making animal masks, working with animals, creating music, dance or performances that revolve around stories of animals or the creative inspirations that they ignite. In every way, students are encouraged in their attempts to revitalize their connections to animals. In the North, the way of myth combines with the way of art to express and bring to life the nature of the relationship of man and animal. Students enact and enliven their animal genes in ways that are profoundly transformative and energizing.

Below

The next orientation is that of the Below upon which we dwell, and her processes of life. The Below is the domain of the Earth Mother and the archetypal elements of earth, wind, fire, water, and air. In mythological metaphor, it is the place of Changing Woman, the earth mounds called mountains, the origin of the winds, and the fire and breath of life and thought. Its characteristic processes and products are symbolized by the dynamic and creative interplay of the elements. The geophysical processes such as hydrologic cycle, volcanic activity, erosion, plate tectonics, the seasons, and all manifestations of weather represent her life and being. The course associated with this orientation is "The Archetypal Elements: Geoscience from a Native American Perspective."

In this orientation, students are introduced to the natural phenomena that sustains all life through an exploration of Native American mythology related to the Winds, Mountains, Seas, Forests, Lakes, Rivers, Plains, and Deserts. The representation of these natural entities in traditional rituals and art forms is studied, along with related manifestations, to gain insight into their nature and characteristics as seen through the eyes and minds of Native people. Concepts and principles of geoscience, physical science, geology, and meteorology are applied to allow students to gain a basic understanding and appreciation of the geophysics of earth processes. This is combined with creative encounters and interpretations of Earth processes through drawing, painting, sculpting, story-ing, and other art forms. Students are encouraged to establish their own relationship with Earth and to creatively express that understanding through art. Students metaphorically root themselves in the Earth and its way of dynamic and creative expression.

Above

The seventh orientation is that of the Above. This is the domain of the Celestial Father, the Great Mystery, the Sun, Moon, and Stars. The course associated with this direction is entitled: "Astronomy: a Native American Perspective". Through this orientation students are immersed in the many cosmological perspectives of Native Americans and their relationship to their environment. Students are introduced to the astronomical knowledge of selected Indian groups of the Americas: the Chumash of California, the Anasazi of New Mexico, the Skidi Pawnee of the Plains, the Aztecs, Maya and Inca of Mexico, Central and South America. These ancient New World astronomies are compared to ancient Old World astronomies of the ancient Britons, the Babylonians, and Egyptians to demonstrate the parallels of approaches and orientation.

Concepts and principles drawn from modern astronomy, physics, anthropology, cosmology, and mythology are applied to help students gain an understanding of modern conceptions of the Universe. Students also make observations of the Sun, Moon, Planets, Stars, and constellations to understand the patterns of celestial bodies. This also helps them appreciate the sophistication and depth of understanding of ancient Indigenous astronomers. Students visit ancient astronomical sites such as those of the Anasazi at Chaco Canyon in New Mexico. They study ancient architecture and art to gain insights into how ancient Americans viewed themselves in relationship to the Cosmos.

Students are encouraged to create their own art in relation to their thoughts and creative inspiration as they study and reflect on the Cosmos. Their creations may include such art forms as calendar sticks, horizon calendars, medicine wheels, star masks, painted star charts as well as poetry, short stories, star mobiles, and jewelry. The creative possibilities are endless!

By tracing the concentric rings of relationship presented in the course, students come full circle in their journey through the orientations of Indigenous environmental understanding and expression. The Cosmos is the grand context and expression of the creative center that is within. Students expand their awareness of the environment and of themselves as creative beings who are part of a greater story of creation, greater than anything that they can even imagine. They become empowered through the realization that they are part of a greater human story of being and becoming. They learn that they can expand their vision of themselves, and that their lives are part of the story of creation and life. They come to "that place the Indians talk about!"

An Indigenous Curriculum Mandala for Science
from a Native American Perspective

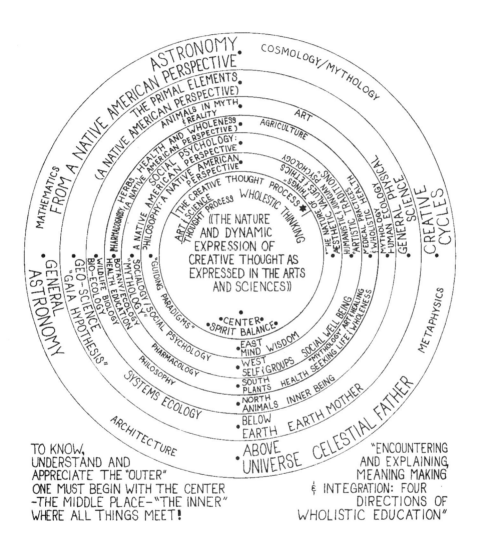

The Sun Dagger: A Cosmological Metaphor For
American Indian Education In A Twenty-First Century World

High atop Fajada Butte in Chaco Canyon National Park, New Mexico is a monument to the ingenuity and sophistication of Indigenous thought. By shaping and precisely placing three sandstone slabs against a concave horizontal indentation facing the sun, and then inscribing one large and one small spiral, the ancient Anasazi inhabitants of Chaco Canyon created the only known solstitial and lunar marker made by an ancient civilization anywhere in the world. This monument to the genius and cosmological perspective of Indian America is appropriately called the "Sun Dagger."

Fajada Butte is a high sandstone mesa rising from the floor of Chaco like a silent sentinel guarding a gateway that leads to the world of an ancient Indigenous past. Chaco Canyon is centrally located in the San Juan Basin of northwestern New Mexico. The canyon is the center of a complex of ancient Anasazi Indian sites that date back over a thousand years. The ruins located in and about the canyon are the most extensive and elaborate expressions of Anasazi culture yet discovered.

From near the top of Fajada Butte one can see the winding course of Chaco Canyon, and the expanse of dry washes, sandstone mesas and horizons that seem to go on into infinity. Fajada Butte, and its location in the Chaco basin, is indeed an appropriate location for an Indigenous marker of the cycles of physical and metaphysical time. The geographical context of Chaco Canyon, the natural form of Fajada Butte and the Sun Dagger—in its elegant simplicity, profound sophistication, and harmonious integration into the natural structure of the butte—presents an extraordinary environmentally based metaphor of the essential perspective that has been achieved by Indigenous education.

The story of the Sun Dagger's discovery is a tale that mirrors the rediscovery of the Indigenous prospective. Anna Sofaer, an artist recording rock art sites located on Fajada Butte, was the first non-Indian to see the unique play of light and shadow created by the Sun Dagger as the sun reaches its noon position around the time of Summer Solstice. What Sofaer witnessed in late June 1977, would change her life and would later force archeo-astronomers around the world to reconsider their preconceived notions regarding the conceptual capabilities and scientific sophistication of ancient American Indian cultures.

Over a period of several years and tireless effort, Sofaer was able to piece together the amazing ways in which the Sun Dagger marked the cyclic movement of the Sun and Moon. The basics of how the Sun Dagger functions may be described as follows:

The site consists of two spirals carved into the rock behind the three horizontal stone slabs. Just before noon on the days surrounding summer solstice, a knife of light bisects the larger spiral. At winter solstice, two noonday daggers frame the large spiral. Finally, during the equinoxes, the smaller spiral is bisected at midday by a lesser dagger, while a larger shaft of light passes to the right of center of the larger spiral.

The large spiral has 19 grooves, which may reflect the Anasazi knowledge of the 19.00-year Metonic cycle of the moon (the time required for the same phase of the moon to recur on the same day of the year). The slightly shorter lunar cycle of 18.61 years corresponds to the time between successive major standstills. At Fajada Butte the moon's shadow bisects the spiral at moonrise during the minor northern standstill and just touches the petroglyph's left edge during major northern standstills. At both places a straight groove has been cut, which is parallel to the moon's shadow.[4]

The Anasazi understood the complementary movement of the sun in relationship to the moon as a visible manifestation of the sacred interplay of complementary opposites expressed throughout the Cosmos. They translated this understanding through various expressions in their ritual traditions and mythology. The Sun Dagger reflects the integration of Anasazi understanding of the movement of the Sun and Moon through time and space with a profoundly spiritual and sophisticated cosmological orientation. The Sun represented the ultimate symbol of light and of life for the Anasazi. They were interested in all aspects of the Sun and traced its journey across the sky throughout the year. They were interested in the relationship of movements of the Sun and Moon to the Earth. The Anasazi strove to resonate their lives, their spirits, and their communities with the natural cycles that they perceived in the Cosmos.

Near midday, during Sun's passage overhead on the summer solstice, a bright ray of sunlight begins to cut through the three positioned sandstone slabs on Fajada Butte. As the Sun moves closer to its highest point in the sky, the dagger of sunlight becomes more pronounced and it points toward the center of the largest spiral. As the Sun reaches its noon time position, the dagger of light spears through the center of the spiral as if heralding, and simultaneously pinpointing, the most sacred and energy-filled time in the Sun's annual pilgrimage across the sky. In a similarly dramatic way, the interplay of light and shadow created by the Sun Dagger also marks the times of winter solstice, the fall and winter equinoxes, and even the major and minor standstills of the Moon, which occur over a cycle of 19 years.

The Sun Dagger metaphorically reflects the connection between time, space, and life on Earth with that of the Sun, Moon, Planets, Stars, and constellations. The play of light and shadow, illumination and orientation, mirroring the cyclic evolution of the Cosmos is recorded by the Sun Dagger. It is a metaphor of the creative learning and honoring of relationship that is indicative of Indigenous education. The Sun Dagger visually shows the drama of the life and movement of time. It represents how the life of the universe is enfolded in the reality of every moment and all life on Earth. The spirals, like miniature replicas of an evolving universe, radiate from a center in concentric rings that show the interrelationship of cycles and a continuity that extends to infinity.

How is the Sun Dagger in its function and its symbolism metaphorically like Indigenous education? Indigenous learning and teaching are developmental processes. They originate with inner experience as a center and radiate out through time and space, forming concentric rings of relationship to other experiences of learning. A cycle of learning is related to the one before and the one after in a continuum of time through the life of the individual and through the generations of a tribe. Learning is also continually moving back and forth between light and shadow through the experiences that occur in one's life. There are times during our lives that a focused point of illumination occurs and the creative energy of the conscious (sun) or the unconscious (moon) come into their fullest potential. There are also seasons and cycles of major and minor standstills of creative focus that characterize human learning and teaching; these must be to honored. Learning in the sunlight (conscious modes) and learning in the moonlight (unconscious modes) complement one another through a process of education. There are pillars of cultural knowledge and context that at times form and illuminate learning and at other times cast shadows, enclose or hide, to contrast one realm of learning from another. The large and small spirals, around which the dagger of light dances with the shadows, may be seen to represent the motion and direction of human thought—one rational, one intuitive—both contained within the same space. Finally, profound learning happens when we climb to a high place, overcoming hardship and obstacles along the way, to gain a perspective that gives us a broader, more expansive, view. Wisdom and important knowledge can be found only through "looking to the mountain" and then rising from a lower plane to a higher one as the physical metaphor of Fajada Butte and its location in Chaco Canyon so magnificently represents.

The Sun Dagger, Fajada Butte, and the ruins of Chaco Canyon have been abandoned for more than eight hundred years. In spite of abandonment, the Sun Dagger has continued to mark the passage of hundreds of sacred time cycles of the Sun and Moon. The discovery of this metaphysical symbol and tool of Indigenous America was greeted at first with great doubt, followed by controversy among Western scientists. This gave way to a flurry of experiments and observation of the site under glass, in the usual tradition of objectified science, in an attempt to fit it to the tacit infrastructure of Western understanding. Just as the natural reality it records, its Indigenous message cultivating a deep understanding of human relationship to the cosmos cannot be denied. The Anasazi understood, as did other Indigenous people, that we are related not only to each other and all other life on Earth, but we are also related to, and a part of, the greater Universe. Therefore, an essential task of Indigenous education continues to be about learning the nature of this relationship and honoring it!

SUN DAGGER
An Ancient Metaphor for A Contemporized Indigenous Education

PHOTO CREDIT: MICHAEL RICHIE

FINAL THOUGHTS

INDIGENOUS EDUCATION AND ITS ROLE IN INDIVIDUAL TRANSFORMATION

IT IS ESSENTIAL THAT THE RELATIONSHIP of Indigenous education to establishing and maintaining individual and community wholeness be seriously considered. Much of Indigenous education can be called "endogenous" education; it revolves around a transformational process of learning by bringing forth illumination from one's ego center. Educating and enlivening the inner self is the imperative of Indigenous education embodied in the metaphor, "seeking life" or for "life's sake." Inherent in this metaphor is the realization that ritual, myth, vision, art, and learning the art of relationship in a particular environment, facilitates the health and wholeness of the individual, family, and community. Education for wholeness, by striving for a level of harmony between individuals and their world, is an ancient foundation of the educational process of all cultures. In its most natural dimension, all true education is transformative and Nature centered. Indeed, the Latin root *educare*, meaning 'to draw out', embodies the spirit of the transformative quality of education.

"A transformational approach to education is distinctly universal, integrative and cross-cultural because it is referenced to the deepest human drives. From this viewpoint all human beings concern themselves with self-empowerment and with whatever enables them to transform their lives and the conditions in which they live; such a viewpoint engenders the intent of people striving to create whole, happy, prosperous, and fulfilling lives."[1]

The goals of wholeness, self-knowledge, and wisdom are held in common by all the traditional educational philosophies around the world. Indeed, even through medieval times all forms of European education were tied to some spiritual training. Education was considered important in inducing or otherwise facilitating harmony between a person and the world. The goal was to produce a person with a well-integrated relationship between thought and action. This idealized outcome was anticipated as following naturally from the right education.

The right education is, of course, a culturally defined construct; its main criteria is socializing the individual to the collective culture of a group. However, this socialization is only one dimension of education, a first step in a lifelong path of learning. Right education causes change that in time creates a profound transformation of self. This transformation is a dynamic creative process that brings anything but peace of mind, tranquillity, and harmonious adaptation. The exploration of self, and relationships to inner and outer entities, require a tearing apart to create a new order and higher level of consciousness. Harmony is achieved through such a process, but it lasts for only a short time before it has to be revised as people and their circumstances change. This is the endogenous dynamic of Tribal education. (See Diagram)

The process begins with a deep and abiding respect for the spirit of each child from before the moment of birth. The first stage of Indigenous education revolves around learning within the family, learning the first aspects of culture, and learning how to integrate one's unique personality in a family context. The first stage ends with gaining an orientation to place.

Education in the second stage revolves around social learning: being introduced to Tribal society, and learning how to live in the natural environment. The second stage ends with gaining a sense of Tribal history and learning how to apply Tribal knowledge in day-to-day living.

The third stage revolves around melding individual needs with group needs through the processes of: initiation, learning guiding myths, and participating in ritual and ceremony. This stage ends with a profound and deep connection to tradition.

The fourth stage is a midpoint in which the individual achieves a high level of integration with the culture and attains a degree of peace of mind. It brings the individual a level of empowerment, personal vitality, and maturity. But it is only the middle place of life.

The fifth stage is a period of searching for a life vision, a time of pronounced individuation and the development of mythical thinking. This stage concludes with a deep understanding of relationship and diversity.

The sixth stage ushers in a period of major transformation characterized by deep learning about the unconsciousness. It is also a time of great travail, disintegration, wounding, and pain that pave the way for an equally great reintegration and healing process to begin in the final stage. The pain, wound, and conflict act as a bridge to the seventh stage.

In the seventh stage deep healing occurs in which the self mutualizes with body, mind, and spirit. In this stage, deep understanding, enlightenment, and wisdom are gained. This stage ends with the attainment of a high level of spiritual understanding. It acts as a bridge to finding one's true center and to being a complete man or woman in "the place the Indians talk about."

The Indigenous Stages of Developmental Learning

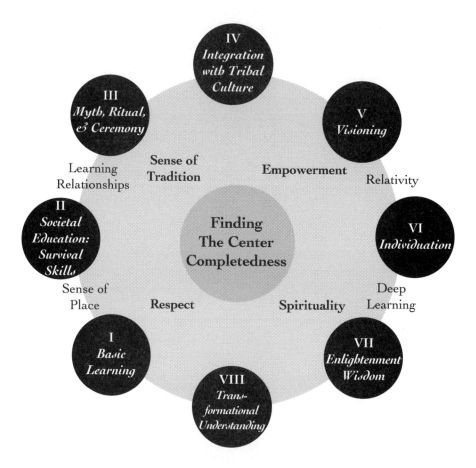

These stages of interrelationship form a creative continuum, lifeway, that helps us to become more fully human as we move through the stages of our lives. Indigenous education traditionally recognized each of the most important interrelationships through formal and informal learning situations, rites of passage, and initiations.

Inherent in Indigenous education is the recognition that there is a knowing Center in all human beings that reflects the knowing Center of the Earth and other living things. Indian elders knew that contacting one's inner Center was not always a pleasant or easily attainable experience. This recognition led to ceremonies, rituals, songs, dances, works of art, stories, and traditions to assist individual access and use the healing and whole-making power in each person. Connecting to that knowing Center was choreographed through ritual preparation to help individuals on their journeys to their own sources of knowledge. The potential for learning, inherent in each of the major stages of a person's life, was engaged and applied to knowing one's Center. This was the essential reason for the rites of passage associated with Indian tribes and various societies within each tribe.

Since the highest goal of Indigenous education was to help each person find life and realize a completeness in their life, the exploration of different approaches to learning was encouraged. This was done with the understanding that each individual would find the right one for them in their own time. But the process of finding one's self and inner peace with its implications of being "adjusted", as it is called in modern circles today, was not the central focus of Indigenous education. Seeking peace and finding self were by-products of following a path of life that presented significant personal and environmental challenges. This "individuation", as Jung called it, did not come easily. It had to be earned every step of the way. In the process of earning it, one learned to put forward the best that one had; one learned the nature of humility, self-sacrifice, courage, service, and determination. Indian people understood that the path to individuation is filled with doubt and trials. They understood that it was a path of evolution and transformation.

> Individuation is a work, a life opus, a task that calls upon us not to avoid life's difficulties and dangers, but to perceive the meaning in the pattern of events that form our lives. Life's supreme achievement may be to see the thread that connects together the events, dreams, and relationships that have made up the fabric of our existence. Individuation is a search for and discovery of meaning; not a meaning we consciously devise but the meaning embedded in life itself. It will confront us with many demands, for the unconscious, as Jung wrote, 'always tries to produce an impossible situation in order to force the individual to bring out his very best.'[2]

There are elemental characteristics that exemplified the transformational nature of Indigenous education. The following are a few important elements for learning goals and the development of content areas.[3]

First, was the idea that learning happens of its own accord, if the individual has learned how to relate with his/her inner Center and the natural world. Learning about one's own nature and acting in accord with that understanding was a preconditioning that prepared the individual for deep learning.

Second, there was the acceptance that experiences of significant hardship were a necessary part of an individual's education, and that such circumstances provided ideal moments for creative teaching. A wounding or memory of a traumatic event and the associated learning provided a constant source for renewal. This transformation enlarged the consciousness if individuals were helped to understand the meaning of these events in their lives.

Third, was that empathy and affection were key elements in learning. Also, direct subjective experience combined with affective reflection were essential elements of right education. Therefore mirroring behavior back to learners became a way that they might come to understand their behavior and how to use experience to the best advantage.

Fourth, an innate respect for the uniqueness of each person created the understanding that each person was their own teacher in their process of individuation. Indigenous education integrated the notion that there are many ways to learn, many ways to educate, many kinds of learners, many kinds of teachers, each honored for their uniqueness and their contribution to education.

Fifth, that each learning situation is unique and innately tied to the creative capacity of the learner. When this connection to creative learning and illumination is thwarted, frustration and rigidity follow. Learning therefore, had to be connected to the life process of each individual. The idea of life-long learning was a natural consideration.

Sixth, that teaching and learning are a collaborative contract between the teacher and learner. In this sense the teacher was not always human but could be an animal, a plant, or other natural entity or force. The teachable moment was recognized through synchronistic timing or creative use of distractions and analogies to define the context for an important lesson. The tactic of distract-to-attract-to-react was a common strategy of Indigenous teachers.

Seventh, that learners need to see, feel and visualize a teaching through their own and other people's perspectives. Therefore, telling and retelling a story from various perspectives and at various stages of life enriched learning, emphasized key thoughts, and mirrored ideas, attitudes, or perspectives back to learners for impact. Re-teaching and re-learning are integral parts of complete learning. Hence, the saying, "Every story is retold in a new day's light."

Eighth, that there are basic developmental orientations involved with learning through which we must pass toward more complete understanding. Learning through each orientation involves finding personal meaning through direct experience. The meaning that we find is subjective and interpretive, based on our level of maturity, self-knowledge, wisdom, and perspective.

Ninth, that Life itself is the greatest teacher and that each must accept the hard realities of life with those that are joyous and pleasing. Living and learning through the trials and pains of life are as important as learning through good times. Indeed, life is never understood fully until it is seen through difficulty and hardship. It is only by experiencing and learning through all life's conditions that one begins to understand how all we do is connected, and all the lessons that we must learn are related.

Tenth, that learning through reflection and sharing experience in community allows us to understand our learning in the context of greater wholes. In a group there are as many ways of seeing, hearing, feeling, and understanding as there are members. In a group we come to understand that we can learn from another's experience and perspective. We also become aware of our own and other's bias and lack of understanding. We see that sometimes people do not know how to use real innovation and that many times people do not know how to recognize the real teachers or the real lessons. We see that a community can reinforce an important teaching, or pose obstacles to realizing its true message. As the Tohono Odum phrase it, "when all the people see the light shining at the same time and in the same way," then a group can truly progress on the path of knowledge.

Survival: An Indigenous Value and An Economic Necessity

Indigenous people evolved ingenious strategies for making a living in even the most inhospitable environments. The ingenuity of Indian people in developing economic systems of trade is a testimonial to their ability to survive and thrive in each place they have lived.

This historic Indian awareness and application of economics are expressed today in the numerous markets and trade fairs that exist in Indian Country. The boom in Native American arts and crafts is a visible expression of this continuing tradition.

Today, Indian people make a living not only in the form of arts and crafts, but in the vocational trades, business, education, government service, and numerous other professions. Economics has always been a part of the social ecology of Indigenous societies. From the earliest times Indian people have engaged in sustainable economic activity in a relatively harmonious relationship with their natural environments.

In the making of a living, Indian people traditionally and historically interjected an ecological attitude, a sense of spiritual ecology, a mutually reciprocal, sustainable relationship. Economics, providing for one's material and physical needs both at the individual and communal levels, was traditionally tied to spiritual, ecological, and communal aims. Traditional Indian expressions of the "give away", the "potlatch", the exchange of food, services, and labor during individual and communal activity are all reflections of an Indian sense of economic ecology.

A mutually reciprocal cycle of giving and receiving established a sustainable form of economics in Indigenous communities. In all Indian communities, material wealth, land, and service (labor) were communally shared to ensure that every member of the community was cared for. This form of economics was an ecological necessity that formed the foundation of long-term serviceability.

From this ecological stance, service, leadership, community responsibility and traditional governance tied individual and community in an intimate and sustainable relationship of interdependence. The individual was the community and the community the individual.

Among the early Chumash Indians, the Antap (traditional high priest), in cooperation with the Alchuklash (religious council), collected food and essential material goods from the various Chumash villages as a form of tax. Food and material were stored in the central village, and during special ceremonies related to the Winter Solstice, redistribution took place—to the old, to widows, to orphans, and other Chumash needy. It was a form of socially conscious economics that ensured the long-term sustainability of the Chumash.

This portrays how economics was done in those times and in "that place Indians talk about". It was an economic system that evolved from a unified understanding that all forms of economics are tied to natural resources and to people in relationship with each other. As with all ecologies, the forms and expressions of Indigenous economics were diverse and multidimensional. There is a foundation of Indigenous economics, complete with ecological orientations and social expressions that may be studied for evolving a contemporary expression of Indian education.

Today, Indian people and Indian communities struggle to be economically viable. In these times, economic survival is associated with accessibility to modern education. Economic development is often tied to the capacity of tribes to be self-determined and self-governed. This capacity is always tied to Western education since it plays the role of gatekeeper to contemporary economic survival. Therefore, a contemporary application of Indian education must creatively integrate the orientation of economic survival and ecological sustainability if it is to serve the needs of Indian people living in contemporary times.

Historically, Indian people were ecological economists who expressed forms of living and using resources that sustained an ecological way of life. The principles of those times and "that place that Indians talk about" are desperately needed by Indian and non-Indian alike if we are to sustain ourselves in this time of true ecological crises.

Indian people have many strengths that are rooted in their traditional ecologically oriented economics. The first step is to re-educate ourselves to these economic understandings and to teach ourselves how to translate them to serve ourselves and our communities.

There are traditionally rooted skills in the areas of agriculture, forestry, trading, politics, governance, environmental sciences, engineering, philosophy, and crafts, to name a few. These are the modern disciplines into which our Indigenous ecological economics may be translated.

The areas of Indian arts and crafts provide a case in point. The creation of sustainable "eco-business" presents another. Art has been integral to the economics of Indian communities since the turn of the century. With its humble beginnings as a curio/tourist trade, the Indian art market has grown into a billion dollar industry supporting individual artists, their families, their communities, and a whole network of art entrepreneurs. In spite of the productivity of Indian artisans, most reap only a small portion of the economic benefit stemming from this industry. Lacking the necessary skills or capital to run their own businesses, many Indian artisans remain essentially art producers, similar to independent farmers producing a crop and selling it at low commodity rates. Indian people must create opportunities to learn the art of business and become the entrepreneurs of their own enterprises.

Ecologically sound business and economic principles can be an expression of Indigenous thought, guided by the contemporary extension of Indigenous ecological ethics and philosophy. The key is to learn how to transfer these principles to making a living in a contemporary context.

Social Consciousness and Indigenous Education

Paulo Freire, Brazilian social reformer and educator, introduces a notion of education that closely parallels the role of Indigenous education. The similarity is in the transformation of the social consciousness of American Indians as they strive for self-determination in the face of the challenges of the twenty-first century.[4]

Freire's thesis is that the critical consciousness of the cultural and historical roots of a People—as expressed and understood from the perspective of the people themselves—is the foundation of their cultural emancipation. The modern struggle of Indigenous people throughout the world has largely been characterized by an attempt to maintain the most cherished aspects of their ways of life, their relationship to their lands, their consciousness of themselves as a distinct People. They are constantly engaged in a dynamic struggle to retain the freedom to be who they are in the midst of subtle, and at times overt, oppression by modern societies.

Freire's central message about education is that one can only learn to the extent that one can establish a participatory relationship with the natural, cultural, and historical reality in which one lives. This is not the same as the Western-schooled authoritarian style of problem solving, where experts observe a situation from the outside and at a distance, then develop a solution or dictate an action or policy. This approach takes the problem out of the context of human experience and leads to a distortion of the problem as an event that has relationship only to itself. This ultra-objectification denies the interrelationship and reduces participation and learning to an intellectual exercise. The result is perpetuation of dependence on an outside authority and the maintenance of the political power brokers behind such authority. Indigenous people who are administered education, extension services, and economic development in these terms usually remain oppressed and gradually become dependent on the authority. Under these circumstances, Indigenous people's ability to revitalize and maintain themselves culturally, socially, and economically through a self-determined process of education is significantly diminished, if not destroyed.

Freire's approach is to begin with the way a group communicates about their world and their experiences in their own social contexts. Then generative words, metaphors, or proverbs are identified: words that evoke thought, feelings, or reveal a historical perspective that has intrinsic meaning to a People and their cultural way of life. These words or phrases are translated into a variety of meaningful images and discussed with the People themselves to "unpack" their meaning. Various stages of dialogue evolve through structures called "culture circles". In the culture circle a group reflects on key generative words and symbols, facilitated by a coordinator who helps form the dialogue. Since the words and symbols being used come from the language, cultural, or historical experience of the group, the people begin to reflect on their collective stories. They do this in ways that stimulate new insights about themselves, their situations, and solutions to problems that they face. Motivation, meaning, and re-searching their cultural roots to find models for viewing their problems are elements built into the culture circle. The group learns by telling and retelling their stories, reflecting on their meaning, and reinforcing the vital elements of their cultural orientation. This learning process stimulates the thinking of "people submerged in a culture of silence to emerge as conscious makers of their own cultures." The group learns how to create new meanings; they learn to apply insights derived from their own culture, history, and social experience to their contemporary life. What they learn about themselves, through themselves, forms the basis for authentic empowerment. It is the beginning of release from imposed authority through a process of education that has become their own. Through such a process the group can truly cease being objects for outside political, economic, or educative manipulation. Instead, they become subjects in making their own stories for the future and controllers of their own destiny.

Freire's method has had a profound effect on increasing the literacy and the social consciousness of, not only rural people in Brazil, but millions of people in third-world nations. It works because it acts to release what is essentially an Indigenous response to learning. It fosters authentic dialogue about what is important to people in contexts of social and political situations that directly affect them. The relevancy of what is being learned and why it is being learned becomes readily apparent, because it is connected to the cultural orientations as the people themselves perceive them. The democratization of knowledge and the educational process perpetuated by Freire's approach mirrors what occurs in Indigenous education. A new relationship among Indigenous people, modern education, and knowledge bases is made possible. The knowledge and orientation of modern educators are changed from an expert-recipient relationship to one of mutually reciprocal learning and co-creation. What is established is a more ecologically sound and sustainable process of education. An education is engendered that frees teachers, learners, and community to become partners in a mutual learning and becoming process.

Freire's method mirrors, at a social level, the ecologically inspired orientation of Indigenous education that I have called "natural democracy." There is a direct communication among all individuals engaged in the educative process. The implicit paternalism, social control, and non-reciprocal orientation between experts and recipients of education give way to authentic dialogue. This dialogue generates a high level of critical consciousness and an educational empowerment that allows Indigenous people to become agents of transformation in their own social and cultural contexts.

The history of American Indian education has largely been characterized by a policy of assimilation. This has been combined with covert attempts at modernization of American Indian communities to fit them into the mainstream profile of American life. For the most part, this has been a technical process of development, combined with intense indoctrination in the political and bureaucratic ways of the federal government. Educational development, like other extensions of federal aid, has occurred through the actions of technicians, bureaucrats, and political manipulators who act to keep real decision-making power outside the parameters of the tribes and individuals affected. Many educators, social reformers, business men, and politicians involved with Indian issues perpetuate this federal and mainstream paradigm. They do this either because they have never questioned their own educational conditioning within this system, or because they have not found or explored alternatives. This situation has prevented Indian people from being the beneficiaries of the exploration of their own transformative vision and educational process. As a result, Indian tribes are still relegated to having to react to their administration by the federal government because of continued dependence on federal aid and extension services. Rather than being pro-active and truly self-determined in their efforts to educate themselves, Indian people continue to struggle with modern educational structures that are not of their own making, but are separated from, and compete with, their traditional forms of education. There continues to be an educational schizophrenia in Indian education as it exists today. Indian people continue to be one of the most educationally disadvantaged and at risk groups in America. This reality exists in spite of the substantive and inventive expressions of traditional education and philosophy that this book has outlined. The essential question is: what needs to happen to reclaim and rename this important heritage, not only for Indian people, but as a contribution to the educational development of all future generations?

I view the next phase of Indian education as requiring the collective development of transformative vision and educational process based on authentic dialogue. This development requires that new structures and practices emerge from old ones through a collective process of creative thought and research. These new structures and practices can only be generated by an ongoing and unbiased process of critical exchange between modern educational thought and practice, and the traditional philosophy and orientations of Indian people.

A new educational consciousness, an "Ecology of Indigenous Education", must be forged that allows Indian people to explore and express their collective heritage in education and to make the contributions to global education that stem from such deep ecological orientations. The exploration of traditional Indian education and its projection into a contemporary context is more than an academic exercise. It illuminates the true nature of the ecological connection of human learning and helps to liberate the experience of being human and being related at all its levels.

From this perspective, education takes on the quality of a social and political struggle to open the possibilities for a way of education that comes from the very soul of Indian people. It also brings to the surface the extent of the conditioning of modern educational processes that have been introjected into the deepest levels of their consciousness. They become critical observers of the modern education to which they have had to adapt, an education that demands conformity to serve certain vested interests of American society. Through the exploration of Indigenous education they learn how to demystify the techniques and orientations of modern education. This understanding allows them to use such education in accord with their needs and combine the best that it has to offer with that of Indigenous orientations and knowledge. They cease to be recipients of modern education and become active participants and creators of their own education.

At a more inclusive level, exploration of Indigenous education liberates the Indian learner and educator to participate in a creative and transforming dialogue that is inherently based on equality and mutual reciprocity. This is a way of learning, communicating, and working in relationship that mirrors those ways found in Nature. It also destigmatizes the Indian learner from being disadvantaged and the educator from being the provider of aid. It allows both the learner and educator to co-create a learning experience and mutually undertake a pilgrimage to a new level of self-knowledge. The educator enters the cultural universe of the learner and no longer remains an outside authority. By co-creating a learning experience, everyone involved generates a critical consciousness and enters into a process of empowering one another. With such empowerment, Indian people become enabled to alter a negative relationship with their learning process. With the reassertion, contemporary development, and implementation of such an Indigenous process at all levels of Indian education, Indian people may truly take control of their history by becoming the transforming agents of their own social reality.

Indian people must determine the future of Indian education. That future must be rooted in a transformational revitalization of our own expressions of education. As we collectively "Look to the Mountain", we must truly think of that seventh generation of Indian children; for it is they who judge whether we were as true to our responsibility to them as our relatives were to us seven generations before. It is time for an authentic dialogue to begin—to explore where we have been, where we are now, and where we need to go as we collectively embark on our continuing journey to "that place that Indian People talk about". I hope that this work will contribute to that dialogue.

Land and Stars, The Only Knowledge

North, West, South, and East.
Above and Below and All Around.
Within knowledge of the land,
We are existent.
Within knowledge of the stars,
We are existent.

Coldness and wind and the snow, northward.
Mildness and mountain and the rain, westward.
Hotness and desert and the hail, southward.
Warmness and mesa and the sun, eastward.
Starshine and sky and the darkness, upward.
Earthsource and stone and the light, downward.

By this Northern Mountain, we live.
On this Western Peak, we live.
In this Southern Canyon, we live.
Upon this Eastern Mesa, we live.
Under this Sky Above, we live.
Above this Earth Below, we live.

We are Existent within knowledge of land.
We are Existent within knowledge of stars.
All Around and Below and Above.
East, South, West, and North.
This is our prayer. This is our knowledge.
This is our source. This is our existence.

Always the land is with us.
Always the stars are with us.
With our hands, we know the sacred earth.
With our spirits, we know the sacred sky.
We are with the land and stars.
We are with the stars and land.

With offering, all around outside.
With offering, all around inside.

This is the knowledge we have.
This is the existence we have.
In thankfulness, we give and we know.
In thankfulness, we receive and we know.

—Simon Ortiz, 1993

❋ APPENDIX ❋

An Outline of Indigenous Teaching and Learning Orientations

Introduction

ONE OF THE MOST IMPORTANT ELEMENTS of Indigenous teaching and learning revolves around "learning how to learn." Learning how to learn is a key element in every approach to education. Therefore, the cultivation of the human capacities — listening, observing, experiencing with all one's senses, developing intuitive understanding, and respecting time-tested traditions of learning — naturally formed the basis for skills used in every process of Indigenous learning and teaching.

Native American people in both North and South America developed a variety of approaches to teaching and learning. These approaches ranged from loosely organized informal contexts in hunter-gatherer tribes, to formally organized academies of the Aztecs, Maya, Inca and other groups of Mexico, Central, and South America. Whatever the approach, there was a continuum of education in Tribal American societies that involved an array of ritual/initiatory practices, closely following the human phases of maturation and development. In each phase of this continuum, an important aspect of learning how to learn was internalized. Learning how to learn in Tribal societies unfolded around the following four basic areas of orientation.

First, the attention to practical needs of the Tribal society, which systematically addressed learning related to physical, social, psychological, and spiritual needs of Tribal members. The most important of these were learning how to survive in the natural environment and learning how to be a productive member of the Tribal society.

Second, the teaching of individuals in individual ways when they showed the readiness or expressed the willingness to learn. The emphasis was on allowing for the uniqueness of individual learning styles and encouraging the development of self-reliance and self-determination.

Third, the application of special intellectual, ritual, psychological, and spiritual teaching tools that facilitated deep levels of learning and understanding. Indigenous teaching was predicated on three basic criteria: flexibility, viability, and effectiveness.

Fourth, the honoring and facilitating of the psychological and transformational process of flowering or opening to self-knowledge and the natural capacities of learning. This was usually accomplished by helping individuals overcome their self-generated impediments to learning.

The list of Indigenous axioms that follows represents the wisdom and creative approaches applied by Tribal teachers in creating an educational process that reflected a sophisticated ecology of education. Indigenous education allowed for a diversity of sophisticated teaching tools that few modern educational approaches are able to duplicate in breadth and creativity. These interpretations of Indigenous teaching axioms are derived from a host of readings and observations related to Indigenous education in American Indian, Sufi, Taoist, and East Indian teaching traditions. They are presented in a simplified form with a minimum of description in the hope that teachers will apply their creative interpretations based on the development of their own lessons and curricula. As processes, these axioms are applicable to the holistic presentation of any content and adaptable to every age level.[1]

1. Tribal teachers begin teaching by building on the commonplace. We have common experiences, understandings, and human traits that can be used to pose a problem in terms, forms, or experiences that are familiar to students.

2. Remember that learning is a natural instinct and that success in learning something new is tied to human feelings of self-worth. Create a learning environment that flows with this natural current of humanness. Enabling successful learning is an essential step in cultivating motivation and enhancing self-confidence in learning.

3. Basic understanding begins with exploring how things happen. Observing how things happen in the natural world is the basis of some of the most ancient and spiritually profound teachings of Indigenous cultures. Nature is the first teacher and model of process. Learning how to see Nature enhances our capacity to see other things.

4. The focus of teaching on perennial phenomena, such as solar and lunar cycles, stimulates the deepest level of learning how to learn and the development of self-knowledge.

5. Indigenous teaching focuses as much on learning with the heart as on learning with the mind.

6. Indigenous teaching facilitates learning how to see how one really is, rather than an image manufactured through one's or other's egos. This

real perception of self helps the student realize that they are essentially responsible for the barriers to their own learning.

7. The real situation provides the stage for most Indigenous learning and teaching. Overt intellectualization is kept to a minimum in favor of direct experience and learning by doing. Teaching through a real situation expands the realm of learning beyond speculation and allows the students to judge the truth of a teaching for themselves.

8. Readiness to learn is considered a basic determinant for the success or failure of a teaching. Indigenous teachers recognize that readiness for learning important things has to be conditioned through repetition and the attunement of the student to the teaching. They watch for moments of teachability and repeat the teaching of key principles in numerous ways and at various times.

9. Placing students in situations in which they constantly have to examine assumptions and confront preconceived notions is a regular practice of Indigenous teachers. Through facilitating this constant examination of what students think they know, they remain open to new dimensions of learning and prepare for higher levels of thinking and creative synthesis.

10. Indigenous teaching is always associated with organic development. Indigenous teaching is planted like a seed, then nurtured and cultivated through the relationship of teacher and student until it bears fruit. The nature and quality of the relationship and perseverance through time determine the outcome of a teaching process. Apprenticeship, and learning through ritual stages of learning-readiness, are predicated on the metaphor of planting seeds and nurturing the growing seedlings through time.

11. Teaching is a communicative art. Indigenous teaching is based on the nature and quality of communicating at all levels of being. Indigenous teachers practice the art of communicating through language, relationship to social and natural environments, art, play, and ritual.

12. Teaching and learning is a matter of serving and being served. Service is the basis of the relationship between student and teacher. This foundation is exemplified most completely in the apprentice-teacher relationships found in all expressions of Indigenous education.

13. Indigenous teaching involves making students think comprehensively and facilitating their awareness of the higher levels of content and its relationship to other areas of knowledge. Such comprehensive thinking forms a firm foundation for the creative process of teaching and learning. Comprehensive preparation and immersion in a learning process invite new understandings. They allow perceptions of dimensions of knowledge that are there all the time but need to be worked before they reveal themselves.

14. Indigenous practices such as creative dreaming, art, ritual, and ceremony help the student externalize inner thoughts and qualities for examination. Such practices help students to establish a connection with their real selves and learn how to bring their inner resources to bear in their lives. Helping students gain access to their real selves is part of the transformative education that is inherent in Indigenous teaching.

15. Indigenous teaching revolves around some form of work. Indigenous teachers recognize that work invites concentration and facilitates a quietness of the mind. This leads to illuminating insights about what is being taught.

16. Tribal teachers understand that all teaching is relative, and each path of knowledge has its own requirements that need to be addressed. Flexibility and learning how to adjust to the demands of the moment are key skills cultivated throughout Indigenous education.

17. Learning about the nature of self-deception is a key aspect of Indigenous preparation for learning. A first step in understanding the nature of true learning is reaching a level of clarity regarding why one is learning. Students become aware that ambition, self-gratification, power, and control as purposes for learning are forms of self-deception. These have to be avoided because they lead to misuse of knowledge and further perpetuation of self-deception.

18. Tribal teachers realize that striving for real knowledge requires a cultivated sense of humility. The human tendencies toward pride, arrogance, and ego-inflation have to be understood and avoided in the search for one's true face, heart, and vocation.

19. Mirroring consequences of a teaching back to students to expand their perspective and deepen their learning is often used in Indigenous

education. Tribal teachers facilitate learning through direct, and at times provoked, perception. They do this by setting up a situation that forces students to see the limitations of what they thought they knew. In this way, students are encouraged to reach deeper into themselves and realize the deeper levels of meaning represented by a teaching. This practice helps students cultivate the humility necessary for maintaining an openness to new learning and the creative possibilities of a teaching.

20. The cultivation of humility prepares a foundation for the students to learn the nature of attention. Attention may be considered a foundation of Indigenous learning in that almost every context—from learning basic hunting and fishing skills, to memorizing the details of ritual, to listening to story, to mastering a traditional art form—relied on its practiced application. Attention in the Indigenous sense, has to do with the focus of all the senses. Seeing, listening, feeling, smelling, hearing, and intuiting are developed and applied in the Indigenous perspective of attention.

21. Learning the nature of appropriate activity is a natural consideration of Indigenous teaching. Activity in Indigenous life always has a purpose. Busy work is not a concept Tribal teachers are interested in perpetuating, since helping students learn to engage in activity appropriate to the situation is a skill required for more advanced Indigenous teaching.

22. Knowledge and action are considered parts of the same whole. Properly contexted and developed knowledge leads to balance in terms of action. Therefore, to assure the integrity and rightness of an action, a great amount of time is spent reflecting and seeking information and understanding before forming an opinion or taking an action. Prayer, deep reflection, patience, and "waiting for the second thought" are regularly practiced in Indigenous decision making.

23. A concept of "each person's work," akin to the Hindu concept of "karma," is honored in the processes of Indigenous education. Indigenous teachers see that each student is unique and has a path of learning that they need to travel during their life. Learning the nature of that path is many times the focus of Indigenous rites of initiation and vision questing. The trials, tribulations, and work that become a part of each individual's learning path constitute the basis for some of the

most important contexts of Indigenous teaching and learning.

24. From the Indigenous perspective, true learning and gaining significant knowledge does not come without sacrifice and at times a deep wound. Indigenous teachers realize that only by experiencing extreme hardship and trauma are some individuals ready to reach their maximum level of learning development. The ritual incorporation of life's hardships into such ceremonies as the Sun Dance transforms the reality of woundedness into a context for learning and reflection. In this way, the wound or traumatic life-event is mobilized to serve as a constant reminder of an important teaching. As long as the wound or the repercussions of an event are used to symbolize something deeply important to know and understand, they provide a powerful source for renewal, insight, and the expansion of individual consciousness.

In summary, a primary orientation of Indigenous education is that each person is their own teacher and that learning is connected to each individual's life process. Meaning is looked for in everything, especially in the workings of the natural world. All things comprising Nature are teachers of mankind; what is required is a cultivated and practiced openness to the lessons that the world has to teach. Ritual, mythology, and the art of storytelling—combined with the cultivation of relationship to one's inner self, family, community, and natural environment—are utilized to help individuals realize their potential for learning and living a complete life. Individuals are enabled to reach completeness by learning how to trust their natural instincts, to listen, to look, to create, to reflect and see things deeply, to understand and apply their intuitive intelligence, and to recognize and honor the teacher of spirit within themselves and the natural world. This is the educational legacy of Indigenous people. It is imperative that its message and its way of educating be revitalized for Life's sake.

Look to the Mountain, Look to the Mountain!

❋ NOTES TO THE TEXT ❋

Preface

1. Vine Deloria, "The Perpetual Indian Message," *Winds of Change 7*, No. 1 (Winter 1992).

2. Nicholas C. Peroff, "Doing Research in Indian Affairs: Old Problems and a New Perspective" (Kansas City: University of Missouri, L. P. Cookingham Institute of Public Affairs, 1989).

3. Ibid., pp. 8-9.

4. David Bohm and F. David Peat in their book *Science, Order, and Creativity* (New York: Bantam Books, 1987) provide a parallel thesis about the "tacit infrastructure" of science and its historic view of itself as being unquestionably objective , thus denying the cultural and social context in which it exists.

5. Ibid.

6. Gregory A. Cajete, "Science, A Native American Perspective: A Culturally Based Science Education Curriculum" (Ph.D. diss., International College, Los Angeles, 1986).

7. Thomas Berry, "The Viable Human," *Revision 9*, No. 2 (1987): p. 79.

Chapter I

1. Fritjof Capra, *Turning Point* (New York: Simon and Schuster, 1982). Presents a similar thesis in this contention that science must evolve a new paradigm of thought, action, and application to meet the challenges of the next century.

2. Eber Hampton, "Toward a Redefinition of American Indian/Alaska Native Education" (Analytic paper, Harvard Graduate School of Education, 1988). Presents an excellent case for the reassessment of Indian education from the standpoint of traditional orientations mentioned. Mr. Hampton also presents an excellent outline of one of the possibilities upon which an Indian philosophy of education may be based. Some of his key categories are listed in this paragraph.

3. Deloria, "The Perpetual Indian Message."

4. Several sources were used as resources for describing these elemental

points of Indigenous education. In the bibliography see the following authors for further explanation: Castle, E. B. (1961); Egan, Kieran (1987); Haines, Joyce; Shah, Idries (1978); Dooling, D. M., and Paul Jordan-Smith (1989).

CHAPTER II

1. P. V. Beck and Anna L. Walters, *The Sacred* (1977), p. 84.

2. Esther Martinez, ed., *San Juan Pueblo Dictionary* (1983), p. 143.

3. Cajete, "Science, A Native American Perspective," pp. 150-165.

4. Beck and Walters, *The Sacred*. See pp. 3-32 for narrative description of the metaphor "Seeking Life" as it is represented in traditional American Indian contexts.

5. Miguel Leon Portillo, *Aztec Thought and Culture* (1963), pp. 3-24.

6. Ibid.

7. Marion Wood, *Spirits, Heroes, and Hunters from North American Indian Mythology* (1982), p. 85.

8. Ray A. Williamson, *Living the Sky* (1984), pp. 281-290.

9. B. Devall and George Sessions, *Deep Ecology* (1985), p. 93.

CHAPTER III

1. Joseph E. Brown, *The Spiritual Legacy of the American Indian* (1982). Provides a basic orientation to these five dimensions of American Indian spirituality.

2. Beck and Walters, *The Sacred*. Provides numerous excerpts describing American Indian people's relationship to the Great Mystery and its applications in the traditional teaching of morals, ethics, and responsibility to Tribal community.

3. Tom Heidlebaugh, "Thinking the Highest Thought" (Unpublished manuscript, 1985). Provides insights into Indigenous thinking as a way of orientation. Heidlebaugh captures something of the sense of "spiritual ecology" shared by Pueblo people as they orient themselves in the center of their world. His essay also illustrates that ecology is a way of thinking and placement relative to the highest and most noble human understanding.

4. James K. McNeley, *Holy Wind In Navajo Philosophy* (1981). Presents one of the most extensive descriptions of Navajo traditional philosophy related to the "Wind soul." Although the concept of holy wind exists in other Tribal philosophies, the greatest amount of written information exists for the Navajo. Therefore, the work of McNeley has been used extensively to illustrate this important Indigenous environmental orientation.

5. McNeley, *Holy Wind in Navajo Philosophy*, p. 1.

6. Benard Haile, *The Holy Way of the Red Ant Way Chant*, told by Hastinn Dijooli (White Cone), 1933, Manuscript 63-15, pp. 97-98, Museum of Northern Arizona, Flagstaff.

7. McNeley, *Holy Wind in Navajo Philosophy*, p. 12.

8. Ibid., pp. 16-17.

9. Ibid., pp. 36-37.

10. Jan Clayton-Collins, "An Interview with Burnam Burnam," *Shaman's Drum*, No. 14 (1988): pp. 29-33.

11. Terry Tempest Williams, *Pieces of White Shell* (1987), pp. 101-104. This story is quoted in its entirety as it was written by the author from the original story told by Claus Chee Sonny, a Navajo medicine man.

12. Primary sources: Grinnell, George Bird, "Scar Face." *Blackfoot Lodge Tales*, pp. 93-103, and Wood, Marion, "Scar Face and the Sun Dance," *Spirits, Heroes and Hunters*, pp. 85-89.

CHAPTER IV

1. J. Donald Hughes, *American Indian Ecology* (1983), pp. 2-3. The work of Donald Hughes is used extensively in this chapter since it provides a repertory of the ecological mindsets and environmental understanding of American Indians before the onset of erosion due to cultural assimilation.

2. Ibid.

3. Oren Lyons, "Our Mother Earth," *Parabola 7*, No. 1 (Winter 1984): pp. 91-93.

4. Eugene Linden, "Lost Tribes, Lost Knowledge," *Time* (September 23, 1991): pp. 46-56.

5. Ibid.

6. Ibid.

7. Ibid.

8. Theodor Abt, *Progress Without Loss of Soul* (1989), pp. 83-90. Theodor Abt presents an excellent synopsis of the repercussions of Western culture's break from the land and the subsequent loss of a part of the soul of human experience and relationship with Nature.

9. Ibid.

10. Dennis Martinez, *Law and Theology Conference* (Boulder: University of Colorado, June 12-13, 1992).

11. Ibid.

12. Ibid.

13. Dolores LaChapelle, *Way of the Mountain Newsletter* (Silverton, Colorado, Autumn, 1992): p. 1.

14. Trebbe Johnson, "Four Sacred Mountains of the Navajos," *Parabola 13*, No. 4 (November 1988): p. 41.

15. Craig D. Goseyun (White Mountain Apache), conversation with the author, Santa Fe, N.M., August 16, 1992.

16. John Young, *Kokopeli* (Palmer Lake: Filter Press, 1990).

17. Hughes, *American Indian Ecology*, p. 28.

18. Ibid., p. 46.

19. Ibid., p. 64.

20. Lowell John Bean, "California Indian Shamanism and Folk Curing," in *American Folk Medicine*, ed. Wayland D. Hand (Berkeley: University of California Press, 1976), pp. 109-123.

21. Donald Sandner, "Navajo Indian Medicine and Medicine Men," in *Ways of Health*, ed. David S. Sobel (New York: Harcourt Brace Jovanovich, 1979), pp. 117-146.

22. Ibid.

23. Ibid.

24. Ibid.

25. Ibid.

26. Ibid.

CHAPTER V

1. Christopher Vecsey, *Imagine Ourselves Richly* (1991), pp. 13-14.

2. John E. Pfeiffer, *The Creative Explosion* (1982). John Pfeiffer provides an extraordinary exploration of the origins of art in pre-historic human societies and its connection to myth and ritual.

3. Naomi Goldenburg, *Changing the Gods: Feminism and the End of Traditional Religions* (Boston: Beacon, 1979), p. 47.

4. D. Feinstein and Stanley Krippner, *Personal Mythology* (Los Angeles: Jeremy P. Tarcher, 1988), pp. 1-8. The work of Feinstein and Krippner in the area of personal mythology reflects the importance of an understanding of mythology to personal growth and transformation.

5. John Stokes, personal conversations with the author, *The Tracking Project*, 5403 Corralles Rd., Corralles, N.M., 87048, fall 1985.

6. Barbara G. Myerhoff, *Peyote Hunt* (1974).

7. There are several versions of this myth recorded in the early 1900s by ethnologists working in the Hopi-Tewa village of Hano and among the Rio Grande Tewa. This particular version of "Water Jar Boy" is similar to that recorded by Elsie Parsons, in her book *Tewa Tales*, The American Folklore Society Memoirs, vol. 19 (1926), p. 193.

8. Elaine Jahner, "Stone Boy: Persistent Hero," in *Smoothing the Ground*, ed. Brian Swan (Berkeley: University of California Press, 1983), pp. 171-186.

9. Portillo, *Aztec Thought and Culture*, p. 140.

10. Jerome Rothenberg, ed., *Technicians of the Sacred* (1985). Presents an excellent description of this characteristic of Indian mythopoetics.

11. Ibid., preface, xvii-xxxiii.

12. Kieran Egan, "Literacy and the Oral Foundations of Education," *Harvard Educational Review 57*, No. 4 (November 1987): p. 451.

13. E. A. Havelock, *Preface to Plato* (Cambridge: Harvard University Press, 1963), p. 29.

14. Ken Wilber, *Up from Eden* (Garden City: Anchor/Doubleday, 1981).

15. Ibid.

16. Ibid.

17. Feinstein and Krippner, *Personal Mythology*, pp. 213-223.

18. Ibid., p. 219.

19. Deloria, "The Perpetual Indian Message."

20. Nollman, *Spiritual Ecology*, p. 198.

21. Cajete, "Science, A Native American Perspective."

22. Joseph Campbell, *Primitive Mythology*, quoted in Sam Keen and Anne Valley-Fox, *Your Mythic Journey* (1989), p. 2.

Chapter VI

1. D. M. Dooling, "Alchemy and Craft," *Parabola 3*, No. 3 (August 1978): p. 24.

2. Arthur Amiotte, "Our Other Selves, the Lakota Dream Experience," *Parabola 7*, No. 2 (May 1982): p. 30.

3. Ibid., p. 32.

4. Patricia Garfield, *Creative Dreaming* (New York: Simon and Schuster, 1974).

5. Linda Marks, *Living with Vision* (Indianapolis: Knowledge Systems, Inc., 1989).

6. Myerhoff, *Peyote Hunt*.

7. Guadalupe Rios de la Cruz (Wife of Ramon Medina Silva, Huichol Mara akame), conversations with the author, Santa Fe, N.M., August 31-September 28, 1990.

8. Ibid.

9. Ibid.

10. Ibid., an English translation of a song by Ramon Medina Silva as related by his wife and presented in "To Find Our Life," a film by Peter Furst, University

of California at Los Angeles, 1969.

11. Marks, *Living with Vision.*

12. Ibid., p. 36.

13. Ananda K. Coomaraswamy, "The Uses of Art," *Parabola 16*, No. 3 (August 1991): pp. 7-8.

14. Jose Argelles, *Mandala* (Boston: Shambhala Publications, 1972).

15. Fredrick Franc, *Art as a Way* (New York: Crossroad Publishing, 1981).

16. Jamake Highwater, *The Primal Mind* (1981), p. 79.

17. Transcendence of consciousness, i.e., taking awareness to the brink of conceptualization and fundamental associations of symbolism through exercises with mind and breath appear in the learning of many cultural art forms. This is because sustaining a level of transcendence of consciousness is inherent in all creative disciplines. Frank Garcia, "The Ceremony of Art," (Unpublished manuscript, Santa Fe, N.M., 1990).

18. This section is paraphrased with permission of Frank Garcia, Santa Fe, N.M. from his unpublished manuscript, "The Ceremony of Art," and personal conversations from 1989 to 1993.

19. Ibid.

Chapter VII

1. Highwater, *The Primal Mind*, p. 172.

2. Nollman, *Spiritual Ecology.*

3. Simon Ortiz, "Surviving Columbus," (Draft manuscript, Santa Fe, N.M., 1992).

4. Nollman, *Spiritual Ecology*, pp. 182-183.

5. Vine Deloria, *God is Red* (New York: Dell Publishing Co., 1973), p. 201.

6. Key sources: McClellan Hall, "Something Shining, Like Gold but Better," (National Indian Youth Leadership Project, 1991); and his "Gadugi: A Model of Service-Learning for Native American Communities," *Phi Delta Kappan* (June 1991): pp. 754-757.

7. Deloria, *God is Red*, p. 200.

8. Simon Ortiz, "Fight Back: For the Sake of the People, For the Sake of the Land," *INAD Literary Journal* (Albuquerque, N.M.) 1, no. 1 (1980): p. 31.

9. Joseph E. Brown, in *I Become Part of It*, D. M. Dooling and Paul Jordan-Smith (1989), p. 20.

10. John A. Sanford, *Healing and Wholeness* (1977), pp. 20-21.

11. Joseph Oxendine, *American Indian Sports Heritage* (Champaign: Human Kinetics, 1988), p. 5.

12. Ibid., pp. 4-5.

13. P. Nabokov and Margaret MacLean, "Ways of Indian Running," *CoEvolution* 26 (Summer 1980): p. 5.

14. Plenty Coups in "Ways of Indian Running," Nabokov and MacLean (1980): p. 6.

Chapter VIII

1. Tribal Sovereignty Associates, *The Power Within People*, (1986).

2. Ibid.

3. All excerpts dealing with Indigenous science are taken from: Cajete, "Science, A Native American Perspective: A Culturally Based Science Education Curriculum," (Ph.D. diss., 1986).

4. J. M. Malville and Claudia Putman, *Prehistoric Astronomy in the Southwest*, (1991), p. 32.

Chapter IX

1. Robert D. Waterman, "Introduction to Transformation."

2. Sanford, *Healing and Wholeness*, p. 22.

3. For further reading related to these maxims of Indigenous teaching and learning read: Hyemeyohsts Storm, *Seven Arrows* (New York: Ballantine Books, 1972).

4. Paulo Freire, *Pedagogy of the Oppressed* (New York: Seabury, 1970).

❋ NOTE TO APPENDIX ❋

1. Idries Shah, *Learning How To Learn* 1978. For Indigenous maxims of teaching and learning that come from the Sufi tradition.

❋ BIBLIOGRAPHY ❋

Abt, Theodor. *Progress Without Loss of Soul*. Wilmette: Chiron Publications, 1989.

Amiotte, Arthur. "The Call to Remember." *Parabola* 17, No. 3 (August 1992).

———. "Our Other Selves." *Parabola* 7, No. 2 (May 1982).

———. "The Road to the Center." *Parabola* 9, No. 3 (August 1984).

Anderson, William. "The Central Man of All the World." *Parabola* 13, No. 1 (February 1988).

Argelles, Jose. *Mandala*. Boston: Shambhala Publications, 1972.

Armstrong, Jeannette C. "Traditional Indigenous Education: A Natural Process." Paper presented at the World Conference, Indigenous People's Education, Vancouver, B.C., June 1987.

Atencio, Tomas. "La Resolana: A Chicano Pathway to Knowledge." Ernesto Galaraza Commemorative Lecture, Sanford Center for Chicano Research, 1988.

Aug, Lisa. "Humans and the Earth." *Turtle Quarterly* 3, No. 2 (Spring/Summer 1989).

Baker, Rob. "A Canoe Against the Mainstream." An Interview with Peterson Zah. *Parabola* 14, No. 2 (May 1989).

Beck, P. V., and Anna L. Walters. *The Sacred*. Tsaile: Navajo Community College Press, 1977.

Berman, Morris. *The Re-enchantment of the World*. Ithaca: Cornell University Press, 1981.

Bernbaum, Edwin. "Sacred Mountains." *Parabola* 13, No. 4 (November 1988).

Berry, Thomas. *The Dream of the Earth*. San Francisco: Sierra Club Books, 1988.

Blackburn, Thomas C., ed. *December's Child*. Berkeley: University of California Press, 1975.

Boas, Franz. *Keresan Texts*. New York, 1928.

Bohm, David, and F. David Peat. *Science, Order, and Creativity*. New York: Bantam Books, 1987.

Brown, Joseph E. *The Spiritual Legacy of the American Indian*. New York: Crossroad Publishing Company, 1982.

Bruchac, Joseph. "The Storytelling Seasons." *Parabola* 14, No. 2 (May 1989).

Caine, R. N., and Geoffrey Caine. *Teaching and the Human Brain*. Alexandria: Association for Supervision and Curriculum Development, 1991.

Cajete, Gregory A. "An Ensouled and Enchanted Land." *Winds of Change* 8, No. 1 (Spring 1993).

———. "Land and Education." *Winds of Change* 8, No. 4 (Winter1994).

———. "Motivating American Indian Students in Science and Math." Las Cruces, N.M.: ERIC Clearing House on Rural Education and Small Schools, 1988.

———. "The Nature of Things and the Things of Nature." Washington, D.C.: KUI TATK, Native American Science Education Association (Spring 1985): 2.

———. "Science, A Native American Perspective: A Culturally Based Science Education Curriculum." Ph.D. diss., International College, Los Angeles, 1986.

———, ed. "Visions and Life Journeys: Contemporary Indian People of New Mexico." Santa Fe, NM: New Mexico Indian Education Association, 1993.

Campbell, Joseph. *The Inner Reaches of Outer Space*. New York: Harper and Row, 1986.

———. *The Way of the Animal Powers*. London: Summerhill Press; San Francisco: Harper and Row, 1983.

Capra, Fritjof. *Turning Point*. New York: Simon and Schuster, 1982.

Castle, E. B. *Ancient Education Today*. New York: Penguin Books, 1961.

Clayton-Collins, Jan. "An Interview with Burnam Burnam." *Shaman's Drum*, No. 14 (1988).

Coomaraswamy, Ananda K. "The Uses of Art." *Parabola* 16, No. 3 (August 1991).

Courlander, Harold. *The Fourth World of the Hopi*. Albuquerque: University of New Mexico Press, 1987.

Cowan, James G. "Aboriginal Solitude." *Parabola* 17, No. 1 (February 1992).

Cronyn, George W., ed. *American Indian Poetry*. New York: Ballantine Books, 1991.

Deloria, Vine. *God is Red*. New York: Dell Publishing Co., 1973.

———. "The Perpetual Indian Message." *Winds of Change 7*, No. 1 (Winter 1992).

Devall, B., and George Sessions. *Deep Ecology*. Salt Lake: Gibbs Smith, Inc., 1985.

Dooling, D. M., and Paul Jordan-Smith. "Alchemy and Craft." *Parabola* 3, No. 3 (August 1978): p. 24.

———. *I Become Part of It*. New York: Parabola Books, 1989.

Egan, Kieran. "Literacy and the Oral Foundations of Education." *Harvard Educational Review* 57, No. 4 (November 1987).

———. *Teaching as Story Telling*. Chicago: University of Chicago Press, 1989.

Erdoes, R., and Alfonso Ortiz. *American Indian Myths and Legends*. New York: Pantheon Books, 1984.

Feinstein, D., and Stanley Krippner. *Personal Mythology: The Psychology of Your Personal Self*. Los Angeles: Jeremy P. Tarcher, 1988.

Ford, Daryll C. "A Creation Myth from Acoma." *Folk-Lore* 41 (1930): pp. 359-87.

Freire, Paulo. *Pedagogy of the Oppressed*. New York: Seabury, 1970.

Garcia, Richard J. "Tohigwu—An American Indian Concept for Sport & Health." Master's Thesis, California State University, Sacramento, Spring 1992.

Garfield, Patricia. *Creative Dreaming*. New York: Simon and Schuster, 1974.

Gill, Sam D. "It's Where You Put Your Eyes." *Parabola* 4, No. 4 (November 1979): p. 91.

———. *Mother Earth*. Chicago: University of Chicago Press, 1987.

Grinnel, George Bird. *Blackfoot Tales*. Lincoln: University of Nebraska Press, 1962.

Haines, Joyce. "From Lao Tse and Hillel to Hart, Freire, and Storm: Celebrating Excellence of Diversity and Diversity of Excellence." Unpublished paper, University of Kansas School of Education, Lawrence, Kansas.

Hall, Edward T. *Beyond Culture*. New York: Anchor Books/Doubleday, 1976.

Hall, McClellan. "Gadugi: A Model of Service-Learning for Native American Communities." *Phi Delta Kappan* (June 1991).

Hampton, Eber. "Toward a Redefinition of American Indian/Alaska Native Education." Analytic paper, Harvard Graduate School of Education, 1988.

Heidlebaugh, Tom. "Thinking the Highest Thought." Unpublished manuscript, 1985.

Heinegg, Peter. "The Agony of Nature." *Parabola* 6, No. 1 (February 1981).

Highwater, Jamake. *Art of the Indian Americas*. New York: Harper and Row, 1983.

———. *The Primal Mind*. New York: Harper and Row, 1981.

Houston, Jean. *The Search for the Beloved: Journey into Sacred Psychology*. Los Angeles: Jeremy P. Tarcher, 1987.

Hughes, J. Donald. *American Indian Ecology*. El Paso: Texas Western Press, 1983.

Hultkrantz, Ake. *The Religions of the American Indians*. Berkeley: University of California Press, 1979.

Johnson, Trebbe. "The Four Sacred Mountains of the Navajos." *Parabola* 13, No. 4 (November 1988).

Jung, C. G. *Mandala Symbolism*. Translated by R. F. C. Hull. New Jersey: Princeton University Press, 1972.

———. "Wilderness and Hearth: The Cycle of the Hunt." *Parabola* 16, No. 2 (May 1991).

Krishnamurti, J. *Education and the Significance of Life*. New York: Harper and Row, 1953.

LaChapelle, Dolores. *Earth Wisdom*. Silverton: Finn Hill Arts, 1978.

———. *Sacred Land, Sacred Sex, Rapture of the Deep*. Silverton: Kivakí Press, 1992.

Lang, Julian. "The Basket and World Renewal." *Parabola* 16, No. 3 (August 1991).

Linden, Eugene. "Lost Tribes, Lost Knowledge." *Time*, September 23, 1991.

Lopez, Barry. "Renegotiating the Contracts." *Parabola* 8, No. 2 (May 1983).

Lyons, Oren. "Our Mother Earth." *Parabola* 7, No. 1 (Winter 1984).

Malville, J. M., and Claudia Putman. *Prehistoric Astronomy in the Southwest*. Boulder: Johnson Books, 1991.

Mander, Jerry. *In the Absence of the Sacred*. San Francisco: Sierra Club Books, 1991.

Marks, Linda. *Living with Vision*. Indianapolis: Knowledge Systems, Inc., 1989.

Martinez, Esther, ed. *San Juan Pueblo Dictionary*. Portales: Bishop Publishing Co., 1983.

Matthiessen, Peter. "Native Earth." *Parabola* 6, No. 1 (February 1981).

McNeley, James K. *Holy Wind in Navajo Philosophy*. Tucson: University of Arizona Press, 1981.

McPherson, Robert S. *Sacred Land, Sacred View*. Brigham Young University, Charles Redd Center for Western Studies, 1992.

Moon, Sheila. *A Magic Dwells*. Middletown: Wesleyan University Press, 1970.

Moore, R., and Douglas Gillette. *King, Warrior, Magician, Lover*. San Francisco: Harper Collins Publishers, 1990.

Myerhoff, Barbara G. *Peyote Hunt*. Ithaca: Cornell University Press, 1974.

Nabokov, P., and Margaret MacLean. "Ways of Indian Running." *CoEvolution* 26 (Summer 1980).

Neihardt, John G. *Black Elk Speaks*. New York: Pocket Books, 1972.

Nollman, Jim. *Spiritual Ecology*. New York: Bantam Books, 1990.

Ortiz, Alfonso. *The Tewa World*. Chicago: University of Chicago, 1969.

Oxendine, Joseph. *American Indian Sports Heritage*. Champaign: Human Kinetics, 1988.

Peroff, Nicholas C. "Doing Research in Indian Affairs: Old Problems and a New Perspective." Unpublished paper, L. P. Cookingham Institute of Public Affairs, University of Missouri, Kansas City, 1989.

Pfeiffer, John E. *The Creative Explosion*. New York: Harper and Row, 1982.

Portillo, Miguel Leon. *Aztec Thought and Culture*. Norman: University of Oklahoma Press, 1963.

Powers, William K. *Yuwipi*. Lincoln: University of Nebraska Press, 1982.

Rivera, George. *Then and Now — Pojoaque Pueblo in Perspective*. Pojoaque Pueblo, N.M., 1992.

Ross, Allan C. *Mitakuye Oyasin, "We are All Related."* Fort Yates: Bear Press, 1989.

Rothenberg, Jerome, ed. *Shaking the Pumpkin*. New York: Alfred Van Der Marck Editions, 1986.

———, ed. *Technicians of the Sacred*. Berkeley: University of California Press, 1985.

Rudolph, Carol P. *Petroglyphs and Pueblo Myths of the Rio Grande*. Albuquerque: Avanyu Publishing Inc., 1990.

Sandner, Donald. *Navajo Symbols of Healing*. Rochester: Healing Arts Press, 1979.

Sanford, John A. *Healing and Wholeness*. New York: Paulist Press, 1977.

San Souci, Robert. *The Legend of Scarface*. Garden City: Doubleday and Company, Inc. New York, 1978.

Shah, Idries. *Learning How To Learn*. San Francisco: Harper and Row, 1978.

Skolimowski, Henryk. *Living Philosophy*. New York: Penquin Books/Arkana, 1992.

Snyder, Gary. *The Practice of the Wild*. Berkeley: North Point Press, 1990.

Sobel, David S., ed. *The Ways of Health*. New York: Harcourt Brace Jovanovich, 1979.

Suzuki, David, and Peter Knudtson. *Wisdom of the Elders*. New York: Bantam Books, 1992.

Swan, Brian, ed. *Smoothing the Ground*. Berkeley: University of California Press, 1983.

Swan, James. *Sacred Places*. Santa Fe: Bear and Company Publishers, 1990.

Tedlock, D., and Barbara Tedlock. *Teachings from the American Earth*. New York: Liveright Publishing Corp., 1992.

Tribal Sovereignty Associates. *The Power Within People: A Community Organizing Perspective*, June 1986.

Tyler, Hamilton. *Pueblo Gods and Myths*. Norman: University of Oklahoma Press, 1964.

Vecsey, Christopher. *Imagine Ourselves Richly*. San Francisco: Harper Collins Publishers, 1991.

Warren, Dave. "New Worlds, Old Orders: Native Americans and Columbus Quincentenary." *ThePublic Historian* 14, No. 4, University of California Press, 1992.

Waterman, Robert D. "Introduction to Transformation." Unpublished paper, Southwestern College, Santa Fe, May 1990.

White, Leslie. *The Acoma Indians*. Washington, D.C., 1932.

Wilber, Ken. *Up From Eden: A Transpersonal View of Human Evolution*. Garden City: Anchor/Doubleday, 1981.

————, ed. *The Holographic Paradigm and Other Paradoxes*. Boulder: Shambhala Press, 1982.

Williams, Terry Tempest. *Pieces of White Shell*. Albuquerque: University of New Mexico Press, 1987.

Williamson, Ray A. *Living the Sky: The Cosmos of the American Indian*. Norman: University of Oklahoma Press, 1984.

Wood, Marion. *Spirits, Heroes, and Hunters from North American Indian Mythology*. New York: Schocken Books, 1982.

Young, John. *Kokopeli*. Palmer Lake: Filter Press, 1990.

❈ NOTE ON THE AUTHOR ❈

DR. GREGORY CAJETE IS AN EDUCATOR, practicing artist, and educational consultant. He is a Tewa Indian from Santa Clara Pueblo, New Mexico, where he lives with his wife Patricia and son, James. Dr. Cajete received a B.A. in Biology/Sociology from New Mexico Highlands University, a M.A. in Education from the University of New Mexico, and a Ph.D. in Social Science Education from International College, Los Angeles.

Dr. Cajete has taught extensively at the Institute of American Indian Arts in Santa Fe, where he was the founding Director of the Center for Research and Cultural Exchange. Additionally, he has lectured widely in schools, universities, and for educational programs throughout the United States, Canada, Europe, and the former Soviet Union.

Currently, Dr. Cajete operates a private educational consulting firm, Tewa Educational Consulting, specializing in environmental education and multicultural curriculum/program development in science, social science, and the arts.